The Journey toward God
in Augustine's *Confessions*

The Journey toward God in Augustine's *Confessions*

Books I–VI

Carl G. Vaught

State University of New York Press

Published by
State University of New York Press, Albany

© 2003 State University of New York

For information, address the State University of New York Press,
90 State Street, Suite 700, Albany, NY 12207

Production by Michael Haggett
Marketing by Jennifer Giovani

Library of Congress Cataloging-in-Publication Data

Vaught, Carl G., 1939–
    The journey toward God in Augustine's Confessions : books I-VI / Carl G. Vaught.
    p. cm.
    Includes bibliographical references (p.) and index.
    ISBN 0-7914-5791-5 (alk. paper) — ISBN 0-7914-5792-3 (pbk. : alk. paper)
    1. Augustine, Saint, Bishop of Hippo. Confessiones. Liber 1-6. 2. Augustine,
Saint, Bishop of Hippo. 3. Spirituality—History—Early church, ca. 30-600.
    4. Christian saints—Algeria—Hippo (Extinct city)—Biography—History and
criticism. I. Title.

BR65.A62 V38 2003
270.2'092—dc22   2003057271

10 9 8 7 6 5 4 3 2 1

For Jane
and Omar

Contents

Preface   ix

Introduction   1
    The Framework of the Enterprise   4
    The Centrality of God and the Soul   8
    Problems of Access to the Text   15

1. Infancy, Childhood, and Adolescence: From Will to Willfulness
    (Books I–II)   21
    The Dynamism of the Text (1.1.1–1.5.6)   22
    Origins and Infancy (1.6.7–1.7.12)   28
    Language and Education (1.8.13–1.18.29)   37
    Personal Defects, *Imago Dei*, and Sin (1.19.30–1.19.31)   51
    Sexuality (2.1.1–2.3.8)   52
    The Pear-Stealing Episode (2.4.9–2.10.18)   54

2. The Philosophical Turn: Seven Stages of Experiential and
    Reflective Development (Books III–IV)   67
    Love, False Images, and Rhetoric (3.1.1–3.3.6)   68
    Cicero and the Bible (3.4.7–3.5.9)   74
    Becoming a Manichaean (3.6.10–3.12.21)   79
    Fragmentation, Illegitimacy, and Astrology (4.1.1–4.3.6)   89
    The Death of a Friend (4.4.7–4.12.19)   93
    The Beautiful and the Fitting (4.13.20–4.15.27)   107
    Categories, Transcendentals, and the Liberal Arts
    (4.16.28–4.16.31)   111

3. Manichaeism, Skepticism, and Christianity (Books V–VI)   115
    The Presence and Absence of God (5.1.1–5.2.2)   116
    The Failure of Faustus (5.3.3–5.7.13)   119
    The Flight to Rome (5.8.14–5.12.22)   126
    Ambrose and the Christian Faith (5.13.23–25; 6.1.1–6.5.8)   134
    Fragmentation and Friendship (6.6.9–6.16.26)   146

Notes	155
Bibliography	177
Index	187

Preface

Augustine's *Confessions* is a difficult book. For many readers, there are too many prayers, too much self-flagellation, and too much philosophy. What other book begins by praising the greatness of God and by calling our attention to the mortality that reflects our separation from him (1.1.1)?[1] Where else can we find an autobiography about the sins of infancy and about an adolescent act of mischief that becomes an obsession (1.7.11), (2.4.9–2.10.18)? Who besides Augustine pictures sexuality as a boiling caldron that seethes and bubbles all around him (3.1.1)? In Book IV, he describes the death of his closest friend as an episode that almost leads him to despair (4.4.7–4.7.12). In Book V, he records his disappointment with Manichean dualism as a way of dealing with his deepest intellectual problems (5.7.12). And in Book VI, he expresses temporal, spatial, and eternal hysteria as he tries to bring the journey of his wandering soul to rest (6.11.18–19). In all these cases, the *Confessions* expresses a range of feelings that is difficult to describe, but it also displays a powerful capacity for reflective discourse. Unlike most philosophers, Augustine can feel deeply and speak profoundly in the same sentence. Indeed, his most famous book poses difficulties for interpretation because it weaves together what most professional philosophers try to separate.

How shall we respond to a book as rich and complex as this? What approach should we take? What questions should we ask? What answers should we expect? What purposes should undergird our inquiry? Without trying to answer these questions prematurely, at least this much should be clear from the outset: we cannot plunge into the *Confessions* without calling ourselves into question. Augustine speaks as a psychologist, a rhetorician, a philosopher, and a theologian; but he speaks most fundamentally from the heart. If we are unwilling to probe the depths of our souls, we will never understand Augustine; for he makes insistent demands that we trace out the path he has traveled in our own spiritual and intellectual development.

In the past two decades, I have tried to respond to these demands; but I have only begun to find the place from which Augustine is speaking in the past few years. If one philosopher pays tribute to another by taking him

seriously enough to criticize, it is even truer that the highest honor we can
pay a great thinker is to try to rise to the level of his thinking. The time has
come to develop a philosophical framework that is rich enough to express a
distinctively Augustinian account of the journey toward God. Only if we do
this is there room for us to stand beside Augustine, and only if we open
ourselves to the fundamental questions he raises can we participate in a
dialogue with him that transcends both hubris and humility.

No one undertakes a project of this kind alone, and I want to thank my
students and colleagues who have participated in it and have helped make it
possible. First, I express my gratitude to the students at Penn State and at
Baylor who have attended my lectures and seminars about the *Confessions,*
and some of whom have been my research assistants. Roger Ward at Penn
State and Chris Calloway and Travis Foster at Baylor have been three of these
students; and I am indebted to all of them for their assistance. In addition,
I am grateful to my student, Kristi Culpepper, for helping with the page
proofs and the index. However, the person who has helped me most is Natalie
Tapken. In particular, she has read many primary and secondary sources and
has helped to prepare the notes for the book. I am also grateful to the thirteen
philosophers who came to Penn State for a week in 1992 to study the *Confessions* with me. We thought and talked until we were exhausted; but in the
process, the text opened up in ways that none of us could have anticipated.
Some of the papers from this conference and from one of my graduate seminars appear in a two-part issue of *Contemporary Philosophy,* vol. 15, published
in 1993. Recently, Baylor University sponsored a Pruitt Memorial Sympo-
sium devoted to the topic, "Celebrating Augustine's *Confessions:* Reading the
Confessions for the New Millenium." Professor Anne-Marie Bowery and I
were the co-directors of this conference, and we intend to publish some of the
papers that were presented in a volume of essays. Finally, I am grateful to
President Robert Sloan, Provost Donald Schmeltekopf, and my colleagues in
the Philosophy Department at Baylor for providing me with a supportive and
exciting academic environment in which to bring this project to completion.
However, I am grateful most of all to Robert Baird, the Department Chair,
who read the penultimate version of the manuscript. He not only made
valuable suggestions about what I have written, but also encouraged me to
turn the manuscript loose after more than a decade of work.

I have presented parts of chapter 1 at a number of institutions and
philosophical meetings: the Graduate Christian Forum at Cornell, the Con-
vocation Lecture Series at Bethel College, the Distinguished Lecture Series
at Baylor, the Philosophy Department Colloquium at the University of Essex,
the Faculty of Divinity in the University of Edinburgh, the School of Philosophy at the Catholic University of America, the Baptist Association of
Philosophy Teachers at Furman University, and the Interdisciplinary Program

at Valparaiso University. I want to thank those who attended these lectures for comments and criticisms that have helped me sharpen some of the issues in this final version of the book. I have also published parts of chapter 1 in a paper entitled "Theft and Conversion: Two Augustinian Confessions," in *The Recovery of Philosophy in America: Essays in Honor of John Edwin Smith.*[2] I want to thank SUNY Press for permission to reprint parts of this paper and to express my appreciation to John Smith for helpful comments about it.

I am grateful to Colin Starnes and James O'Donnell for their encouragement. I met Colin at his farmhouse near Halifax in the summer of 1992 soon after his book about Augustine's conversion appeared; and I participated in a session of James's NEH Seminar at Bryn Mawr the following summer, where teachers from a variety of disciplines discussed a wide range of problems and raised questions about his three volume text and commentary about the *Confessions.* I value the work of these classical philologists because it is the most encouraging sign that Augustinian scholarship is beginning to move beyond the place where Pierre Courcelle left it in 1950. I am pleased to add my philosophical voice to their attempts to reorient the discussion of Augustine's most influential book.

Finally, I want to express my gratitude to Professor Richard Swinburne in Oxford, who helped me find an academic home at Oriel College while the first draft of this book was written. I also want to thank Professor Rowan Williams at Christ Church for allowing me to participate in his course about Augustine; Christopher Kirwan at Exeter College for discussing some philosophical problems about the *Confessions* with me; and Robert Edwards, a medievalist and colleague at Penn State, for making detailed comments on an earlier version of the manuscript. My wife, Jane, accompanied me to Oxford during what will always be one of the most memorable years of our lives. I never think about that year without thinking about her and about the liberating comfort it brought her day after day. I am also grateful for our dog, Omar, who "studies" with me, and who is a source of joy for both of us. This book is for them.

Introduction

This book is a detailed analysis of the first six Books of Augustine's *Confessions*, and it comes to focus on two central themes: the first is the relation between God and the soul, and the second is the language we must learn to speak to deal with this relation appropriately. At a time when philosophy and theology are moving in so many directions, I have chosen to explore these problems, not because they are fashionable, but because they are fundamental. This is true when Augustine raises these questions in some of his earliest writings; and it is still the case today, however reluctant many of us may be to fasten our attention on these issues.

My own version of Augustine's questions is that the relations among God, the soul, and language are the most important problems a philosopher can consider, that religion is the region where all the enigmas of the world converge,[1] and that solitude is the place where the ultimate issues of life intersect.[2] Yet we must never assume that the problem of God and the soul and the subtle uses of language it requires are either resting-places or private problems with which we must struggle alone. When we confront these issues, we face enigmas to be pondered rather than problems to be solved; but when we speak about them, we must not only speak in private, but should also address the public context in which our life and thought are embedded.

What draws me to Augustine's *Confessions* is that I see myself on almost every page. As the Renaissance poet, Petrarch, is the first to notice, the *Confessions* is not only Augustine's story, but also the story of Adam and Eve, and hence the story of us all.[3] It is a microscopic expression of a macroscopic theme: in a single life the relation between God and the soul unfolds as a sustained encounter between an individual and the ground of its existence,[4] where the experiences that emerge from this encounter demand the richest linguistic responses of which we are capable. As Augustine says himself, "What can anyone say when he speaks of thee? But woe to them that keep silent—since even those who say most are dumb" (1.4.4).

Augustine's account of his journey toward God presupposes a metanarrative of creation, fall, conversion, and fulfillment in the light of which he believes

1

that the lives of all his readers can be understood. This does not mean that each of us moves through every stage Augustine traverses, that all of us do so in the same way, or that the particularity of our unique situations can simply be subsumed within a universal pattern. Augustine is convinced that the pattern is there, and one of his most important tasks is to call our attention to it. However, the author of the *Confessions* not only addresses us as tokens of a type, but also as unique individuals. In doing so, he stands in between the global human situation and the particular modifications it exhibits. The *Confessions* thrusts us into the hyphenated place among the universal and the particular, the past and the future, the community and the individual, and God and the soul, challenging us to listen, not only to what God says to Augustine, but also to what God says to us.

The interaction between God and the soul unfolds within a temporal, spatial, and eternal framework, mobilizing the language of the restless heart as a way of bringing space, time, and eternity together. The relation between time and eternity is expressed most adequately in metaphorical discourse, while the relation between eternity and space requires analogical uses of language for its appropriate articulation. In both cases, figurative discourse is the key for binding God and the soul together.

This pivotal relation involves both unity and separation and expresses itself in creation *ex nihilo,* in the fateful transition from finitude to fallenness, and in the quest for fulfillment that attempts to reestablish peace with God. All these stages of the cosmic drama require figurative discourse for their adequate expression, but they also involve a performative use of language that reflects the dynamism of God, the discord of our fragmented spirits, and the vibrant interaction that can develop between the soul and the one who brings it into existence. Performative discourse is the language of creation, the language of the restless heart, and the language that permits God and the soul to confront one another in the space that opens up between them.

The two strands of our inquiry come together because the primary mode of interaction between God and the soul is linguistic and involves speaking and hearing as its fundamental expression. However important seeing may be, speaking and hearing generate the context in which the ultimate issues of life can be addressed. If these issues are to be dealt with adequately, the language of God and the soul must not only be figurative and performative, but must also be sufficiently intelligible to bring stability to the human situation.

Figurative language points to the mystery of God and to the separation between God and the soul; performative utterances point to the power of God and to the space between the creator and the creature in which they can disclose themselves; and intelligible discourse points to the Word of God, to the self-transcendent structure of consciousness, and to the hope that both God and the soul will have something to say when they meet. In this book, this hope is grounded in Augustine's existential and ecstatic language about God and the soul and by the conviction that its figurative, performative, and intelligible dimensions will enable it to leap across the centuries to speak decisively in the postmodern world.

Augustine stands like a colossus for more than a thousand years, casting his shadow over the development of the Middle Ages. As one of the translators of the *Confessions* reminds us, "every person living in the Western world would be a different person if Augustine had not been or had been different."[5] The story of Augustine's life reveals the secret of its impact: though he is one of the most original philosophers and theologians in the Western tradition, he is also a person in whom powerful feelings, strength of will, and greatness of intellect converge. Augustine is one of the greatest psychologists since Plato, the greatest rhetorician since Cicero, and the greatest Christian thinker before the birth of Thomas Aquinas. In all three domains, the greatness of his soul expresses the complexity of his life, the power of his spirit, and the profundity of his thinking.

The most important fact about Augustine is that he combines philosophy and passion in equal proportions. Yet his passion pours into his philosophy, not to confuse or distort it, but to give it impetus. Augustine not only gives us his thought, but also gives us himself. "He does not skim the truth off the [surface of] experience and give us that"; instead, "he gives it [to us] in the [concrete] context in which he learned it."[6] Augustine's head and heart interpenetrate and sustain one another, and his experience and his thinking are equally important because they express inseparable sides of the same person. Though he presents himself as a rhetorician, a psychologist, and a philosopher with unquenchable passions, what he wants most is truth about God. Augustine seeks the ground of truth as the light in which all other truth exists; and to find it, he not only undertakes a philosophical journey, but also speaks to God from the center of his being.

On more than one occasion, Augustine says that he is not telling the story of his life to inform God about it, but to speak to other men and women in God's presence (5.1.1), (8.1.1), (10.1.1–10.4.6). Though he could scarcely have foreseen the impact that his book would make on future generations, in addressing "that small part of the human race who may come upon these writings," he makes it clear that he wants to bring his readers into the vertical relationship between God and the soul from which he speaks (2.3.5). Augustine's deepest wish for the *Confessions* is that those who read it may understand "what depths there are from which we are to cry unto thee" (2.3.5).

In this book, my way of responding to Augustine's intentions is to retell the story of his journey toward God, to interpret it in terms of the philosophical framework that I am about to introduce, and to indicate how Augustine's development finally brings him to the place where ecstatic encounters with God are possible. As this book unfolds, I will not only present my interpretation of Augustine's journey and my arguments for it, but will also attempt to immerse myself and the reader in Augustine's narrative. Otherwise, the existential dimension of the journey toward God will be compromised, and the first six books of the *Confessions* will be reduced to concrete occasions for mere abstract reflection.

THE FRAMEWORK OF THE ENTERPRISE

Augustine's *Confessions* develops within a three-dimensional framework: the first is temporal, the second spatial, and the third eternal. These dimensions generate three axes along which it moves, and each axis exhibits two orientations that point in opposite directions. The temporal aspect of Augustine's life moves forward and backward; the spatial side of his existence points outward and inward; the eternal horizon in which he lives stretches upward and downward; and when these axes converge, they establish a place where his life and thought unfold, both for himself and for his readers.[7]

The two orientations of Augustine's temporal development are important because they allow him to embrace the future and to recover the past. His life is a sequence of episodes that develops toward a culmination, but he also plunges beneath the flow of his experience in a courageous effort to remember the most significant stages of his psychological, spiritual, and philosophical development. He does this, not because he loves the past or because he is proud of his achievements, but because he wants to remember the sins that separate him from God, and by reliving them, to allow himself to be gathered up from the fragments into which he has fallen (2.1.1). Augustine's recollection of the past and his expectation of the future are ways of finding God, where what he remembers and what he anticipates give him access to what would otherwise remain beyond his grasp.

The spatial side of Augustine's life also points in two directions, not only moving outward toward the cosmos, but also moving inward toward the soul. The story of his life begins with his parents, nurses, friends, and education and moves through crucial stages of his philosophical development. This development permits him to transform the narrow spatial context with which he begins into a way of thinking that gives him access to a larger world. Yet the most significant episodes of his life occur within the depths of his soul, where it is not so much what happens to him, but how he responds to his circumstances that matters. The internal space in which Augustine comes face to face with himself, the marks his interactions with others make on him, and the ways in which these encounters point toward God are the most important elements of his spatial development.

The eternal axis along which Augustine moves makes the interplay between the soul and the ground of its existence possible, pointing upward toward God and pointing downward to his fruitless attempts to flee from God's presence. In the first case, Augustine seeks to bring himself into a positive relation with the source of power that creates and sustains him. In the second, he tries to flee from God in a downward movement that implicates both his will and his intellect. The upward movement is an intellectual ascent with a volitional dimension. By contrast, the flight from God is an intellectual attempt to escape the searching light of truth and a desperate effort to insist on his own willfulness in opposition to the will of God.

An adequate attempt to understand the *Confessions* must move within temporal, spatial, and eternal dimensions simultaneously. The temporal side of the discussion gives us access to Augustine's historical development and to the narrative devices he uses to express it. The spatial aspect of the inquiry allows us to take up the relation between Augustine and his surrounding context and points to the problem of the individual and the community. And the eternal horizon of the enterprise enables us to deal with the existential and the religious components that his journey toward God exemplifies.

The temporal, spatial, and eternal dimensions of the *Confessions* are not only schematic and categorial, but also exhibit a descriptive richness that allows us to approach the text in concrete terms. The temporal aspect of Augustine's life expresses itself in the narrative stages of the book, in its plot and cast of characters, and in the concept of human development that underlies it. The spatial side of his experience points to the problem of the private self and the larger world, to the relation between the individual and the community, and to his attempts to understand the connection between them. Finally, the eternal axis along which he moves leads to the formula that becomes the motto of his life: as he tells us on more than one occasion, "Unless you believe, you shall not understand."[8] This formula allows Augustine to express the spatial and temporal sides of his development from an eternal point of view, to speak to God from the center of his being, and to bridge the otherwise unbridgeable chasm between God and the soul.

In approaching Augustine's narrative as an intersection of temporal, spatial, and eternal dimensions, we can make the temporal aspect of his story accessible by reflecting on the psychological structure that it exhibits. This is possible because Augustine builds the account of his life around an explicit conception of human development, distinguishing six stages in the life of a typical individual: infancy, childhood, adolescence, youthful maturity, adulthood, and old age. Augustine moves through the first three stages of this sequence in Books I–VI of the text; and since he writes the book between the ages of forty-three and forty-seven, what he says about these stages is formulated from the perspective of adulthood.

Augustine also makes a definitive appraisal of the book only two years before his death, placing a stamp of approval on it from the standpoint of old age.[9] On eight occasions in Books I–VI (2.2.4), (2.3.6), (2.6.12), (3.15.27), (4.1.1), (4.16.28), (5.3.3), and (6.11.18), Augustine mentions one of these stages of human development, underscoring his awareness of the importance of chronology in giving us access to the temporal stages of his journey. However, the stages of Augustine's development are not accidental temporal episodes, but exhibit an intelligible structure that allows us to bring his story into relation with the story of us all. He builds the *Confessions* around the stages of creation, fall, conversion, and fulfillment because he believes that his temporal journey displays a logical progression, not only in his own case, but also in the case of Everyman. This allows us to understand it as more than a random sequence of events and to use it as a framework within which we can map our own development.[10]

It is also important to notice that every stage of Augustine's existential development has a social component, permitting us to come to terms with the relation between the individual and the community within which his life unfolds. This communal element points beyond a linear approach to the *Confessions* to the interpersonal dimension that must be acknowledged in any adequate appraisal of the text; and it moves us beyond time to space and to a logic of spatial interaction that cannot be analyzed in temporal terms alone. This logic is dialogical rather than dialectical and is exemplified most clearly in the verbal interaction between Augustine and members of the community with whom he converses. Augustine's concern with language begins with his attempts to communicate in infancy, develops into his preoccupation with becoming a rhetorician, leads to a dialogue between God and the soul, and culminates in metaphorical and analogical discourse that describes the significance of his journey toward God.

As the contemporary psychologist Erik Erickson has suggested, each of the significant stages of a person's life is not only temporal and spatial, but also poses an existential crisis that demands a resolution.[11] This crisis mentality is appropriate to Augustine, for he understands his life as a series of conflicts that he must resolve to become who he is. The crises that define Augustine's development are important, not simply as episodes, but because they allow him to understand and to embrace the meaning of his life. It is here that the stages of his life and the crises to which they point have a bearing on the vertical dimension of his experience.

The resolution of the crises that Augustine undergoes brings him fulfillment in time and space by bringing him into relation with the eternal axis along which he discovers the meaning of his life. Indeed, each stage of his development points beyond history by implicating the meaning of his being. As an infant, Augustine begins to sense that he is what he has been given. This generates hope and expresses itself later as a capacity to embrace a life of faith (1.6.7).[12] In childhood, he learns that he is what he wills to be and that he is what he can imagine (1.8.13), (1.9.14).[13] Later, he discovers that he is what he can learn (1.18.28–29);[14] and when he faces a prolonged identity crisis that begins in adolescence, he finds that he must choose what he is to become (2.3.6–8).[15] Because all these stages point not only to the development of life within a social context, but also to what each stage means, they mobilize Augustine's awareness of the vertical dimension of existence. This leads him from time, to space, to eternity, pointing to the need for all these elements in any adequate approach to the problem of God and the soul.

Though psychological considerations help us understand the temporal, spatial, and eternal dimensions of Augustine's journey, it is not sufficient to deal with them in psychological terms alone. If we are to gain a richer understanding of the framework they generate, the rhetorical facet of each axis must also be taken into account. The temporal aspect of Augustine's rhetorical strategy is exemplified most forcibly in his willingness to emphasize the elements of dissonance in his story in contrast with the continuities that it exemplifies.

Though it is appropriate to follow Neoplatonic commentators in looking for coherence in Augustine's development,[16] his rhetoric underscores the importance of temporal discontinuity as he moves from stage to stage. Floggings by his teachers (1.9.14), stealing pears with adolescent friends (2.4.9), the sudden death of his closest companion (4.4.8), sexual addiction (8.5.10–12), (8.7.17), and a series of professional disappointments bring his temporal development to a standstill. The powerful rhetorician's depiction of these episodes and his explanation of the conditions that make them possible not only allow him to underline the negative elements that interrupt his progress, but also permit his readers to pause in their linear progression through the text. In doing so, we are permitted to brood over the incidents that Augustine depicts and to confront the episodes that bring him face to face with radical discontinuity.

The spatial dimension of Augustine's rhetoric is expressed most clearly in his use of gardens to generate open spaces in his journey toward God. Gardens punctuate the metaphor of a journey with "spatial" moments that often display a dimension of eternal significance. For example, the pear-stealing episode that occurs in an orchard (2.4.9) and that reminds us of the Garden of Eden[17] brings Augustine face to face with the problem of sin, not only as the preference of a lower for a higher good (2.5.11), but also as the enjoyment of a negative act for its own sake (2.7.15), (2.8.16). In this case, Augustine's rhetoric permits him to bring the spatial and eternal dimensions of his journey together in a single episode.

Gardens also play a crucial role in Books of the text that will be discussed in a subsequent book. For example, the place where Augustine is converted to Christianity (8.8.19) is analogous to the garden of Gethsemane;[18] and the garden at the center of the house where Augustine and his mother participate in a shared mystical experience (9.10.23) is analogous to the Paradise they long to enter.[19] In both cases, Augustine stands apart from the temporal flow of his story to participate in a spatial context that gives him access to eternity.[20]

The eternal facet of Augustine's rhetoric is reflected most obviously in the motto that we have considered already. However, his claim that unless we believe, we shall not understand is not simply a label for a method of inquiry, but an attempt to persuade his readers that unless we undertake a journey of faith, we will never achieve the understanding we seek. This familiar phrase is a reflection of Augustine's basic way of thinking, and it propels us beyond ourselves to speak about the ground that creates and sustains us.

If we keep the temporal, the spatial, and the eternal dimensions of the text in view, and if we pay careful attention to the psychological and the rhetorical aspects it displays, we can approach Books I–VI of the *Confessions* in the following way. First, we can understand them as important parts of the life story of its author that develops in temporal stages, sustained by the community and subject to unpredictable incursions that interrupt the continuity of its flow. As his narrative unfolds, commitment to his friends brings the temporality of Augustine's experience into relation with a spatial community, and his developing orientation toward what lies beyond space and time gives his life eternal significance. Second, we can notice how Augustine acquires technical tools that enable him to become a psychologist, a rhetorician, a philosopher, and a theologian. The first persona allows him to give a profound analysis of himself; the second helps him persuade his readers to share his journey; the third makes it possible for him to generate a comprehensive theoretical framework within which his life unfolds; and the fourth permits him to inquire about the role God plays in his temporal, spatial, and eternal development. Finally, we can retrace Augustine's discovery that however important the intellect may be, the ultimate issues of life are problems of the will and of the intersection of the will and the intellect in a sustained attempt to respond to the human predicament. If we understand this, we might also come to recognize the fact that Augustine is not simply an existential traveler, a detached speculative thinker, or a self-fashioning and desiring subject, but more than anything, a decentered self in search of the language of redemption—a language that will permit him to express himself in experiential and reflective terms simultaneously.

THE CENTRALITY OF GOD AND THE SOUL

On more than one occasion, Augustine tells us that God and the soul are the central themes of his philosophical reflections. This is especially clear in the early formulation of his views in the *Soliloquies*—a book he writes soon after his conversion. In this book, Reason asks Augustine, "What do you wish to know?" When he answers that he wants to know God and the soul, and when his interlocutor asks, "Nothing more?" Augustine replies decisively, "Nothing whatever."[21] In this single sentence, the author identifies the crucial issues around which his experiences and reflections turn.

Important ambiguities in Augustine's approach to these questions are visible in this early text, and both these and related ambiguities continue to surface in his later writings. The title of the *Soliloquies* suggests that it is a monologue, but it unfolds as a dialogue between Augustine and Reason. Near the end of his life, Augustine complicates the situation by saying that the book is "written as a dialogue between myself and Reason, as if there were two of us present, though actually I was alone."[22] Yet even a casual examination of the text reveals that it begins in a much more subtle and interesting way. Writing when he is recovering from his last feverish days as a professor of rhetoric, Augustine tells us that he has been trying to understand himself and to discover the highest good to which he ought to commit himself. Then he says, "Suddenly someone spoke to me, whether it was myself or someone else from without or from within I know not. Indeed, to know that is my main endeavor."[23] Does the voice to which Augustine responds speak from his heart or from beyond his consciousness? Is the richest form of community the dialogue of the soul with itself, or do the *Soliloquies* point to a conversation in which two interlocutors must be distinguished? The voice of Reason might simply be Augustine's better self; but it might also be the voice of God, speaking from within or without. As Augustine says, "to know that is my main endeavor."

Soon after he becomes Bishop of Hippo, Augustine focuses his attention on the problem of God and the soul and on the language appropriate to it by moving in a more personal and poignant direction. The text in which he does this is the *locus classicus* of his treatment of these issues, and it approaches them from both existential and reflective perspectives. The first six books of the *Confessions* are saturated with prayers and biblical quotations; they overflow with autobiographical sketches and with rhetorical questions; and they focus on theoretical issues, the most important of which are the nature of God and the problem of evil.[24] In all these ways, Augustine's text fills the middle ground between God and the soul where the temporal, spatial, and eternal dimensions of his life intersect.

Nevertheless, a cluster of ambiguities is present even in Augustine's richest treatment of the relation between God and the soul; and two of these ambiguities surface in his perplexing attitude toward nature. When the author of the *Confessions* turns his attention to the problem of making access to God, he first turns outward toward the world, then turns inward toward the soul, and finally turns upward toward God.[25] Nature is present as a content of consciousness, and Augustine never hesitates to affirm its independent existence. Yet he begins with nature as a domain of symbols that points beyond itself toward God; and he moves toward God through sensation, memory, and reason as a hierarchy of stages that leads to truth as a transcendent standard of judgment (10.6.8). This generates an ambiguity about whether the symbolic status of nature is more important than its independent existence in the soul's relentless quest for wisdom. If it is, nature as an independent realm might seem to drop away as a significant element in Augustine's reflections, and the soul's awareness of nature would become the first stage in the spiritual journey that gives him access to God.

A related ambiguity about the status of nature arises from Augustine's commitment to the doctrine of creation *ex nihilo*. According to this doctrine, God creates the soul, the body, and the world as really distinct from himself, where they are not parts of something larger, but stand over against their creator as irreducible elements of the real order.[26] This suggests that nature does not collapse into the source from which it emerges, but comprises a domain of its own whose symbolic richness Augustine is willing to acknowledge. This makes it possible for him to say that the whole creation praises God without ceasing and that the soul climbs toward its creator by leaning on the things he has made (5.1.1). However, we still might wonder whether the independence of nature is primary or whether the symbolic relation between nature and its source is fundamental. Augustine's repeated claims that God creates the world *ex nihilo* (12.3.3), (12.7.7), (12.8.8) suggest the first, while his equally important claims that nature is a cluster of symbols for God suggest the second (7.10.16), (13.9.10), (13.19.28).

If we return to Augustine's claim that the only problem that concerns him is the relation between God and the soul, the awareness of nature and its symbolic status appear to be the most important factors to consider. The journey of the soul toward God is mediated by its awareness of nature, and it begins with the natural order as a dependent realm of symbols that gives it access to its creative ground. On the other hand, since Augustine believes that God creates the world *ex nihilo*, the created product should be expected to play an important role in Augustine's reflections about the relation between God and the soul. Indeed, the relative independence of the soul is a necessary condition for the freedom with which it can preserve its integrity.

Another important ambiguity in the *Confessions* emerges from Augustine's complicated attitude toward the body as one of the most significant aspects of the natural order. If the only problem with which he is concerned is the relation between God and the soul, and if God creates both the soul and the body and says that they are good, how does Augustine's preoccupation with God and the soul take the bodily dimension of creation into account? Were he simply a Neoplatonist, it would be appropriate for him to say that the body is a prison house and that one of our most important moral, religious, and philosophical tasks is to free the soul from its bodily entanglements.[27] Yet in spite of attempts to reduce Augustine to his Neoplatonic dimension, the created goodness of the entire person makes it impossible for him to move in this direction for long. Somehow, Augustine must remain focused on the relation between God and the soul without denying the goodness of embodied existence to which the Christian faith commits him. His attempts to do this lead to some of the most difficult problems with which he tries to come to grips in the *Confessions*.

On more than one occasion Augustine says that a human being is a composite of a soul and a body and that an individual is a complex entity that can be analyzed into parts.[28] Second, he claims that the soul is primary, that the body is secondary, and that the soul rules the body through the will.[29] Finally, he says that the will can become willful and that when this occurs, the corrupted soul corrupts the body.[30] A crucial part of Augustine's Neoplatonic legacy is his belief that though the soul can act on the body, while the body can never act on the soul. This aspect of his position surfaces most clearly in his theory of sensation, according to which the soul uses the organs of sensation to see, hear, touch, taste, and smell without requiring any reciprocal action of the body on the soul.[31]

One of the clearest places where linguistic subtlety is required is in framing an adequate account of Augustine's complex attitude toward sexuality. According to popular misconceptions of his thought, he is preoccupied with this issue because he believes that the soul is inherently good and that the body is evil—sharing this assumption with his Manichaean opponents, the Stoic rhetorician who converts him to the love of wisdom, and the Neoplatonic teachers who attempt to persuade him to embrace their metaphysical system. To be sure, Augustine claims that sexual discord is a clear expression of the negative effects of the disordered soul on the body (8.5.10). This suggests that sexual activity is frequently an expression of willfulness and apparently confirms the Neoplatonic distinction between the inherent goodness of the soul and the negative orientation that precipitates its fall into the body.

However, careful reflection should prevent us from accepting this explanation of Augustine's views about the issue. The best explanation for his preoccupation with sexuality is not that he regards it as evil, but that he sees it as an expression of the most severe addiction from which he and many others suffer (8.11.25–26). When Augustine speaks about loving the world as fornication against God (1.13.21), he is describing a problem of spiritual attachment, where what is illegitimate about it is that it expresses an infinite attachment to something finite rather than a (finite↑infinite) attachment to the infinite richness of God.[32] The first kind of attachment is illegitimate, not because it is sexual, but because it places infinite demands on something finite that it can never satisfy. By contrast, the second kind of attachment can never be misdirected because God is infinite, because he can bear the infinite demands we make on him, and because he can lead us beyond other contents of cognition to the infinite richness of his own nature. Though it is true that the ground of our existence can only be found in the present, it is equally clear that only idols can be fully present to consciousness. As Augustine expresses the point, God is "more inward than my inmost self, and higher than my highest reach" (3.6.11). This interplay between immanence and transcendence frustrates illegitimate attachment, which is the target of Augustine's diatribes against fornication.

The second point to notice is that if unregulated sexual activity is a serious problem for Augustine, this fact points to a more intimate relation between the soul and the body than the standard account of Augustine's epistemology suggests. Can Augustine be redeemed from sexual addiction by repudiating the body, or will it not also be necessary for his body to be transformed for salvation to occur? If the soul leaves the body and is never reunited with it as the Neoplatonist maintains, this does not cancel the sin it could not have committed without being embodied. Rather, it simply prevents sins of the same kind from occurring in eternity. Small wonder that Augustine hints at the need for the resurrection of the body when he claims that the soul that has been following the body must be converted so the body can follow the soul (4.11.17). This can occur, not through the metaphysical separation of two parts of the individual, but through the resurrection of the body, where the transformed body is set free from the chains in which both the soul and the body have become entangled.[33]

Finally, the figurative sensory language Augustine uses in reference to the soul is an epistemic indication that there is a greater unity between the soul and the body than might otherwise have been expected. In the words of an analytical philosopher who would have never thought to use them with reference to Augustine, there is a semantical solution to the problem of the soul and the body that becomes a pervasive theme in the *Confessions*.[34] Augustine's complex semantics not only presupposes that the person is a composite of a soul and a body, but also incorporates both metaphorical and analogical discourse as essential elements.[35] Metaphors bind the soul and the body together in an open-ended unity, while equally fundamental analogies hold them apart (4.10.15–4.11.16), (7.15.21), (11.30.40). Indeed, the hyphen that connects the soul and the body, the interplay between them to which metaphors and analogies call our attention, and our linguistic capacity to move back and forth between these two dimensions of the person require figurative discourse as an irreducible element. Though Augustine is concerned primarily with the problem of God and the soul and with the language appropriate to it, one of our central tasks will be to show how figurative language also gives him access to the problematic relation between the soul and the body.

Augustine's journey toward God unfolds within a temporal, spatial, and eternal framework; presupposes the centrality of the relation between God and the soul; and points to the linguistic dimension of the problems before us. Yet what more should we say about the linguistic pathway that the author traverses in binding God and the soul together and about the figurative uses of language that make it possible for him to do so? These questions are important, not only because they focus on the language of God and the soul, but also because they call our attention to speaking and hearing as primordial phenomena.

One of the most important things to notice about Augustine's use of language is that he often employs sensory metaphors to point beyond the fragmentation of time toward the stability of eternity (4.10.15–4.11.16), (7.15.21), (11.30.40). In doing so, he establishes a linguistic pattern that ties language about God to sense perception rather than the transcendental categories usually preferred by the scholastics. As his frequent reliance on the category of substance and on the concepts of being and truth suggest, Augustine is not indifferent to the power of categorial and transcendental discourse.[36] However, in following the Platonic rather than the Aristotelian tradition, he is aware that the richest language about God is rooted in the senses, linking the lowest level of cognition to the highest place the soul can reach in its efforts to give an adequate description of eternity.[37] In this coincidence of opposites, the depths of experience meet the heights of eternity, and the language of God and the soul becomes the language of the heart.

Augustine follows the Platonic tradition by emphasizing the importance of visual metaphors. However, only a few have noticed that auditory images are equally important in his account of the relation between God and the soul.[38] This is evident even in his early book about the freedom of the will, where Augustine places seeing and hearing on the same level because they are the only senses for which the corresponding object is accessible to everyone who seeks it.[39] Publicity is one of the most important marks of truth, and the fact that seeing and hearing open out on a public world, and on the creative source to which it points, suggests that both of them are privileged modes of access to what lies beyond us.[40]

Augustine uses auditory images throughout his writings, but their crucial role in his search for God is especially evident in the *Confessions*. It is tempting to assume that the predominance of auditory language in Augustine's most well-known book derives exclusively from his numerous quotations from the Psalms. Yet he uses auditory symbols, not only when he echoes the words of the Bible, but also when he speaks in his own voice.[41] The problem is not whether auditory images saturate the *Confessions*, but how we are to relate them to the more familiar visual metaphors that are so clearly present there. Indeed, the problem of relating visual and auditory ways of speaking is a linguistic version of how to connect Neoplatonism and Christianity in Augustine's thinking.

The Neoplatonic path to God depends on visual metaphors and attempts to unify God and the soul, while Augustine's Christian conversion allows him to respond to the voice of God with the voice of his heart. Augustine uses visual metaphors to express the significant role of the intellect in the search for God (7.17.23), (10.5.7), (10.23.33). He also begs God not to hide his face from him and says, "Even if I die, let me see thy face lest I die" (1.5.5). Yet the great rhetorician uses equally powerful auditory symbols to express the longing of his soul for transformation. First he asks, "Let me learn from thee, who art Truth, and put the ear of my heart to thy mouth" (4.5.10). Then he writes: "Accept this sacrifice of my confessions from the hand of my tongue. Thou didst form it and hast prompted it to praise thy name" (5.1.1). Finally, he implores God to "trim away" all "rashness and lying" from his lips, to harken to his soul, and to "hear it crying from the depths" (11.2.3).

We can understand the story of Augustine's life most adequately by reading it aloud rather than by moving our eyes from place to place along a printed page. This way of proceeding allows the cadences of his discourse to resonate in our ears, reflecting the original linguistic situation in which he speaks, and mirroring the linguistic interaction between God and the soul to which he responds. The richness of Augustine's rhetoric and the power of his thinking moves us most when we hear him speaking; the oral culture in which he lives and the circumstances in which he dictates the *Confessions*[42] come to life as we listen to his story; and the conversation between God and his soul becomes accessible to us when we repeat the words he speaks and hears as he enters God's presence. The *Confessions* is not a theoretical account about God that Augustine formulates from a distance, for he knows that God has spoken to him directly and that he must respond to the voice of his creator from the center of his being. The response he makes to what he hears presupposes two kinds of word: on the one hand, it is the intelligible structure of the world that makes his reflections about God and the soul possible; on the other hand, it is an act of speaking in which God reveals himself to Augustine's fragmented heart.

The *Confessions* is a sequence of acts of speaking, some of which are divine and some of which are human. Augustine says, "Speak that I may hear" (1.5.5) but he also exclaims, "Who shall bring me to rest in thee? Have mercy that I may speak" (1.5.5). The author of the *Confessions* responds to the voice of God not only by listening to what it says, but also by presenting himself to God as a person who has something to say. What sets human beings apart from other creatures is their capacity to transcend their finitude. One of the most important ways in which this dimension of Augustine's nature expresses itself is the forcefulness with which he responds to the utterances of God. The resulting conversation allows him to plumb the depths of creation, to confront the human predicament, to embrace the new creation that brings reconciliation to his soul, and to anticipate the resurrection in which he will not only see God, but will also be like the incarnated word that makes this vision possible.

PROBLEMS OF ACCESS TO THE TEXT

With the framework for interpreting the first six Books of the *Confessions* before us, and with the theme of God and the soul at the center of our attention, several important problems about Augustine's enterprise require special consideration. The first pertains to the attitudes of typical readers to Augustine's journey toward God; the second concerns the truth of what Augustine has written; and the third focuses on the relevance of the *Confessions* to the postmodern predicament. Let us consider each of these issues in turn.

The most important thing to say about our initial attitude toward the text is that we are perhaps too close to what Augustine has written or too far away from it. On the one hand, we have heard his story before and believe we understand it without further reflection; on the other hand, his problems are unfamiliar or offensive, turning us away from them toward other questions that seem to be more pressing or congenial. As a consequence, a radical opposition emerges between positive and negative attitudes in almost any audience that Augustine addresses. When we read the *Confessions* for the first time, read it again because we know that it has an indispensable place in the Western tradition, or return to it with philosophical and theological maturity, it either arouses or irritates us by bringing us face to face with the problem of God and the soul.

Augustine deals with this problem by finding a middle ground between the divine and human realms and by speaking from it. In the process, he challenges his readers to find a place of their own between pious fascination and intellectual antagonism. The writer of the *Confessions* speaks in the first person singular; he does not simply talk about God, but addresses him directly; and when he speaks about the stages of his life, he asks us not only to understand what he means, but also to feel what he feels. Augustine encourages his readers to move back and forth between the immediacy of his experience and his attempts to describe it as a series of intelligible stages, making it possible for us to participate in the journey he undertakes at both experiential and reflective levels.

When we turn to the problem of the truth of what Augustine has written, we find a delicate interplay between memory, reconstruction, and the vertical dimension of experience that sustains his journey. The episodes Augustine recounts presuppose the power of his memory to recover the incidents he has experienced. To this extent, his book is a recollection of previous events rather than a reconstruction of them and purports to be true in a relatively conventional sense. On the other hand, Augustine describes only some of the circumstances of his life, restricts himself to crucial episodes, and builds his story with such rhetorical power that the result is an account of a unified life. In this respect, the *Confessions* is a reconstruction rather than a recollection.

It is also important to notice that the events Augustine describes are not merely episodic. Rather, they are what they are and mean what they mean because they are expressions of the providential hand of God, weaving the stages of his life into a pattern. The relations among recollection, reconstruction, and the activity of God are interwoven in the text; the receptive and creative powers of the soul point to a ground that gives them ultimate significance; and the dimension of depth that lies beyond history and interpretation binds them together and holds them apart. When this occurs, God discloses himself to the rational agents he creates, demands an authentic response from those who become aware of his presence, and points to the possibility of a truthful relationship with his creatures within the vertical place his creation of the world establishes. In this sacred space, truth as disclosure illuminates the intellect, truth as authentic existence mobilizes the will, and truth as correspondence brings the will and the intellect together into an imagistic relation with God.

With the problem of our attitude toward the text and the problem of the truth of what Augustine has written in the background, the final problem we must face is to indicate how a contemporary reader can gain access to a text saturated in the thought forms of the late Roman Empire. It is easy to assume that the problems Augustine discusses are unfruitful ways of engaging in philosophical reflection; for whatever else may be said about the contemporary situation, it is clear that God and the soul no longer establish the context in which most of us live. Language is the new horizon for philosophical inquiry, and most philosophers have turned away from the problem of God and the soul toward the world reconstrued as a text. Though this "text" calls for interpretation, it is more a construction than a discovery; and it can be deconstructed only because an act of construction generates it.

If the world is a text, it is not a book written by someone who exercises authorial control over it; and it is not a book to be deciphered by anyone who can expect to encompass it. The shift toward language presupposes that the autonomous self of modern philosophy has been decentered, that the text with which we are confronted is as much absent as present, and that the meaning we can extract from the *Confessions* is not grounded by an interplay between signifier and signified that would give our approach to Augustine's intentions semantical stability. As a consequence, any contemporary approach to the *Confessions* faces a cluster of difficult questions: How can we interpret a text of which neither the author nor the reader is the master? How can we acknowledge the fact that the text hides as much as it reveals? And how can we appraise Augustine's preoccupation with God and the soul without presupposing that what he says depends on a referential connection between signified and signifier that anchors his enterprise?

A careful reading of the *Confessions* points to several significant features about Augustine's use of language that permit him to answer these questions, and by doing so, to address contemporary readers. First, he uses language to address his readers directly, speaking from his own fragmentation to ours and acknowledging that neither he nor his readers can ever be in complete control of what we say or do. Second, his text is saturated with figurative discourse because he knows that both God and the soul are always present and absent, forcing him to stretch language to the breaking point to convey hints and suggestions about their meaning and proper relationship. Finally, he uses allegorical interpretation as a way of indicating that even God and the City to which he often calls our attention never anchor our lives univocally. Instead, they open us up to the radical otherness of what will always lie beyond us, point to the infinite richness of our origins, and resist reduction to static contents of consciousness that would be incompatible with the ecstatic dimension of experience and reflection upon which Augustine's enterprise depends.

As we approach the *Confessions*, we can understand Augustine's language from a descriptive point of view, watching his drama unfold before us as if we were spectators. Commentators often deal with the *Confessions* in this way, placing the text in quotation marks and insisting on preserving a proper measure of theoretical detachment. This is appropriate in a scholarly analysis of the book, for a bracketing device is necessary if we are to consider Augustine's way of understanding God and the soul as one approach among others. However, the author of the *Confessions* writes without quotation marks, not simply because Latin does not have such a device, but because his language resonates with figurative and performative richness. Augustine does not give us a theory about God, but God himself; he does not provide a theoretical account of the soul, but points to its need for deliverance; and he does not provide a systematic account of the relation between God and soul, but gives us a linguistic pathway that permits us to approach it only through figurative discourse. The most serious question about the text is the proper relation between the scholarly discussion of Augustine's intentions and their figurative and performative dimensions.

We might choose to maintain our academic distance, discussing the book in merely abstract terms. However, the quotation marks we place around the text might drop away, asking us to face the philosophical and religious implications of Augustine's life and thought directly. This is the existential and reflective risk one must take in any serious effort to study the *Confessions*. Since Augustine's deepest problem is not cognitive, but personal, a merely theoretical response to his fragmented condition is inappropriate. Our central questions become: What power can make the quotation marks fall away, and what will allow us to respond to Augustine's journey as active participants? Adequate answers can be found only if God speaks again in the words through which he speaks to Augustine, shattering our attempts to control our destiny, hiding in the moments in which he reveals himself, and challenging us to turn away from attempts to capture what is ultimate by using language as a tool to reduce it to a stable content of consciousness.

I agree with Kenneth Burke's suggestion that language is the key to the *Confessions*. However, Burke is wrong when he insists that we can leave Augustine's language about God in quotation marks and that we can approach it from a rhetorical point of view that ignores the existential claims it makes on us.[43] Since the most persuasive aspect of the text is its evocative and performative dimensions, my book about it does not focus simply on the typically philosophical aspects of Augustine's undertaking, but draws experience, reflection, and evocative discourse into an account of the relation between God and the soul that can never be frozen into a cluster of doctrines. Augustine breaks beyond the web of words to give us access to the presence and absence of God; and I will try to show how he does this by interpreting the *Confessions* in an Augustinian spirit.

In Books I–VI, Augustine is both a sinner and a saint; but he is also a writer who confesses his sins and praises God as the source of redemption. In the process, he plunges beneath the contrast between two sides of his consciousness: the first is the nonverbal dimension of feeling and intuition; the second is the verbal dimension of thinking and articulation. Augustine feels his predicament before he can describe it, but his description of it also captures its richness without sacrificing the clarity of detailed and disciplined reflection. He brings these two dimensions of his life together by finding a dynamic way of speaking about God and the soul and by embracing figurative, performative, and intelligible discourse about their relationship. The figurative dimension points to the transcendence of God, the performative dimension expresses the activity of God, and the intelligible dimension reflects the immanence of God.

As Augustine binds the two sides of his consciousness together, he leads us toward eternity; and as his journey begins to reach its culmination, the spatial and temporal interaction between the two aspects of himself points to a place where they meet. In a physiological formulation, it is the corpus callosum; in religious language, it is the Holy of Holies; and in philosophical terms, it is the Place of places. This Place is first a place of silence, then a place of power, and finally a place of speech; and as these facets of it interpenetrate, the mystery of our origins, the power of their self-expression, and the word that permits us to speak about them intersect. In the first six books of the *Confessions*, Augustine moves from the enigma of his origins, through his resistance to education in childhood, to the turmoil of an emerging adolescent; but he also begins to enter the place where the mystery, the power, and the intelligibility of God converge. If we choose to follow him there, we will face the problem of God and the soul; enter the temporal, spatial, and eternal matrix that gives us access to it; and hear the language of the heart that places us at the center of Augustine's restless journey toward God.

1

Infancy, Childhood, and Adolescence
From Will to Willfulness (Books I–II)

Augustine's *Confessions* exhibits an interplay between two competing dimensions: on the one hand, the dynamism of creation and a desire to return to his origins motivates his inquiry; on the other hand, a radical discontinuity separates him from God and makes his longing for peace problematic. A corresponding interaction between desire and discontinuity pervades his experience. Though he is an image of God, original sin separates him from his sustaining ground; and though he longs to recover his origins, he turns away from them to embrace a world of his own. A conflict emerges from these competing orientations that points to two directions in which Augustine develops: the first moves from fragmentation to unity, and the second contracts into itself and disintegrates.

The author implicates his readers in his inquiry by immersing us in the dynamism of the text, by focusing on his origins, childhood, and education, and by analyzing an adolescent pear-stealing episode in which he falls away from God to become a negative reflection of omnipotence. In all these cases, a confrontation surfaces between will and willfulness that specifies the more general contrast between desire and discontinuity. Augustine's will expresses a desire for peace that points beyond itself toward God, but his willfulness generates a separation from God that causes him to turn away from the center of his being.

In Books I and II, Augustine binds his experience and his capacity for philosophical reflection together by giving equal weight to both dimensions of his nature. This allows him to move back and forth among the stages of infancy, childhood, and adolescence and a penetrating analysis of their

21

significance, exploring the relations between the individual and the community, and reflecting on his desire to plunge beneath the spatial and temporal dimensions of his experience in a restless attempt to escape from God. As these first two Books unfold, Augustine moves through determinate stages of temporal and spatial development; but he also falls along the vertical axis of experience from original innocence into an abyss from which he is unable to extricate himself. After a brief consideration of the framework that the author develops for understanding his own enterprise, we shall turn to the pivotal episodes he relates and to his reflections on their religious and philosophical significance.

THE DYNAMISM OF THE TEXT (1.1.1–1.5.6)

The *Confessions* begins with its own introduction. Like Virgil's *Aeneid,* where the opening lines introduce the entire text rather than the first book,[1] and like the *Divine Comedy,* where the first Canto introduces the text as a whole rather than its first part,[2] Augustine's first five chapters are intended to give us access to his comprehensive intentions. It is tempting to pass over these chapters in silence by turning directly to Augustine's account of his infancy, but doing so misses the opportunity to allow the author to speak for himself by expressing his basic intentions. The greatest rhetorician since Cicero should be expected to choose the pathway into his *Confessions* carefully, and our first interpretive task should be to understand how he does this.

Augustine's introductory remarks point to the dynamism of the text rather than to the abstract philosophical structure that undergirds it. This is not to say that he is indifferent to systematic considerations, but to suggest that his fundamental objective is to undertake a journey that leads to dynamic and transforming interaction between God and the soul. Augustine begins with the dynamism of God, the dynamism of praise, the dynamism of sin, and the dynamism of the restless heart; moves to faith seeking understanding as the basic pattern of his inquiry; embraces the power of reflection by asking rhetorical questions about the relation between God and the soul; uses paradoxical adjectives to point to a dynamic dimension in the nature of God; and prays that the transforming activity of God will enlarge and restore the "house of his soul" (1.5.6). In all these ways, he seeks the middle ground between God and the soul where a dynamic interplay between them can occur.

The first sentence of the book calls our attention to the greatness of God: "You are great, O Lord, and greatly to be praised; great is your power, and to your wisdom there is no limit" (1.1.1). Yet having begun with God, Augustine also begins with us by claiming that though we are only a part of creation, we desire to transcend our place in nature by praising our creator.

The author tells us that human beings, both individually and collectively, wish to rise beyond our limitations and to praise the one who has brought us into existence; and he says that we desire to do this in spite of our sin and in spite of the mortality that results from it. As Augustine expresses the point in the most memorable sentence in the book: "You have made us for yourself, and our heart is restless until it rests in you" (1.1.1).

The restless heart expresses a longing for God that binds individuals together into a community and mobilizes us to reach beyond ourselves to what will always remain beyond our grasp. However, the passion that Augustine shares with his readers reflects an initial contrast between Neoplatonic and biblical strands in his thinking. This apparent opposition expresses itself when he wonders whether he should first invoke God or praise him, and whether he should first know him or call on him. Like a typical Neoplatonist, Augustine suggests that he cannot invoke a being that he does not know, and that unless he knows him, he might invoke him as other than he is. On the other hand, he considers the possibility that he must call on God in order to know him, where calling on God is a way of reaching out toward him in an act of self-transcendence. In this case, calling on God would be prior to knowing him, at least in some sense of this considerably elastic expression (1.1.1).

At this stage of his inquiry, Augustine remembers Paul's questions, "How shall they call on him in whom they have not believed? Or how shall they believe without a preacher?"[3] These questions seem to suggest that faith is a way of knowing God, where calling on God presupposes knowing him in this fideistic sense of the term. In this case, the knowledge of God is prior to the search for understanding, where knowledge (*scire*) of God and faith (*credere*) in God are identical, at least at the outset.[4] Yet even if this should prove to be the case, the Neoplatonic and the biblical strands in Augustine's thinking still seem to diverge on the issue before us: in the first case, the author has cognitive access to the concept of God before he can believe in, call for, or search for him; in the second, his quest for a knowledge of God presupposes faith in him, where hearing someone speak on his behalf mediates the relation between them.

Despite initial appearances, Augustine is not forced to choose between beginning with knowledge and beginning with faith; and this is not due to the fact that faith itself may be a way of knowing God. As the *Confessions* unfolds, Augustine finds a way of embedding the Neoplatonic path of recollection within the biblical path of faith. Since we are made in the image of God, epistemic access to God is presupposed by the soul's awareness of its own nature. Yet since the transformation of the will requires a reorientation of the person for which the intellect is a necessary but not a sufficient condition, Augustine subordinates the intellect to the will by claiming that he will seek and call on God in the faith that God has given him. Thus he concludes the first paragraph of the text, not by mentioning the natural knowledge of God, but by referring to the speaking word that injects itself into history, and by suggesting that he makes access to it, not through recollection, but by listening to Ambrose and Paul, the Neoplatonic bishop and the Christian theologian who are preachers.[5]

Against the background of a vague awareness of the nature of God, Augustine begins with the incarnation as the spoken word of God, turns to preaching as the verbal expression of its existential significance, and embraces hearing as the way in which preaching about the divine word becomes accessible. Though faith presupposes the natural knowledge of God, it also rests on the incarnation, and on preaching and hearing as ways of access to him; calling and seeking are the mediating links that lead to understanding; and understanding emerges as the final step in a progression from hearing and believing, to calling and seeking, to finding and praising the one with whom we begin. In this case, knowledge is not simply identical with the natural knowledge of God (*scire*), or with faith (*credere*) as the knowledge presupposed by our search for him, but with the understanding (*intellegere*) that results from our attempt to comprehend the one we seek. At the beginning of Augustine's attempt to do this, we hear about the incarnation in which God speaks to his fragmented heart; at the end, we hear about a song of praise in which his knowledge of God can begin to celebrate its consummation.

In the auditory space defined by the beginning and the end of his journey toward God, Augustine expands the scope of his inquiry by developing the tensions that arise when we call on God; and he does this by asking questions about the relation between God and the soul, the paradoxical nature of which places us at the center of reflective excitation. The dynamism of creation and desire and the emergence of faith seeking understanding issue in reflective tension, and this tension reveals itself most clearly when the author moves beyond questions about the priority of faith and knowledge to unanswerable questions about the relation between God and the soul. The questions he asks put our souls in motion; and in doing so, they invite us to participate in the perplexity generated by pondering the impenetrable mystery of God, who not only creates heaven and earth, but also establishes a reflective interplay between God and the soul into which Augustine wishes to lead us.

The author of the *Confessions* wonders why we should call God into ourselves where there is not enough room for him to live. Suppose the creator responds to our call; suppose he appears; suppose his answer is a way of being present. How could we be sufficiently rich to contain the ground of our existence? What happens to the center of the soul if God reveals himself to the restless heart? If he discloses himself and appears within it, would the finite container that seeks to contain him explode? Everything God creates has some capacity to receive him. Yet if God is present in us because he is present in everything else, why should we call on him when he is present already? Within the middle ground between God and the soul, Augustine's disorientation pushes him to the limits of reflection; and he exclaims in desperation, "I am not now in hell, yet you are even there. For 'If I descend into hell, you are present' " (1.2.2). Augustine cries for redemption out of the depths of his soul; but if wherever he goes God is present already, why does he continue to call? Once more, the philosopher asks a paradoxical question only to leave it unanswered.

We might try to resolve these perplexities by suggesting that God is not so much in us as we in God. Yet Augustine remains unsatisfied with a theoretical answer to his paradoxical questions and continues to press them home with relentless intensity: "If we live in God, why do we call him to come to us?" "From whence can he come?" "Where do we stand when we call?" "And why is it not enough to exist in God instead of calling him into us?" (1.2.2). The philosopher who suggests that to be is to be in God has no easy answers to these questions.

Augustine faces these problems by transcending the part-whole framework presupposed by his earlier questions and by embracing a more dynamic conception of the relation between God and the soul than the concepts of whole and part can express.[6] Though he knows that we exist "in" God, he also knows that we have turned away from our creator and that we must call to God from the depths of our fallen predicament. As a consequence, he suggests that God and the soul are related to one another as dynamic centers of power that often move in radically different directions. This allows him to indicate that the *orientation* of the soul matters more than the place of the soul within a larger context. Our "place" in relation to God is our orientation toward him, where being close to God is turning toward him in faith, and being far away from him is turning away from him in disobedience.[7] Augustine also calls our attention to the limitations of the concept of place in describing our relation to God by pointing to the fact that there is more reality in God than any finite context can contain, and by insisting that God is not only greater than we are, but also present and absent at the same time. In this way, he suggests that the concept of omnipresence subverts the category of mutual containment as a literal conception and points to the need for a flexible mode of discourse to describe the relation between God and the soul (1.2.2).

To express the dynamism of God and the omnipresence to which it points, Augustine resorts to figurative discourse, claiming that the vessels God fills do not contain him, and that even if they break, he does not pour out. When God pours himself out, he does not descend, but lifts us up. God does not scatter himself, but gathers us together. Thus, the relation between

God and the soul is richer than a literal conception of the relation between a part and a whole, pointing to the omnipresence of God and to the figurative discourse necessary to speak about it (1.3.3).

Some familiar Parmenidean questions underscore Augustine's paradoxical conception of the relation between God and the soul: When God fills all things, does he fill them with his whole being? Do singular things contain God singly? And do larger things contain more of him and smaller things less? (1.3.3) Augustine tries to answer these questions, but even here his answers lead to a further perplexity: Is it not rather that you are wholly present everywhere, yet in such a way that nothing contains you wholly? This pivotal question undermines a literal conception of the part-whole relation between God and the soul, pointing to the irreducible transcendence of God and to the linguistic flexibility that is required to understand the relation between God and what he has created. In doing so, it moves beyond univocal discourse, exploding the concept of place as a way of locating God, and moving toward a more vibrant account of the interplay between God and the soul than conventional expressions of this relation permit (1.3.3).

God is wholly present everywhere, but nothing can contain him wholly. When we attempt to speak about our relationship with God, something always slips through and moves beyond the containment relation. It is this something to which Augustine points. God frustrates our attempts to capture him because he is too close to our hearts for us to hold him at a distance and because he is too far from our understanding for him to become a determinate content of cognition. As we stand in the middle ground between God and the soul and seek to respond to his voice, we do not find unequivocal answers to theoretical questions. Rather, we are drawn into a persistent activity of questioning that expresses the reflective dimension of our restless hearts and that points beyond us to the omnipresent being whose dynamism permits it to be present and absent at the same time.

The dynamism of faith seeking understanding reflects the dynamism of the nature of God, and Augustine expresses the dynamism of his creator by attributing paradoxical adjectives to him: "[God is] most merciful and most just; most hidden and most present; most beautiful and most strong; stable and incomprehensible; unchangeable, yet changing all things" (1.4.4). He loves, but without passion. He is jealous, but free from care. He is angry, but remains serene. He changes his ways, but leaves his plans in tact. He recovers what he has never lost; owes men nothing, but pays them as if he were in debt; and when he cancels debts, he loses nothing (1.4.4).

No doubt, Augustine chooses many of these adjectives to perplex and irritate his Manichaean critics. How can God be jealous, angry, change his ways, and cancel his debts as if he owes us something? These are attributes of the Old Testament deity that a sophisticated Manichaean reader would surely repudiate.[8] Yet in claiming that God changes his ways, but leaves his plans in tact, the resourceful rhetorician prepares the way for a distinction in Book III between the permanence of justice and the variability of custom that undermines Manichaean objections to the behavior of the Old Testament patriarchs (3.7.12–3.9.17). By placing perplexing characteristics of God in opposition to others that negate them, he also begins to subvert Manichaean literalism, affirming but pointing beyond determinate attributes of God to the mystery and the majesty of the One who sustains him.

The author of the *Confessions* cannot plumb the depths of the relationship between God and the soul by speaking univocally; and he knows that God must have mercy on him if he is to continue to speak, however inadequate his attempts to do so may be. First he exclaims, "Have pity on me, so that I may speak"; and then he cries, " 'Say to my soul: I am your salvation.' Say this, so that I may hear you" (1.5.5). Both God and the soul have roles to play in the drama unfolding before us; and though Augustine asks God for permission to speak, he also listens for God's reply. It is in the interplay between what he says and what he hears that the reflective dimension of the *Confessions* develops, and it is the interaction between speaking and hearing that gives him access to the one who brings redemption.

Augustine prays that the dialogue between God and the soul will have dramatic consequences: the house of his soul is too narrow for God to come into it, and he asks his creator to enlarge and rebuild it so he will be able to stretch out toward God's infinite richness (1.5.6). To speak about God and the soul in the language of containment does not capture their explosiveness because both concepts transcend our efforts to express them in ordinary discourse. If Augustine is to sustain his role in the conversation, God must transform and enrich him so he can learn to speak a new kind of language that is adequate to the existential matrix within which he is embedded.

Augustine's soul is in ruins; he asks God to restore it. He knows there is much about him that is offensive; he quickly confesses it. In the process, he returns to the faith that animates his inquiry by insisting that he can speak to God only because he believes (1.5.6). The dynamism of creation and desire leads to the dynamism of faith seeking understanding, and the dynamism of faith seeking understanding generates discourse that is equally vibrant. As he begins to speak, Augustine not only participates in the reflective excitation of paradoxical questions about God and the soul, but also suggests that these questions reflect the paradoxical nature of God. Yet when he faces this paradox, he does not accept merely theoretical answers, but asks God to speak so he may hear, to enlarge the house of his soul, and to restore the ruins into which he has fallen (1.5.6). In doing so, Augustine embraces faith seeking understanding as the maxim of his life,[9] enters a pathway that leads to a new way of speaking about God and the soul, permits the voice of God to expand the constricted boundaries of his soul, and asks God to gather up the fragments of his fragmented heart.

ORIGINS AND INFANCY (1.6.7–1.7.12)

Augustine carries the dynamism of his introductory comments into a brief but important account of the first stage of his life. This account, in turn, rests upon a humble entreaty that God permit him to speak. Augustine cries from the depths of his fragmented predicament, "Grant me to speak before your mercy, grant me who am dust and ashes to speak." This way of referring to himself displays what Rudolf Otto calls a feeling of nothingness when one stands before the majesty of God.[10] Thus, it is appropriate that what Augustine says about himself at this early stage of his reflections tells us more about his ignorance than it does about his knowledge. The first paradox in his narrative is that he begins by speaking about his origins—an original condition that is prior to speech, transcends his capacity to remember, and remains shrouded in mystery. As he expresses his perplexity, "What do I want to say, Lord, except that I do not know whence I came into what I may call a mortal life or a living death. I know not" (1.6.7).[11]

Whatever the solution to this problem may be, Augustine knows that his origins do not provide a foundation from which to ask the question of the meaning of his life, but point to a cognitive abyss that he cannot transcend by his own efforts. The word *infans* means "one who is not yet able to speak," and by implication, "one who cannot remember." Augustine begins the autobiographical section of his book, not only by telling us about a time when he cannot speak, but also by speaking about a stage of life that he cannot remember. This initial stage of his life is opaque, and it points to the opacity of the origins from which he emerges.

Augustine cannot find an adequate response to questions about his temporal origins by recollecting them directly, and he must depend on what others teach him about what he cannot discover for himself. His parents assure him that God has brought him into existence, fashioning him in one of them and by means of the other; and though he does not remember this, he is willing to accept what they say (1.6.7). Even though his life begins with death, Augustine is convinced that it also begins with the even more important fact that God fashions him in time. This suggests that the first word to be said about the human situation is not original sin, but original innocence, and that however surprising this might seem, original innocence and original sin stand side by side at the earliest stage of Augustine's development.

Depending once more on the testimony of others, Augustine concludes that though his mother and nurses nourish him, they do not fill their own breasts, but dispense the "food of infancy" from God. At this initial stage of his life, the "father" who creates him becomes the "mother" who sustains him;[12] and God the creator plays both roles by giving his nurses the will to care for him and the impulse to sustain him by instinctive affection. These important facts give Augustine stability, but they also imply that he must depend on others for sustenance. Thus, his reflections about the absolute dependence of infancy point to a positive community as his natural condition and to an ultimate ground without which he would have been unable to survive.

It should not be surprising that the great rhetorician deals with the problem of origins by focusing on his infancy; for in doing so, he places himself in a condition of weakness and innocence that all of us share. Beginning the discussion in this way rather than with a metaphysical inquiry into the problem of origins allows him to identify himself with his readers and permits us to identify ourselves with him. During this first stage of his journey, he asks us to stand on common ground with him and addresses us as participants in a common enterprise. Augustine's fascination with infancy makes the question of origins a human question; and by starting there, he generates a context that allows us to see ourselves in his story. However, he also weaves the problem of his temporal and his ultimate origins together by calling our attention to the fact that life is a gift, where this central fact points to the grace on which his temporal existence depends. At the beginning of his story, the rhetorician, the psychologist, and the theologian focuses our attention not only on infancy, but also on the creative source out of which he emerges, and on the condition of original innocence that all of us share.[13]

Beginning with infancy also places Augustine in contrast with others and in contrast with God, and he expresses this fact by claiming that he must learn about his origins from others (1.6.10). Thus, the innocence of infancy quickly becomes the dependence of finitude. Augustine focuses on the earliest stage of his life as a way of recovering his origins and of binding himself to his readers, but the radical discontinuity generated by his incapacity to remember his original condition brackets what he says about it. His inability to remember emphasizes his limitations; and this deficiency seems to cut him off, not only from his historical beginnings, but also from his mythological origins.[14] When Hegel asks, "How shall we begin?" he answers that we have begun already and that the first task of systematic reflection is to understand this fact.[15] When Augustine asks the same question, he is unable to answer in the light of his own experience; and as a consequence, he shudders in the face of an abyss he cannot outstrip.

Finitude is a positive condition; and Augustine acknowledges this fact by saying that the ones on whom he depends to prepare comforts for him, satisfy his needs, and see him smiling, both when he sleeps and when he is awake.

As Aristotle reminds us, man is not only a rational animal, but also an animal that imagines, an animal that imitates, and an animal that laughs.[16] It scarcely matters whether rationality, imagination, imitation, or laughter can be found in infancy, even though recent research suggests that a tendency to smile expresses itself in a typical infant between the sixth and the eighth weeks of life.[17] What matters is that the "smile" of the infant points to a state of innocence in which we stand before God as creatures that have been made in God's image.[18]

The traditional view that the smile of an infant is caused by an angel passing over is comparable to the scientific claim that it is due to flatulence,[19] for both hypotheses move beyond the evidence of spontaneous smiles in infants found in every culture. Yet what is crucial for our present purposes is Augustine's suggestion that by smiling when he is asleep and awake, the infant participates in a positive community during the earliest stage of his life. Though he complains that he cannot remember his infancy and must learn about it from others, his parents and nurses inform him that a created community sustains him from the beginning, where within this context, he knows "how to suck, to lie quiet when [he is] full, and to cry when in pain—nothing more" (1.6.7).

God is not present as a thematic element in Augustine's account of his origins and his infancy. Yet he acknowledges God's unspoken presence by using what others teach him to paint a placid picture of his original condition that reminds us of a garden of innocence. The purpose of this description of infancy is theological rather than historical, and Augustine moves to the vertical dimension of experience by pointing to a state of innocence in which all of us participate.[20] Yet instead of doing this in merely theoretical terms, the great rhetorician describes the early weeks of infancy *as if* he lives in paradise, speaking about his relation to God and to his nurses *as if* the spatiotemporal matrix in which he exists is free from negativity. The problem that remains at the center of Augustine's narrative is that he cannot remember this infant "paradise," making it necessary for him to depend on the reports of others to understand his infancy and on analogies between himself and other infants to confirm what they say.

The "paradise" Augustine describes contains individuals who stand over against one another, and his description of his original state of innocence has irreducible difference in it. Yet the differences that separate the members of this original community from one another also bind them together. To be finite is to be determinant and to stand in contrast with others, but determination is not simply a negative condition. From an Augustinian point of view, Spinoza's definition of finitude as limitation by negation is mistaken.[21] It is tempting to believe that finitude is a negative condition that we must overcome; but if this were so, the desire of finite beings to become gods would be inevitable. A negative appraisal of our finitude would drive us beyond ourselves, pressing us to outstrip our limitations in an erotic quest for satisfaction. Though he is captured by eros at crucial stages of his life, the mature Augustine responds to this problem by embracing the biblical view that God looks at the created order and declares that it is good. This divine declaration points to the positive value of finitude in contrast with the obvious deficiencies of fallenness.[22]

Though his description of "paradise" reflects a positive appraisal of finitude, Augustine does not deny his self-transcendence. This dimension of his nature expresses itself in the power of his will to reach beyond itself toward other individuals who stand alongside him in the historical and the mythological communities in which he exists. In the community he shares as an infant, Augustine's will distinguishes him from others; but this community is also a harmony of wills that presupposes the tacit presence of God. Augustine's uniqueness expresses itself in the will as a principle of individuation, as a source of self-transcendence that brings him into a positive relation with others, and as a way of pointing beyond space and time to his eternal relation with God. From a temporal point of view, the power of his will individuates him; from a spatial perspective, it brings him into relation with the community that sustains him; and within an eternal horizon, it links him with God at the initial stage of his development.

Augustine does not simply depend on the reports of others to learn something about his infancy, but confirms what they say by observing other infants (1.6.8). In this case, seeing is more important than hearing because hearing is only hearsay. In addition to common goals to which many individuals may be oriented, analogies between one individual and another are crucial links that bind members of the community together. Without them, we would be separate individuals, cut off from others in a world of our own. From a metaphysical point of view, analogy is a principle of unity and separation that makes a community of individuals possible; from an epistemic perspective, it is a principle of inference that allows Augustine to generalize from his observation of infants to conclusions about his origins that confirm what others teach.

In the first year of his life, Augustine begins to realize where he is, to notice distinctions between himself and others, and to want to express his wishes to the adults who can satisfy them (1.6.8). However, he cannot do this because his wishes are within and his parents and nurses are beyond his reach. Thus, a bifurcation emerges between inner and outer dimensions of his consciousness that mirrors the earlier distinction between himself and others. This second contrast is important because it drives the spatial distinction between self and others back into the structure of consciousness, where the difference between the outer and the inner worlds not only separates Augustine from others, but also separates him from himself.

In its initial efforts to communicate, the infant flings its arms and legs about and makes cries and sounds that reflect its wants and wishes. Yet when its nurses do not satisfy its needs because the signs it makes are not similar to them, it becomes indignant, reminding us that Augustine's original condition is not altogether positive (1.6.8). In its futile efforts to find the gratification it seeks, the frustration of its will externalizes itself; and its consequent outbursts point to a radical discontinuity that disrupts the positive community out of which it emerges.

By pointing in this direction, Augustine does not intend to suggest that an infant first has a concept and then thrashes about to express it. He does not need a Wittgensteinian to tell him that communicating his wishes is a social activity and that a child develops the capacity to do so only gradually through training in practical contexts. In fact, all the sounds and bodily movements that reflect Augustine's predicament can be traced to volitional roots (1.6.8), implying that the psychology of infancy should be more concerned with practice than with epistemology, and more interested in the will as a principle of interaction with others than in the understanding as a pathway to truth. In the first twelve months of life, infants live in a practical rather than a theoretical world; and far from being miniature adults, they are dependent beings whose emotional lives develop stage by stage, manifesting only a minimal continuity with the intelligent individuals they will become.

Augustine's purpose in describing his efforts to satisfy his needs is not to develop a theory of emotion or cognition, but to place the infant in a practical context of communal interaction and to emphasize the ambiguities it faces (1.6.8). An infant can have feelings and impulses to express them through natural signs before it has concepts corresponding to the inclinations and tendencies that generate them. The infant's struggles to express its desires reflect a fundamental opposition between positive and negative elements in its nature, and it is out of this internal conflict that a negative community of fallen individuals emerges. In this case, the finitude of innocence becomes the fallenness of alienation; and this alienation manifests itself, not only in relation to others, but also in relation to ourselves.[23]

As an individual who is alienated from himself, Augustine returns to the problem of origins at a more fundamental level. He has sounded the crucial theme already by asking whence he comes into this mortal life or living death, but now he begins to develop it by asking whether his infancy follows another stage of life that has passed away before it. Did he spend such a period in his mother's womb, as others have suggested, and as his own observation of pregnant women seems to confirm? Yet what precedes *this* period of his life, leading him to ask in frustration, "Was I, indeed, anywhere, or anybody?" (1.6.9) No one can explain these things to him—neither his father, nor his mother, nor anyone else; and since his memory cannot extend even to the earliest stages of life, it can scarcely give him an adequate understanding of a mode of life that is prior to conception. In this case, the limitations of Augustine's memory not only separate him from his infancy, but also cut him off from eternity.[24]

However this may be, it is tempting to believe that Augustine's question about preexistence reveals a tacit commitment to Neoplatonism and that this commitment is a secret doctrine that he will gradually unveil to the attentive reader as the text unfolds.[25] According to one of the most important stands in the Neoplatonic doctrine of the soul, a person is a fallen soul whose task is to return to its origins through a process of recollection and purification that culminates in a contemplation of the truth.[26] When the slave boy in Plato's *Meno* works out a mathematical problem in the sand, his recollection of structural truths leads to the hypothesis that the soul exists before birth, where it acquires the knowledge it recalls after its embodiment in space and time.[27] In the light of this tradition, could Augustine's question about preexistence be a way of pointing to the Neoplatonic myth of the fall of the soul into the body as an explanation of the forgetfulness that makes recollection necessary?

Augustine seems to point in this direction by praising the creator of heaven and earth for his "first being" and for his infancy, where *primordia* appears to be a way of calling our attention to an original condition of innocence in which the soul exists with God prior to its appearance in history. Indeed, Augustine's use of this word, together with claims he makes at later stages in the text, has led Robert O'Connell to conclude that he is a Neoplatonist, not only when he writes the *Confessions*, but even in the systematic and polemical treatises of his philosophical maturity.[28] What response should we make to this thesis, at least as it pertains to Augustine's richest account of the relation between God and the soul?

The most straightforward way of understanding Augustine's comment about *primordia* is to construe it as referring to life in the womb. In the Roman tradition, the period before birth is the first stage of life, where *primordia* refers to the time between birth and conception rather than to a place where a disembodied soul exists prior to its fall into the body.[29] Augustine suggests this conventional interpretation by claiming that he learns about both his *primordia* and his infancy from women who have had experience of both stages (1.6.9). On the other hand, it would be a mistake to deny that there is a "place" of creation that is "prior" to our fallen predicament and that makes recollection and the use of *primordia* as a philosophical concept possible.[30] However, this place need not be construed as a kingdom of disembodied beings, but may be understood as a "paradise" where the souls and the bodies of individuals are created in unfallen space and time "before" their expulsion into the discord of a fallen spatiotemporal medium.[31]

Fallen and unfallen souls are two sides of the same person, where the first word to be said about the person is original innocence, and the second word is original sin.[32] When Augustine asks the question, "Whence do I come?" he is not asking about a disembodied soul, but about a person understood as a composite of a soul and a body.[33] Augustine follows the Neoplatonic tradition in claiming that the soul is superior to the body,[34] that it is the *higher* man,[35] and that it only uses the body;[36] but he also suggests that the *true* man is not the soul, but the soul and the body understood as a unity (10.9.6). When Augustine says "I," he usually refers to himself; and only against this background does he use the same word *derivatively* to point to the soul or the body.[37] Augustine presupposes a complex semantics that allows him to move back and forth between the metaphorical unity of the soul and the body and their analogical separation, reserving the primary use of the indexical expression to point to himself as a composite being. The great rhetorician uses bodily predicates for the soul and spiritual predicates for the body to bind them together (5.1.1), (9.1.1), and he uses spiritual predicates for the soul and physical predicates for the body to hold them apart (10.2.2), (10.7.11). However, he points to the unity of the person as a composite being when he says "I" without qualification.[38]

At this stage of his reflections, Augustine introduces the theme of time and eternity, suggesting that the times through which we pass would have no way of moving on unless they were contained in God's eternal present (1.6.10). One of the crucial differences between Augustine and most contemporary philosophers is his conviction that time without eternity is meaningless. This does not mean that eternity is a lifeless standard of intelligibility on which temporality depends, but a dynamic source of power from which it emerges, by which it is measured, and through which it can be transformed into an ecstatic pathway that brings things in time into a positive relationship with God.

Against the backdrop of the relation between time and eternity, Augustine returns to the analysis of his fallen predicament by insisting that God is not responsible for sin. Sin is a pervasive dimension of Augustine's experience; and as we have noticed already, he believes that we would stand under judgment if we had lived for only a day (1.7.11). As with almost every other crucial passage in the book, this reference to the sins of infancy has raised a flurry of scholarly disagreements. Some commentators say that the sins Augustine has in mind are sins that he commits from the beginning of life, while others claim that the sins of infancy are a reflection of the original sin we "inherit" because of our participation in the sin of Adam.[39] Some combine the two positions by suggesting that sins of the soul are committed individually, while the mortality of the body is a constant reminder of our participation in Augustine's fallen condition.[40] Mediating positions of this kind are often dualistic, emphasizing the separation between the soul and the body, and parceling out the responsibility for sin by tracing bodily mortality to Adam and spiritual degeneration to acts of our own.

My view about this issue occupies the middle ground between the soul and the body and is to be articulated from the ontological and the metaphysical "hyphen" that binds them together and holds them apart. On the one hand, the sins of infancy reflect the fact that both our souls and our bodies participate in the sin of Adam; on the other hand, the sins that we commit as embodied beings are distinctively our own, even though they presuppose Adam as the type of which we are tokens. Augustine's most profound response to the problem of sin parallels his response to the problem of innocence, where both sin and innocence are functions of our unity and separation from Adam.

Though Augustine claims that he does not remember his infancy, he says that every child serves as an illustration of his predicament: when infants cry for the breast, custom and common sense do not allow adults to rebuke them because they would not understand; but since parents discourage this kind of behavior as children grow older, it must be objectionable from the outset (1.7.11). Again, we find that sin is primarily a phenomenon of the will rather than a cognitive condition that can be dealt with at the level of theoretical understanding. This becomes clear when we notice that this passage is the first place where Augustine uses a distinctively cognitive word to reflect on the status of infancy. When he says that it would be useless for adults to chastise infants for their behavior because they would not *understand* what their elders mean, he places cognition in stark contrast with the volitional malady that characterizes him, even at the earliest stage of his development (1.7.11).

Augustine develops this volitional theme by claiming that it is inappropriate for an infant to cry for what would have been harmful if someone had given it to him; says that he sins when he becomes indignant at those who do not indulge his "capricious desires"; blames him for trying to harm his nurses for not obeying him; and concludes that the innocence of the infant reflects the weakness of its body rather than the purity of its mind (1.7.11). His assessment of this issue is confirmed by the fact that the Latin *innocens* means, "causing no harm," which is not the case with the kind of behavior to which he calls our attention. This conclusion becomes virtually inescapable when Augustine sees an infant become livid as it watches another baby nursing at the breast, leading him to ask whether it is innocent for one infant to deny another access to the fountain of life, where the milk it has tasted flows freely for all (1.7.11).

We might quibble about whether an infant can be described as indignant, as trying to harm its nurses, or as livid when it observes another infant nursing in its place. Perhaps we should say that the infant behaves *as if* it were indignant, *as if* it were trying to harm its nurses, and *as if* it were livid at the sight of the behavior of another baby. Recent research about these issues is inconclusive, though much of it suggests that Augustine is more accurate in describing the behavior of infants than our more tentative reformulation of his claims implies.[41] However, to focus on these problems in a scientific way misconstrues Augustine's intentions. He knows that original sin has as much to do with our mature choices as with a defect we inherit and express in the first twelve months of life. As Paul expresses the point in the *Epistle to the Romans*, "Just as through one man sin entered into the world, and death through sin, so death spread to all men, *because all sinned.*"[42] The will is the center of human existence;[43] and in every person who participates in the human predicament by standing alongside Adam, it is the source of a willful distortion of our positive condition.

The distinction between will and willfulness points to a contrast between finite power and infinite self-accentuation, expressions that are present even in the earliest stage of life. Two modes of human existence stand in radical opposition: one is positive and defines our finitude; the other is negative and generates our fallen predicament. Yet even though Augustine maintains that fallenness is a problem for which our participation in the sin of Adam is ultimately responsible, he insists that we ought to praise our creator for the gift of finitude. He reminds us that God not only gives life to the infant, but also gives it a body, "equipped with limbs, beautified with a shapely form, and for its complete good and protection, endowed with all the powers of a living being" (1.7.12). These remarks suggest that God expresses his perfection, not only by creating souls, but also by creating embodied beings that are good and in whom original innocence is prior to original sin.

Augustine is reluctant to dwell on his infancy because he must trust what others say about it and must depend on his own observation of other infants to have some grasp of it. Thus he confesses, "although such testimonies are most probable, this age I hesitate to join to this life of mine which I have lived in this world." Infancy "belongs to the dark regions of forgetfulness [and] is like that [period] which I lived in my mother's womb," where the hiddenness of infancy, like the hiddenness of sin, invites Augustine to ask, " 'If I was conceived in iniquity,' and if my mother nourished me within her womb in sin . . . ,[44] where or when was your servant innocent?" (1.7.12)

Again, the deepest and the most sophisticated answer to this question is not that the soul preexists in an innocent state before it falls into the body, but that both the soul and the body have an innocent dimension in the "paradise" in which they have been created.[45] Yet in this shadowland which is the deepest substratum of human existence, created beings also participate in Adam's sin, embrace it by making choices of our own, and make the fateful transition from the unfallen spatiotemporal context in which we are created to the fallen spatiotemporal matrix in which we are separated from God.[46] Because he understands this so clearly, Augustine recoils from the negative side of his origins, shudders when he looks at original sin, and moves beyond his infancy with the plaintive cry, "What matters that now to me of which I recall no trace?" (1.7.12)

LANGUAGE AND EDUCATION (1.8.13–1.18.29)

Augustine is anxious to move away from the discussion of infancy to a region where his memory extends; and to make this transition he asks, "Did I not advance from infancy and come into boyhood? Or rather, did it not come upon me and succeed my infancy?" (1.8.13) His infancy does not go away, but is no longer present; and he is no longer an infant who cannot speak, but becomes "a chattering boy" (1.8.13). In the Roman world, the passage from infancy to childhood is marked by the transition from an incapacity to speak to verbal interaction; and Augustine follows this tradition by claiming that at the close of his infancy, he is learning signs to communicate his feelings to others. In the judgment of a rhetorician for whom language is so important, the transition from inarticulate gestures to spoken discourse is one of the most important moments in the life of every individual (1.8.13). Augustine's ultimate purpose is to understand the relation between God and the soul and the language appropriate to it; but he also suggests that learning to speak is a significant step in his temporal development, and the most important way of developing spatial and temporal interaction between himself and others.

Augustine emphasizes the role of language in his transition from infancy to childhood by describing how he learns to speak. His account of this process is a familiar part of the philosophical tradition and has become the standard picture of the way in which language is acquired.[47] Yet the picture Augustine sketches is much less simple and straightforward than familiar caricatures of his position suggest. For example, he not only uses language in a richly polymorphous way, but also gives an account of learning to speak that reflects the complexity of the figurative, performative, and intelligible uses of language in which he engages. The great rhetorician knows that referential uses of language arise within a context of dynamic social interaction; and he also understands that referring to something, to say nothing of pointing to matters of ultimate significance, is an achievement of considerable subtlety and linguistic complexity. Thus, it is important to discuss his account of the acquisition of language, not only as significant in its own right, but also as a way of laying the groundwork for his approach to the language of God and the soul.

In describing how he learns to speak, the first thing Augustine tells us is that he remembers himself as a babbling boy and that afterward, he reflects on the process that makes learning a language possible (1.8.13). This suggests that memory is an essential element in what he has to say about the acquisition of language and implies that the stage about which he is giving a reflective account can scarcely be earlier than the second or third years of life. Augustine also claims that adults do not teach him how to speak as they teach him the alphabet when he is older, but that with the mind God has given him, he expresses his feelings spontaneously through cries, sounds, and bodily movements so he will be obeyed (1.8.13). Thus, volitional and theocentric rather than abstractly theoretical elements are at the center of the process of language acquisition he describes.

When the child is unable to express his or her wishes, those around the child sometimes name a certain thing and point to it, permitting the child to observe the object and to grasp the fact that it is called by that name. Yet in doing so, its parents and nurses use a "natural language, common to all nations," which expresses itself through changes of countenance, glances, gestures, and intonations, indicating a practical rather than a theoretical concern with "the affections of the mind in seeking, possessing, rejecting, and avoiding things" (1.8.13). *Little by little* Augustine begins to gather (*colligere*) that words he hears frequently, set in their proper places in sentences, are signs of things; and when his mouth becomes accustomed to the signs, he uses them to express his wishes. Thus, he understands referential terms as parts of a larger linguistic context, and on this basis, not only communicates what he wishes to say, but also plunges more deeply into the "the stormy fellowship of human life" (1.8.13).

This Augustinian picture of the acquisition of language has been the target of considerable philosophical criticism. Most of it derives from the fact that Wittgenstein ridicules a truncated version of it in the opening pages of the *Philosophical Investigations,* suggesting that Augustine's theory of linguistic development emphasizes the referential aspect of language illegitimately.[48] No one who is sensitive to Augustine's subtle uses of language, his careful account of how language is acquired, and his struggles to learn how to speak the language of God and the soul can fail to object to this inadequate understanding of his intentions.[49] However, before we develop our criticisms, let us remember the central strands of Wittgenstein's influential indictment against him.

First, Wittgenstein claims that pointing to a thing and using a name to denote it leaves the meaning of the name linguistically underdetermined for a child who does not understand it already.[50] For example, when we point to a bottle, how is the child to know whether we are pointing to its shape, its texture, the milk it contains, or the bottle itself? Ostensive definitions are inadequate as a way of learning the meaning of a word because they fail to allow a child who hears them for the first time to pick out the objects to which they point. Second, Wittgenstein claims that Augustine focuses only on words as names and ignores other uses of language that are equally important in social contexts. These other linguistic activities include asking questions, giving orders, making promises, and assessing the value of a course of action from a normative point of view. Whatever else they involve, these ways of speaking do not bring us into a simple referential relation between language and the world. Finally, Wittgenstein suggests that the contrast between an inner realm of names and an outer region to which these names refer belies the complexity of our interaction with the world. Consciousness and the world do not stand over against one another in stark referential contrast, but interact as elements of a complex social process in which language has multiple uses. As a consequence, Wittgenstein claims that philosophers should focus on the manifold uses of language rather than restricting themselves to the relation between words and objects.[51]

Wittgenstein also implies that Augustine believes that he can think before he can speak.[52] If this were so, it would mean that he possesses an inner language before he acquires the language he uses to communicate with others. Wittgenstein rejects this view by insisting that thought as inner speech presupposes a public context of communication and cannot occur until a person can engage in verbal interaction with others.[53] This view has become such a commonplace in contemporary philosophy that to question it seems like blasphemy. However, Augustine's account of how he learns to speak is closer to the truth than Wittgenstein's insistence that the ability to think is totally dependent on the capacity to speak within a social context.

Augustine not only focuses on what he wants to say, but on his spontaneous urge to communicate; and though he implies that he has something to convey, he does not claim that it is perfectly determinate and that he simply lacks the words to express himself. Instead, he tells us that whimperings, grunts, gestures, and the sounds at his disposal are not sufficient to allow him to make the transition from silent frustration to intelligible communication (1.8.13). At this stage of his life, there is a twilight zone of partial indeterminacy where Augustine dwells in virtual isolation because he is not yet able to express his needs.

What he has to say is not what he thinks clearly and distinctly, but something of which he has a vague apprehension without the capacity to make it more determinate either in thought or discourse. This is evident from the language he uses to describe his initial condition, ranging from willing, wishing, and grasping, on the one hand, to the affections of the mind and collecting things together on the other (1.7.11–1.8.13). These words point to an infant's struggle to communicate at a relatively primitive volitional level rather than to a fully developed cognitive condition that it cannot express because of physical limitations. In this respect, Augustine is closer to the author of the *Philosophical Investigations* than to the author of the *Tractatus*:

the clear, univocal, and determinate relation between word and object that characterizes Wittgenstein's first book, and which he repudiates so forcefully in his later philosophy, is also rejected in Augustine's account of a child's attempts to learn how to speak.[54]

As he develops the point in the *Confessions*, the place of indeterminacy between silence and speech is mediated by hearing the adults around him using names for the things to which they point (1.8.13). However, Augustine never suggests that the act of pointing uniquely determines the referent to which an adult is attempting to call his attention. Rather, ostensive definition is only one of the vehicles through which he learns to identify the objects to which the words he hears refer (1.8.13). The natural language his parents and nurses use to teach him how to speak involves a subtle range of facial, bodily, and vocal indications of what they intend, all of which eventually allow Augustine to grasp what they seek to convey (1.8.13). For example, he insists that our earliest uses of language enhance our capacity to seek, possess, reject, and avoid significant items in our immediate environment (1.8.13). As we might formulate the point, practical words are the "metaphors" and "analogies" with which Augustine begins; and he moves only gradually from contexts of action in which words of this kind are appropriate to contexts of cognition in which literal discourse emerges as a medium for cognitive interaction.

The fact that learning how to speak happens step by step not only points to the developmental dimension in Augustine's account of learning a language, but also separates him from the later Cartesian tradition in which speech is merely the externalization of a prior act of thinking. Augustine's impulses and frustrations are prelinguistic, and having these feelings does not presuppose that he possesses the corresponding concepts as parts of his mental vocabulary. The natural language of gestures precedes the referential use of language, and Augustine must learn how to participate in it before reference can occur.

Even in referential contexts, Augustine is more impressed by the indeterminate dimension of the "objects" to which he refers than the determinate structure that transforms them into frozen contents of cognition. For example, he insists on countless occasions that God and the soul are both present and absent, acknowledging an indeterminate dimension in the two terms to which he is most concerned to refer (1.2.2), (1.3.3), (1.4.4), (4.5.10), (6.3.4). Because the world in which he lives is a symbolic universe,[55] he is prepared to extend this dimension of indeterminacy to all the things to which he refers, suggesting that they stretch out beyond their determinate boundaries toward their creator (5.1.1), (7.13.19), (13.33.48). Only figurative discourse that outstrips the univocal framework in which his critics have attempted to imprison him will permit us to acknowledge this aspect of his experience.

Augustine is more interested in performative uses of discourse than in giving an account of learning how to correlate words with objects. The point of his description of the acquisition of language is not to develop a theory of reference, but to place himself in a community of linguistic and social interaction. This description presupposes the natural language of gestures common to all nations and points to a complex interplay of figurative, performative, and intelligible uses of language within a community of spatial and temporal interaction (1.8.13). Augustine's place in the community is a necessary condition for learning how to speak, and this linguistic community presupposes the community of parents and nurses in which he participates as an infant. The author of the *Confessions* takes the "paradise" of his origins up into the context of language as a communal activity,[56] which presupposes a framework of social conditioning with which he is more familiar than most Wittgensteinians imagine. Indeed, it almost seems that Augustine is a proto-Wittgensteinian in his account of this aspect of acquiring a language.

We must also pay careful attention to Augustine's claim that however important his place in the linguistic community may be, he does not ultimately depend on others to teach him to speak, but teaches himself with the aid of divine illumination. M. F. Burnyeat makes this point in an article intended to counter familiar Wittgensteinian objections to Augustine's account of the acquisition of language.[57] As he translates the relevant sentences from the *Confessions:* "For it wasn't that my elders had been teaching me. . . . Rather, I had been teaching myself with the mind which you, my God gave me." In his recent commentary on the *Confessions,* James O'Donnell suggests a variant reading of the text, which can be rendered, "My elders taught me not . . . , but I myself, with the mind which you have given me, . . . grasped (*prensabam*) [words] with my memory."[58] O'Donnell's variation makes it clear that Augustine is functioning at a primitive, volitional level, rather than in the rarified cognitive atmosphere of a Cartesian consciousness. However, the most important point about both translations is that they point to the autonomous capacity to speak in the light that flows from God, where the creative source of our existence is understood as a divine teacher.[59]

After he has learned to communicate, Augustine continues to move in a religious direction by suggesting that the linguistic paradise from which he emerges quickly becomes "the stormy fellowship of human life" that he must try to navigate. This is made difficult by the fact that his parents imitate the behavior and the language of the Serpent when they encourage him to learn tricks of speech that bring honor and success. Augustine's teachers thrust him in the same direction by urging him to use language to mislead and subvert a submissive audience. They also force him to learn what they teach against his will and without understanding the value of his studies; and when he resists, they flog him. Augustine speaks of his early education as a "sorrowful road on which we are compelled to travel, multiplying labor and sorrow upon the sons of Adam" (1.9.14). This all too obvious reference to the Fall, and to the trickery that makes it possible, undergirds the insistence of Augustine's teachers that he embrace linguistic deception in school. As a consequence, the "paradise" with which he begins and the natural language that he embraces become the fallenness of linguistic duplicity that he is encouraged to imitate.

Laboring under the burden of an education he despises, Augustine sees men praying; and he begins to move in a positive direction by conceiving of God as an invisible being who can free him from the misery he suffers at the hands of his teachers. The positive aspect of the community of nurses and of natural language expresses itself in a positive concept of God, which leads, in turn, to his first attempt to speak the language of God and the soul. Praying "unties the knot of his tongue," permitting him to move beyond the acquisition of language and the rhetorical purposes it serves to words that point beyond themselves to the ground that sustains him (1.9.14). Yet when he prays that his teachers will not flog him, and when God does not intervene, his elders and parents treat the stripes he receives as a joke.

The negative dimension of Augustine's early education counterbalances the "paradise" of his earlier experience; punishment in school and joking parents reflect the discontinuities of his incapacity to remember his origins and his frustration and willfulness as an infant; and his experience with his teachers leads from a positive community of nurses to a negative community of childhood misery (1.9.14). This journey occurs, not only in space and time, but also in the vertical place opened up by the presence and the absence of God. Yet when Augustine tries to enter this place by praying to a powerful being that he cannot see, God remains silent as the boy makes the lonely transition from the positive to the negative aspects of childhood (1.9.14).

When he enters the classroom, Augustine carries the habits of the earlier stages of childhood with him: he continues to play rather than to study, and he stubbornly refuses to embrace the transition from what he can imagine to what he can learn. The structure of his early education also makes it difficult for him to move from one stage to the other because those who punish him for playing rather than learning are engaged in playful activities themselves. As he formulates the point so bitterly, "The idling of our elders is called business; the idling of boys, though quite like it, is punished" (1.9.15). Even the bishop cannot understand why an adult should punish a child for playing ball instead of learning how to play in rhetorical contests in which his teachers are so proficient (1.9.15).

Augustine realizes that playing is definitive, not only of the life that he is about to leave behind, but also of the career that he will soon embrace: imagination will be an important part of his work, and one of his most important tasks will be to discipline himself so playing games with words will not become the last word about the meaning of his life. Throughout the *Confessions,* play will always be the most serious competitor to work, tempting Augustine to regard his life as a game. For example, playing as the most important work of childhood,[60] playing instead of studying in school (1.9.15), playing ball and learning how to play at rhetoric (1.9.15), and playing as a way of binding a community of adolescent companions together (2.3.8) are all important aspects of Augustine's experience.

Despite his fascination with games, both the saint and the writer insist that he should have studied harder in school. He knows that he is not only what he can imagine, but also what he can learn;[61] and he acknowledges that what he could have learned about language from his teachers could have been put to better use later. The familiar Neoplatonic theme of utility emerges at this stage of the narrative, suggesting that some things are good, not in themselves, but for what they enable us to accomplish. Thus, Augustine maintains that he should have learned as much as he could from his teachers, even though they blur the distinction between imagination and knowledge that he must learn to draw for himself (1.10.16).

The reference to the usefulness of language to achieve a higher end introduces a hierarchy of value that places the language of God and the soul at the center of Augustine's thinking. His educational development begins with a universal natural language, moves to the knowledge necessary to construct persuasive speeches, and culminates in a religious purpose that discourse can accomplish. This Neoplatonic ladder undergirds Augustine's education; and it provides an intelligible structure that allows him to develop from infancy, through childhood and adolescence, to the larger world in which he becomes the most influential Christian thinker until the development of scholasticism in the thirteenth century.

Two serious impediments stand opposed to the positive stages of Augustine's linguistic development: though he enters the domain of natural language willingly, he dislikes the formal training that enables him to speak persuasively; and though he delights in charming an audience with rhetorical mastery, he refuses to embrace the end toward which his education points (1.10.16). The development of Augustine's will is an inverted image of a hierarchy of content that develops through an ordered series of linguistic stages. In the first case, he moves from natural language toward the highest Good; in the second, he embraces willfulness that traces out a negative pattern of its own. The positive and negative dimensions of his experience are mirror images of one another, one of which points to the development of the intellect, while the second calls our attention to the degeneration of the will. This contrast leads Augustine to appeal to God for relief from the conflict between his will and his intellect, pointing once more to the eternal dimension of experience that undergirds the psychological and rhetorical dimensions of his journey.

The deliverance Augustine seeks begins in childhood. Along the vertical axis of his experience, he hears about eternal life; and when he is an infant, a priest marks him with the sign of the cross and seasons him with salt. When he is ill in childhood, he begs his mother for baptism, which would have made it possible for him to turn away from the stormy fellowship of human life that he has entered to the cleansing waters of salvation that he longs to embrace. However, when he begins to recover from his illness, his mother decides to defer his baptism; for she is convinced that the sins Augustine might commit after baptism are more serious than the ones he commits beforehand. Monica foresees the temptations that wash over him as he grows out of childhood and prefers that he face them as "unformed clay" rather than as Christ's image (1.11.18).[62]

Given the cultural situation, the decision to postpone Augustine's baptism is understandable;[63] but in appraising it from the perspective of the saint who writes the *Confessions*, Augustine suggests that his mother's choice expresses the same willfulness he ascribes to himself in childhood (1.11.17). Willfulness is a universal problem, and we do not find it only in childhood expressions of frustration. In this case, it issues in his mother's decision to follow custom and tradition rather than to obey the biblical command to follow Christ. Yet even here, Augustine points beyond time and space to eternity by telling us that he believes in God, along with his entire household except his father (1.11.17).

Many commentators emphasize the fact that one of Augustine's parents is a Christian and the other is a pagan. This suggests that his natural origins are ambiguous and that he must choose between the two strands of his family if he is to come to himself. Because she understands this so clearly, his mother wants Augustine to acknowledge God as his father. The psychoanalytic implications of this desire are painfully evident,[64] but the analysis of Monica's relation to her son should also recognize the theological dimension of her wishes. Though a psychological interpretation might suggest that she wants both God and her son for herself, Augustine's mother knows that it is more important for him to become God's child than to remain the child of his parents. This finally occurs when he is thirty-three, where as we shall see in a later book, he points beyond genetic and psychological considerations by describing his conversion in a garden in Milan.

At this early stage of his life, Augustine does not undergo the conversion that will make his adoption possible. Instead, his willfulness remains the dominant aspect of his development, expressing itself in resistance to what his parents want him to learn. He hates his teachers for forcing him to study; and though he admits that good will come from it, he insists that no one does well against his will. Thus, he points once more to an opposition between the task of the intellect and the orientation of the will: though the Neoplatonic ladder of education leads him toward a higher good, he orients himself away from it, where even the teachers who force him to learn share his negative condition. As he expresses his predicament somewhat theatrically, "I was a great sinner for so small a boy" (1.12.19).

In a familiar section of Book I, Augustine wonders why he hates the Greek literature he studies from childhood (1.14.23). When he writes the *Confessions* in his mid-forties, he still cannot use the language effectively,[65] though he loves Latin literature from the beginning. Yet even in his study of the language he loves, he finds elementary grammatical and mathematical lessons oppressive and speaks about his attitude toward them in two voices: from the perspective of childhood, the rudiments of reading, writing, and reckoning in Latin are burdensome; but from the point of view of a writer, these early lessons are better than fiction because they allow him to read and write what he wishes (1.13.22).

In childhood, Augustine is enthralled when his teachers encourage him to learn about the wanderings of Aeneas and to weep about the fate of Dido; and he loses himself in the stories he hears about these fictional characters. Yet when the sinner appraises this state of affairs from the standpoint of the saint and the confessor, he complains that false images attract him in childhood and that he sheds tears for Dido rather than for his own predicament. By focusing on fictions rather than on his fallen condition, the precocious child commits fornication against God, seeks the lowest rung of creation, and falls back to the earth from which he is struggling to separate himself (1.13.21).

This concern with fornication and with imprisonment on the earth appears to be a clear example of the influence of Plotinus on Augustine. Indeed, such an explicitly negative reference to sexuality and to the body seems to point in this direction. According to Porphyry, Plotinus never mentions his parents, is ashamed to be trapped in the body, and identifies it with the lowest level of creation from which he wants to escape.[66] One of the reasons that Plotinus never allows a statue to be made of him is that he identifies himself so completely with the soul that he will not permit an artist to create a visual representation of him.[67] In all these ways, it might seem that Plotinus prepares the way for Augustine by suggesting that the soul is divine and that its ultimate destiny points beyond the body to a region that transcends it.[68]

However, another interpretation of Augustine's apparent agreement with the founder of Neoplatonism is possible. According to this alternative, fornication against God is not turning away from the soul to the body, and the earth is not profane because it is the lowest level of creation. As a consequence, Augustine not only mentions his parents, his birthplace, and the early stages of his development, but also reverses Neoplatonism when he claims, "I forsook you, and I followed after your lowest creatures, I who was earth, turning to earth" (1.13.21). The earth with which he identifies himself is the earth of creation, while the earth to which he sinks points to the negative orientation of the soul and to the fallen condition it seeks to embrace. Four paragraphs later Augustine says that man is made of dust, pointing not to the Neoplatonic myth about the fall of the soul, but to the biblical story of creation *ex nihilo* (1.16.25).

As he understands the conception, fornication against God is an individual's attempt to lose itself in its finitude rather than a tendency of the soul to fall away from God into the body. Augustine identifies the temptation to become infinite with sensuality, where the sensual consciousness attempts to attach itself to a finite content that is unable to bear its infinite weight. Returning to the earth does not point to the negative status of matter, but expresses the disorientation of the will that leads from an appropriate attachment to God to an addictive attachment to the lowest order of creation. Augustine is acutely aware that he suffers from a sexual addiction that influences his approach to every aspect of his life, and it is this addiction that expresses his fallen condition most clearly.

Augustine, the sinner, tells us that a "veil" hangs over the entrance to the grammar school that seems to point to the wonderful mysteries concealed there.[69] The legendary wanderings of Aeneas stand at the center of this secular Holy of Holies, inviting the students who enter it to embrace the richness and power of the Latin literary tradition. Yet Augustine has discovered that the veil he must penetrate to gain access to this tradition is not so much a covering for mystery as a curtain for error (1.13.22). This becomes clear when he remembers that the story of Dido and Aeneas is false, even though anyone who has learned the language knows how to spell their names (1.13.22). At this stage of his recollections, Augustine invokes once more the familiar Neoplatonic contrast between higher and lower levels of reality, where this contrast points to the superiority of structure to the false images that attract him.

As his education unfolds, Augustine turns away from the necessary conditions for discourse to their contingent and evanescent expression. His will not only expresses the capacity to learn, but also exhibits the power to reject what is universal. Augustine's restless will cannot find rest in knowledge alone, but tries to come to rest at the center of its own restlessness. Though his intellect recognizes the value of the quest for truth, he also knows that he will never find satisfaction in what is lifeless and unchanging. If he is to come to himself, he must drive beyond images, linguistic structures, and the attempt to find rest in the infinite dimension of himself to embrace the one who has brought him into existence.

Augustine continues to probe his hatred of Greek, claiming that his negative attitude toward the language puzzles him because Greek literature contains as many false images as Latin: Homer's poetic images are as skillful as Virgil's, and the writer cannot understand why they repulse him. His answer to the question hinges on the priority of the will to the intellect as it expresses itself in the difference between two ways of learning a language: learning Greek requires formal instruction in an alien tongue, while mastering Latin happens naturally as he gradually begins to converse with those around him (1.14.23). Augustine learns the language of the Romans by conversing with his nurses, while he learns Greek from his instructors in a formalized context. The child assimilates Latin in a rich linguistic interplay with other people, but he tries to grasp the elements of Greek by taking a reflective stance on a language others generate (1.14.23).

Like the later Wittgenstein, the author of the *Confessions* emphasizes the positive role of the community in acquiring a language; and he identifies the negative element of linguistic instruction with an abstract structure that merely stands over against him. He learns Greek didactically and turns away from it; he learns Latin in a linguistic community and reembraces the paradise with which he begins (1.14.23). One way to remain in "paradise" is to be part of a community of conversation and of spatial interaction, but acquiring a language by trying to learn its vocabulary and the linguistic rules that govern it is a different thing altogether. The foreignness of a foreign tongue is a function of its distance from us, and we can traverse this distance only if we learn to speak it as if we were children.

In the Roman world of his day, boys pay fees to learn how to speak persuasively rather than truthfully; and in describing the context in which this occurs, Augustine mobilizes a cluster of metaphors that develops his earlier reference to the stormy fellowship of human life in contrast with the cleansing waters of baptism. First, he invokes the terrors of the ocean from which only the death of Christ can rescue him:

> Woe to you, O torrent of men's ways! Who will stand against you? How long will it be until you are dried up? How long will you sweep the sons of Eve down into that mighty and hideous ocean, over which even they who are borne upon the tree can hardly cross? (1.16.25)

Second, he speaks of the "hellish flood" into which his rhetorical training throws him; and in recalling his career as a rhetorician, he imitates himself in the forums of Carthage, Rome, and Milan by using the metaphor of the ocean to depict his own behavior:

> You beat against your rocky shore and roar: "Here words may be learned; here you can attain the eloquence which is so necessary to

persuade people to your way of thinking; so helpful in unfolding your opinions." (1.16.26)

Finally, he reminds us that the rhetoricians under whom he studies approach the subject from a purely practical point of view rather than from the theoretical perspective of Cicero; and as adherents of the Second Sophistic, they believe that a student can understand words best by hearing actors utter them in a dramatic context.[70] Augustine does not object to words like "thunder," "rain," or "golden shower," but blames his teachers for forcing him to learn useful words in useless ways. Later, he will use these words to depict the human predicament; but now he is drowning in the "ocean" he is learning to describe and in the rhetorical education that makes his linguistic access to it possible (1.16.26).

Augustine makes a decisive and unexpected transition at this stage of his account by indicating that his teachers encourage him to speak, not only persuasively, but also correctly (1.18.28). Here he moves from imaginative activity to linguistic structure, from play to work, and from what he can imagine to what he can learn.[71] In the process, the grammatical forms that he hated at the beginning of his education become a topic of academic interest, where this shift of focus is rooted in the normal pattern of human development. Whereas a younger child hates grammatical abstractions in contrast with imaginative stories, an older child often takes pride in his or her ability to handle the syntactical dimension of language with clarity and precision.[72] Yet even in this context, Augustine's tutors reveal their limitations by being more concerned with structural correctness than with the value of their students' actions. In terms of the familiar image of Plato's *Republic*, the transition they encourage from false images to grammar affirms the third level of the divided line, but it places this third level of the line higher than the normative conditions that lie beyond it.[73] In doing so, they fail to teach their students to embrace the priority of goodness, allowing the ethical and spiritual dimensions of experience to be subordinated to merely structural considerations.

Along the vertical axis of his experience, Augustine can feel God drawing him upward, even though the voice of God does not speak to him directly at this stage of his development. The interplay between speech and silence tilts toward silence at the vertical level, while discourse dominates the spatial and temporal dimensions of the world he is beginning to enter. Within the silent space that surrounds Augustine's love of language, and in response to the hiddenness of God that overshadows this stage of his life, he compares himself to the Prodigal Son who is far away from God because his heart is darkened (1.18.28).

Courcelle has emphasized this passage as the first indication that Augustine adopts the model of the wanderings of Odysseus, and the fall of the soul to which it points, about which he learns from listening to a sermon by Ambrose in 386 (2.10.18).[74] Presumably, this is the occasion on which Augustine begins to become a Neoplatonic Christian, adopting the philosophical vocabulary of Ambrose and Plotinus to articulate the heart of the Christian gospel. However, it is not by accident that Augustine mentions the Prodigal Son instead of Odysseus in the *Confessions* and that he emphasizes nonplatonic dimensions of the story in his use of it.[75] For example, Augustine is clear about the fact that in the case of the Prodigal Son, the journey from will to willfulness does not involve the fall of the soul into the body as punishment for sin. Rather, it expresses an act of the will in which the soul turns away from God,[76] seeking to wander in the "desert" of a far country rather than to become a "field" that God can cultivate.

Let us gather up the metaphors that express Augustine's resistance to the upward journey toward God. By learning how to speak, he plunges into "the stormy fellowship of human life." By not being able to persuade his mother to secure baptism for him, he is left unwashed by the "cleansing waters of salvation." By being caught in the "torrent of men's ways," he is swept down into "a mighty and hideous ocean, over which those who are borne upon the tree can hardly cross." By participating in the "hellish flood" of fictional discourse, he internalizes the ocean by dashing against the "rocks" of his soul, and by "roaring" out the words that are intended to deceive his audience. By learning words like "thunder," "rain," and "golden shower" in rhetorical contexts, he embraces useful words in useless ways. And by undertaking a "journey" that is neither geographical nor epistemic, but a volitional way of falling away from God, he is a "desert" rather than a "cultivated field" that will make it possible for him to return to the "garden" of his father. However, only God can reverse this process of degeneration when he breaks his silence and speaks to Augustine's fragmented heart.

The linguistic particles that are mobilized by the metaphors Augustine uses are as important as the metaphors themselves. He is *in* a storm, *in* a torrent, *in* an ocean, *in* a hellish flood, and *in* the thunder, rain, and golden showers of the discourse he learns from the rhetorical flourishes of the poets he reads and the teachers he obeys. He is *on* a journey in a far country, but as he crosses the waters to get there, he is not borne up *on* the tree that will enable him to secure safe passage to dry land. As a consequence, he *becomes* a roaring ocean that dashes against the rocks of his soul; and he *becomes* a desert rather than a cultivated field that God is able to transform. Yet this will become possible only when God leads him *into* a garden where salvation becomes possible, and as a consequence, *into* the waters of baptism that will finally set him free. *In, on, becomes, into*—this is the path Augustine traces out in his journey toward God and in his attempt to reflect on its significance in the story unfolding before us.

Augustine complains that he and his teachers follow the conventional rules of grammar, but neglect the eternal rules of salvation and that they are more ashamed to mispronounce a word than to hate those who speak incorrectly (1.18.29). His teachers encourage him to move away from false images toward structural stability, permitting Augustine's psyche to turn toward the truth he seeks eventually. There is a similarity between rules of grammar and rules of conduct, for both serve as indispensable standards by which utterances and actions are measured. Yet neither Augustine nor his teachers grasp the superiority of goodness to structure that will finally transform him into a unified being (1.18.29).

Though discourse and the objects about which Augustine communicates presuppose a structural dimension, the distinction between good and evil transcends the structural elements that are subordinate to it. Augustine makes judgments about the goodness of things, but he can never explain these judgments in structural terms alone. God the creator is the highest end to which the soul can orient itself, where a divine ground is both the arche and the telos of the psyche. Though Augustine asks his readers to join him in climbing a Neoplatonic ladder, he also insists that we face the problem of the relation between God and the soul at both the beginning and the end of our journey. As a result, the thrust of the will toward God becomes the undergirding theme of the *Confessions* and the ground from which Augustine addresses those who read it.

Augustine's account of his early development involves an interplay of positive and negative dimensions. The positive elements are learning a natural language at the appropriate stage of development, an early awareness of God, a natural belief in him, and learning Latin through natural conversation in spatial interaction. These positive factors are developments of the paradise in which he participates as an infant and of the community that sustains his existence. The negative elements are the alien character of Greek that stands over against him, his failure to make the transition from what he can imagine to what he can learn, and his preference for false images in contrast to grammatical structure. Though these dimensions have temporal implications, they also point to his fallen predicament and to his participation in a negative community whose power he must learn to transcend.

Augustine moves up a Neoplatonic ladder to affirm the value of intelligible structure, but he continues to embrace the dramatic context where he learns to speak and where his love for fictional discourse is sustained. As a consequence, one of his most important educational tasks is to bring the figurative, the performative, and the intelligible dimensions of language together. Though Augustine must discard the falsity of fiction for structural stability, he must also integrate a structural element into the dramatic account of his life and into the conversations with his friends that undergird his journey.

One of the most important problems in Books I–VI of the *Confessions* is to bring space, time, and eternity together and to reflect their unity in a positive interplay among the intelligible structure of discourse, performative acts of speaking, and figurative uses of language that make access to a source of transformation possible. Augustine develops through temporal stages and is part of a community where the power of his will binds its members together. However, as he will also try to teach us, only the language of God and the soul can unify space, time, and eternity, and only the language of the heart can knit the act, the structure, and the value of speaking together.

PERSONAL DEFECTS, IMAGO DEI, AND SIN (1.19.30–1.19.31)

At this relatively early stage of his development, Augustine plunges into the community that he enters as a boy, calling it a "wrestling arena" in which he is more afraid of perpetrating a barbarism than of envying those who have not (1.19.30). He lies to his tutor, masters, and parents; steals from his parents' cellar and table; and seeks dishonest victories and desires preeminence (1.19.30). The disclosure of these defects is important because the situations to which they point contrast so radically with the pear-stealing episode with which he will soon be preoccupied. In these cases, there are determinate reasons for his actions, however inadequate they may be to justify his behavior; in *that* case, there is no reason for the act but the negative dimension of the act itself. In calling our attention to actions for which reasons can be given, the great rhetorician sets the stage for our appreciation of the more radical character of the episode that he is about to consider.

In spite of original sin, Augustine points to original innocence by claiming that thanks would be due to God even if he had not survived his childhood. Even then he exists, lives, is anxious about his own well-being, and is an image of the mysterious source of unity that brings him into existence (1.20.31).[77] There are several evidences of this: he keeps watch with his inner sense over the deliverances of his outer senses, takes pleasure in the truth, has a vigorous memory, is able to speak, enjoys his friends, and shuns sorrow, meanness, and ignorance (1.20.31). Earlier Augustine praises God for his infancy and gives thanks for the body to which the sensitive soul (*anima*) is conjoined. Now he praises God for both the *anima* and the *animus*, pointing to the soul that God has brought into existence. To the extent that his use of these capacities is positive, he is still in "paradise," enjoying the created status his participation in Adam makes possible.

Yet having praised God for the gifts of finitude, the author of the *Confessions* also reminds us that he moves from finitude to fallenness and that sin is an inappropriate attachment to finite things (1.20.31). Human life is positive when it expresses a natural concern for its own existence and is a trace of the image of God the fall never obliterates. Yet when the will turns away from what is infinite toward what is finite as if it were a realm to which it could devote itself completely, this transition contradicts the natural development of consciousness toward structural stability and toward the love of God.

Sin is an infinite attachment to a merely finite good rather than an appropriate attachment to what is infinite, and it is this boundless attachment to what is finite that accounts for the resistance of the psyche to deliverance. If Augustine is to move beyond his willful predicament, he must turn away from anything finite that cannot bear the weight of the infinite demands he makes on it; and he must accept the transformation this reversal promises. Looking forward to the context in which this occurs, Augustine concludes his reflections about childhood by pointing to the indispensable role God plays in preserving his life, to the transforming work God does in developing and perfecting the spiritual and bodily gifts he has given him, and to the redemptive grace God expresses as the source that creates and sustains him. This process of transformation also enables him to anticipate the time of fulfillment in which life *in* God will be life *with* God, where we will not be absorbed into something larger, but will live alongside one another in the City of God we are created to inhabit (1.20.31).

SEXUALITY (2.1.1–2.3.8)

Augustine begins to move away from childhood into adolescence by focusing on a year of idleness and adolescent mischief and by describing a pivotal episode that reflects his fallen predicament. This episode is important, not only because it occurs at such a critical moment in his temporal development, but also because it generates a space in which he interacts with "unfriendly friends" and points in a decisive way to the vertical axis along which he falls away from God. The temporal, spatial, and eternal axes of Augustine's life intersect in the pear-stealing episode more clearly than in any incident that he has related thus far, incorporating in a single situation the multiple directions in which his journey toward God unfolds.

Before he uses these directions to elaborate one of the most memorable episodes in the text, Augustine tells us that the reason he wants to confess his sins is not because he loves them, but because acknowledging and reliving them will enable him to love God (2.1.1). In a remarkable anticipation of contemporary psychology, the philosopher suggests that we can recover what is positive about ourselves only by remembering and reexperiencing what is negative. The account of Augustine's journey toward God immerses him in the negative dimension of experience, but the purpose of his story is to allow him to use his sins as a vehicle for reestablishing a positive relation with God. Behind his fallen predicament stands original innocence; but in order to reembrace it, he must move through the sins he confesses to the fulfillment he seeks. One of the most important reasons for recounting the story of Augustine's life is to indicate how the stages of his development are reexperienced in the text. If we do not do this, but approach the text instead from an exclusively theoretical point of view, the existential richness of his enterprise will be lost in a tissue of abstractions.

Augustine tells us that when he is a sixteen-year-old boy, he wants to love and to be loved; but he also needs someone to gather him up from the fragments into which he has fallen. Together with the founder of psychoanalysis, the patristic theologian knows that the cry for love expresses the deepest longing of the human heart. Yet almost sixteen hundred years before Freud, he also knows that love is the place where the conflicts of life reach their most passionate and most tortuous expression. Thus, the saint, looking back on the sinner, elaborates his predicament in an explosive barrage of sexual metaphors:

Clouds arose from the slimy desires of the flesh and from youth's seething spring. They clouded over and darkened my soul, so that I could not distinguish the calm light of chaste love from the fog of lust. Both kinds of affection burned confusedly within me and swept my feeble youth over the crags of desire and plunged me into a whirlpool of shameful deeds. I wandered farther from you, and you let me go. I was tossed about and spilt out in my fornications, and I flowed out and boiled over in them, but you kept silent. (2.2.2)

Augustine makes it clear that he had several options for dealing with the problem of adolescent sexuality. First, he could have found a wife, even if he could not have restricted himself to sexual activity intended solely for the purpose of producing children. Second, he could have married and tried to be content with using sexuality for procreation, since this is the way God softens the thorns of suffering in fallen space and time that have no place in the unfallen spatiotemporal matrix in which Adam and Eve are created.[78] Finally, he might have renounced sexual activity altogether, sublimating his erotic powers into a vehicle for seeking the kingdom of heaven (2.2.3). Yet it is not surprising that the young adolescent does not avail himself of any of these possibilities, choosing instead to unleash his natural impulses without concerning himself with their spiritual consequences.

Augustine follows "the sweeping tide of [his] passions" and departs from God by breaking his laws. Yet he is unable to escape God's anger and punishment, which are intended to lead him back to the "place" from which he has fallen away. In the "sixteenth year of [his] body's age," the young man is exiled from the "joys of [God's] house," which points to the fact that he has turned away from a state of original innocence to the "the madness of lust" as an existential condition (2.2.4). Augustine mentions the age of his body rather than the age of himself, not because of a commitment to a metaphysical dualism, but because the fundamental problem with which he is concerned at this stage manifests itself in sexual terms. This problem is his separation from God, where an infinite attachment to what is finite replaces an original attachment to what is infinite.

Augustine's parents do nothing to constrain him because they want him to be a student of grammar and rhetoric and because their ambitions for their son rival his own. As the lust of adolescence rages within him, both Monica and Patricius stand in the background, dreaming about the worldly prospects of their sixteen-year-old prodigy. His father wants him to study rhetoric to become a lawyer; his mother wants him to continue his education so he will return to God; but both parents are more concerned with his rhetorical education than with his spiritual development (2.2.4).

Once more, Augustine suggests that God remains silent while he continues to turn away from him by moving in a downward spiral that threatens to issue in destruction. However, God is also beginning to speak to him through his mother, who warns him to refrain from fornication and adultery, even though she is unwilling to secure a marriage for him because she believes that it will interfere with his career. It is unlikely that he would have consented in any case; for in matters that pertain to sexuality, he ignores everything she says because he is ashamed to be less shameless than his friends (2.3.7). It is as if he had fallen into a Babylonian exile, where everything he does is motivated by a desire for either praise or pleasure. Unfortunately, he also walks "the streets of Babylon" with his Babylonian friends (2.3.8), participating in a theft that seems innocent on the surface, but that epitomizes his fragmented condition. In committing the theft, Augustine moves beyond an infinite attachment to what is finite to an infinite attachment to his own infinitude, where the act in which he participates is the root from which sin in the more traditional sense emerges.[79]

THE PEAR-STEALING EPISODE (2.4.9–2.10.18)

The pear-stealing episode at the end of Book II is one of the two most important events in the first six books of the *Confessions*.[80] When Augustine steals the pears, he falls into an abyss that separates him from God, and only the voice of God will be able to extricate him from it. Yet the pear-stealing episode not only points to Augustine's need for redemption, but also raises fundamental questions about the aesthetic, ethical, political, and religious aspects of human experience. These lenses filter and give us access to the human predicament, bringing us face to face with one of the most puzzling philosophical problems we will ever encounter.

The details of Augustine's story are deceptively simple. Late one night, he and his friends steal pears from a neighbor's vineyard. They slip under the fence, shake and rob the tree, and slip away again with an enormous load of pears, barely tasting them before they feed them to the swine (2.4.9). What could be more innocent than this? Almost everybody does it. Adolescent acts of mischief happen as a matter of course; it is not surprising that Augustine participates in one; and most of us must admit that we have engaged in similar acts ourselves. Yet this is precisely the point. The pear-stealing episode is not simply Augustine's story, but also our own. What *is* surprising is not that the reader stands on common ground with Augustine, but that in sharing it with him and in understanding the significance of our actions, we enter a forbidden place that brings our spatial and temporal development to a standstill.

The most obvious thing to notice about the pear-stealing episode is its aesthetic significance. Though Augustine says that the pears he steals are not as good as the ones in his own vineyard and that nothing about their color or flavor draws him to them, he admits that they are pleasing and attractive (2.4.9), (2.6.12). This gives the stolen fruit a positive place in the order of creation, allowing the beauty it has to reflect the infinite beauty of God. Yet Augustine cannot explain the pear-stealing episode from an aesthetic point of view: he steals something that he has already in sufficient measure, where the motive for his action is not to savor what he steals, but to enjoy the theft itself. As Augustine suggests at a number of places in his writings, "to use" (*uti*) contrasts with "to enjoy" (*frui*), where enjoyment (*fructus*) transcends usefulness (*utilitas*) and points beyond desire (*appetitio*) and delight (*delectatio*) to the blessedness (*felicitas*) that comes from God.[81] When Augustine participates in a negative act that he performs for its own sake, the fruit (*fructus*) of the action is not only negative in itself, but also an inversion of the enjoyment (*fructus*) of God that he has been created to share.

Augustine's description of the pear-stealing episode makes it sound like a crime; and for the saint who is once a Manichaean, it is. Manichaeans believe that trees spring from the semen of demons and are a rich source of particles that have escaped from the Kingdom of Light. A Manichaean would never pluck their fruit; and even if he did so accidentally, he would ask one of the Manichaean elect to ingest it to release the light. From a Manichaean perspective, giving the fruit to an animal would increase the disgrace of the crime, embedding the goodness of the particles in it in creatures lower in the chain of being than trees. When Augustine reminds us that the theft occurs at night as the powers of darkness reign, the episode becomes even more reprehensible for a man who has been a Manichaean for nine years.[82]

However persuasive this interpretation may be, Augustine places his initial description of the episode within an ethical framework rather than within a cosmological context. From the outset, he insists that a theft is not only a violation of the positive law the Ten Commandments codify, but also an encroachment on the natural law that God has written on our hearts (2.4.9). The attitude of a professional thief confirms this: he will not tolerate the theft of his possessions, and even a rich thief will not permit a poor one to steal from him (2.4.9). Yet Augustine wants to steal from his neighbor's vineyard because of his failure to appreciate the demands of justice and his contempt for appropriate behavior, and eating a few bites of the pears pleases him and his friends because it is forbidden. Thus, he characterizes the theft as a violation of both natural and positive laws and as an occasion for pleasure in eating forbidden fruit, generating the expectation that he might try to explain it in ethical terms that have aesthetic implications.

Yet having begun to move in an ethical direction, Augustine undermines this kind of explanation quickly. First, he suggests that there is no moral reason for stealing forbidden fruit: he is neither poor nor hungry, nor is this a case of stealing bread for starving children. The theft he commits is a gratuitous act that does not point beyond itself, but has a negative character that he loves for its own sake. As Augustine formulates the point, he is "evil without purpose"; and there is "no cause for [his] evil but the evil itself" (2.4.9). Second, the needs that drive Augustine to steal the pears issue in desires that are just as negative as stealing itself. If he had been poor and hungry, his desire for food would have been positive because what he sought would have been substantial and good. Yet when he steals the pears simply to be stealing, the desire to steal is negative because what he seeks is insubstantial and evil in its own right (2.4.9). Third, Augustine's evaluation of the act mentions shame rather than guilt, insisting that he is "seeking nothing from the shameful deed but shame itself." If guilt is a moral category, and if it is sometimes associated with the aesthetic delight we take in doing what is forbidden, shame drives deeper, exposing us for what we are rather than for what we do. In doing so, shame makes it possible for us to look at our infinite attachment to our finitude, which is the root of sin in the familiar sense of the term. Finally, Augustine suggests that if the act were primarily ethical, it would involve a preference for a lower to a higher good. In moral contexts, we explain a crime by pointing to a desire for something good that overrides our commitment to something better; but in the pear-stealing episode, there is no logical space for excuses (2.5.11). In stealing the pears with his adolescent companions, and in finding his sole gratification in the theft itself, Augustine falls into a bottomless pit that lies beneath unethical behavior.

The political dimension of the theft surfaces in Augustine's reference to the companions with whom he commits it. As he says himself, "the bond of human friendship has a sweetness of its own, binding many souls together" within a larger community (2.5.10). Friendship arises from a shared orientation toward common objects of affection (2.5.10), making it understandable that Augustine says seven times that he would have never stolen the pears alone (2.8.16–2.9.17). Perhaps the explanation for the pear-stealing episode is communal and hence political in the traditional Aristotelian sense. Might he not simply blame his behavior on others, suggesting that when they say, "Let's go, let's do it" (2.9.17), he cannot resist? Evocative language is often the penultimate cause of political action, sweeping our isolated individuality up into collective action that reflects the will of a larger community.

Having claimed that he would not have stolen the pears without his friends, Augustine seems to embrace this political explanation of his action, underscoring the point by insisting that he still recalls how he felt about this then: "I could not have done it alone" (2.8.16–2.9.17). This allows him to conclude that he loves the negative character of the act, not only for itself, but also because of the companionship of the accomplices with whom he commits it. Yet at the last moment, he rejects this conclusion with these puzzling remarks:

> Then it was not only the theft that I loved? No, truly, nothing else, because *my association with the others was itself nothing* [my emphasis]. But what is it in all truth? . . . If I had then merely liked the pears that I stole, and merely wished to eat them, I could have done so by myself, were doing that wrong deed enough to lead me to my pleasure. . . . But my pleasure lay not in the pears: it lay in the evil deed itself, which a group of us joined in sin to do. (2.8.16)

The pear-stealing episode reminds us of an original garden where Adam and Eve face an absolute prohibition. God gives them all the food they need, but he demands that they not eat fruit from the tree of the knowledge of good and evil.[83] When they refuse to obey, they reach beyond their natural limits as (finite↓infinite) beings to encroach on the divine mystery through infinite self-accentuation.[84] This does not mean that God objects to their acquisition of speculative knowledge, as romantic poets and philosophical idealists have tried to persuade us. Rather, it implies that he wants to lead his creatures toward wisdom gradually and that he wants to protect them from a life in which good and evil alternate in an unending cycle of frustration.[85]

In the biblical tradition, the knowledge of good and evil has practical rather than theoretical implications, plunging the finite beings that possess it into a maelstrom of positive and negative values that they are never able to harmonize. It is this mystery that only God understands until the willful acts of Adam and Eve give them access to it. The practical knowledge they acquire subjects them to the judgment of God and exposes them to the harsh realities of a cyclical life, lived out in the perpetual interplay between good and evil. Life in the garden is an unfallen time of innocence before the contrast between good and evil emerges, and God forbids his children to eat fruit from the tree at the center of the garden to make it possible for them to avoid the hardships knowledge of this contrast generates.[86]

Augustine and his friends transform an orchard of innocence into a garden of willfulness; and in the process, they not only place themselves beside Adam and Eve in the Garden of Eden, but also pitch the pears they steal to the hogs (2.4.9). In doing so, they stand beside the Prodigal Son in the hog trough, eating the husks of their adolescent enthusiasm with the swine.[87] This is the tragic consequence to which the rejection of Paradise and the acceptance of the perpetual alternation between good and evil lead. Augustine's most penetrating account of the pear-stealing episode characterizes it as a negative act that he performs gratuitously. As he says over and over: "I stole the pears, not for their sake, and not for my sake, but for the act's sake." The end of the act is not beyond it, but the act itself; and stealing the pears is not an expression of a desire for determinate objects, but an act of the will without an object that turns back on itself and that points to the frozen abyss of the bottomless pit. As Augustine says in confessing this sin to God:

> Foul was the evil, and I loved it. I loved to go down to death. I loved my fault, not that for which I did the fault, but I loved my fault itself. Base in soul was I, and I leaped down from your firm clasp even toward complete destruction. (2.4.9)

When someone commits a crime, we often ascribe the act to a desire for subordinate values. For example, when a person commits murder, he does not commit the act for its own sake, but because he desires the other man's wife, covets his property, or wants revenge. Thus Augustine asks, "Would a man commit murder without a motive, taking delight simply in the act of murder? Who would believe such a thing?" (2.5.11). Even Catiline, the notorious enemy of the Roman Republic whom Cicero denounces, has some motive for his actions, justifying his behavior by saying that he acts so he will not grow inactive. The ruthless politician commits his crimes so that having gained possession of the city, he will gain honors, empire, and wealth. This frees him from fear of the laws and from financial hardship, providing a motive for his outrageous behavior (2.5.11). Morality is the context to which we usually appeal in assessing actions of this kind, and it is appropriate that Augustine turn toward it to understand the pear-stealing episode.

Nevertheless, Augustine insists that his act is not motivated primarily by ethical or aesthetic considerations. His motive for stealing the pears is not that he prefers one good to another, or that he seeks pleasure in doing what is forbidden, but that he enjoys stealing for its own sake. When the will prefers a lower to a higher good, we object from a moral point of view, where acts of this kind are sinful in a broad sense. And when we engage in an action simply for the pleasure of breaking a taboo, the negativity of the action is reflected in the smirk on our faces as we plunge into it. Yet Augustine knows that a degeneration from will to willfulness expresses the human predicament in an even more radical way, generating a definition of sin as embracing a negative act for its own sake.[88] Sin in this sense is the root of the more familiar conception of sin as the preference for a lower to a higher good. In the first sense, sin is an infinite attachment to a finite good; in the second, it is the attempt of a (finite↓infinite) being to become infinite without qualification. In this second case, willfulfulness plunges beneath the continuum of finite goods, displaying an infinite attachment its own infinitude. This predicament is the ground from which sin emerges, not only as a moral issue, but also as an ontological problem.

Since the act in question is intrinsically evil, a serious problem arises about its ontological status. As Augustine formulates the point, "Beautiful you were not, for you were a theft. But are you anything at all so I could speak to the point about you?" (2.6.12). This pivotal question points in two directions: on the one hand, it asks whether we can make an intelligible response to an act that is inherently evil and that reflects the absolute nothingness toward which it is directed; on the other hand, it suggests that Augustine wants to approach the problem as if it were a case in a courtroom to which he can make a rhetorical and juridical response. Postponing consideration of the ontological aspect of the question for the moment, let us turn to the rhetorical and juridical issues it raises.

Augustine is a rhetorician, whose original ambition is to become a lawyer and a government official.[89] One of the classes of cases that he has been trained to argue are those that seem trivial on the surface, but which he must persuade both the judge and the audience to take seriously.[90] In this case, God is the judge, we are the audience, Augustine is the prosecutor, and both he and his adolescent companions are the defendants. When he asks, "Are you anything at all so I could speak to you?" he acknowledges that the episode we are considering might not only seem trivial, but also so negligible that it would be absurd to argue about it.

From a human point of view this might be so; but since God is the judge, and since the offense is serious when it is considered from a vertical perspective, Augustine has no doubt that he must plunge on with the case as both ardent prosecutor and reluctant defendant. The task of persuading his audience to take the issue seriously is problematic, but it is also important because Augustine believes that we stand alongside him as defendants in analogous situations that deserve prosecution and judgment of their own. Thus he continues with the case, implicating both himself and his readers in an issue, the seriousness of which eventually shines through its apparent triviality.

One of the reasons this case is important is that when Augustine admits that he has stolen the pears simply to steal, he makes a transition from will to willfulness. The original discontinuity that separates him from his origins becomes doubly discontinuous: Augustine is not simply a person separated from origins that he cannot remember, but also a creature who deliberately turns away from them. There are two abysses to be considered here, one cognitive and the other volitional. In the first case, Augustine's unaided intellect cannot transcend the epistemic barrier that cuts him off from his origins; in the second, his willfulness turns away from the one who creates and sustains him.

The orchard where Augustine steals the pears is an image of the garden where pride produces the Fall. Augustine and his friends reflect the efforts of Adam and Eve to transcend their finitude, only to embrace the endless interplay between good and evil that defines their fallen condition (2.6.14). Oliver Wendall Holmes asks how a grown man can focus so much attention on such a harmless act.[91] Yet what the great jurist fails to notice is not only that an intricate legal case is unfolding before him, but the more important fact is that Augustine's act of adolescent mischief expresses the radical disorientation of the human will.

Embracing sin for its own sake turns Augustine away from God, and stealing pears with adolescent companions expresses an attempt to become infinite by imitating the omnipotence of which he can become only a shadowy likeness. If Augustine and his friends had stolen the pears to eat them, it would have been a finite act. If they had stolen them to respond to a craving that several bites would satisfy, it would have been a bounded episode. Stealing pears in such a case would have embedded the act in a determinate context that would have made it intelligible and would have permitted Augustine and his friends to make excuses for their behavior. However, when they steal the fruit simply to be stealing, their theft becomes an infinite act that separates them from God.

The separation from God that the pear-stealing episode represents has two sides. On the one hand, God and the soul that falls away from him are on opposite ends of an ontological continuum. Augustine suggests that this continuum binds its poles together, for putting ourselves far away from God and rebelling against his law is a perverse imitation of the creator that presupposes his existence. From this perspective, the imitation of God is a negative reflection of omnipotence, which implies that there is no place where we can depart from God completely. On the other hand, participation in the theft of the pears is an act that lies beneath the continuum that connects God and the soul in an intelligible relation. As Augustine expresses the point, the theft has no beauty of its own, not "even that flawed and shadowy beauty found in the vices that deceive us" (2.6.12). From this perspective, the act is lower than the lowest level of the continuum of goods, pointing to an abyss that is discontinuous with the intelligible dimension of the problem before us.

What more can be said about the dimension of discontinuity in the childish prank that Justice Holmes refuses to adjudicate, but with which Augustine continues to struggle at the concluding stage of his argument? The sinner, the saint, and the confessor gives the answer by claiming that since "the theft itself was *nothing*, I was all the more wretched in that I loved it so" (2.8.16). Combining this quotation with the claim that the companionship of his accomplices is also *nothing* leads to the heart of Augustine's problem. The saint looking back on his sin trembles as he faces the two *nihils* with which his recollection of the pear-stealing episode confronts him.

Aesthetic, ethical, political, and religious considerations converge in Augustine's explanation of the act; and he brings these dimensions together when he says, "But my pleasure lay not in pears: it lay in the evil deed itself, which a group of us joined in sin to do." Pleasure, crime, companionship, and sin stand together in Augustine's pantheon of explanatory principles. He also mobilizes these principles when he claims, "We laughed because our hearts were tickled at the thought of deceiving the owners, who had no idea of what we were doing and would have strenuously objected" (2.9.17).

The laughter that delights Augustine and his companions is aesthetic, deception is ethical, ownership is political, and since the ultimate owner of the vineyard is God, deceiving the owners has inescapable religious implications. Nevertheless, the problem of nonbeing, both in the act he commits and in the companionship he shares, remains at the center of Augustine's perplexity, inviting us to make a final effort to plumb the depths of his predicament. Augustine suggests that the two *nihils* and the relation between them are the central elements of his problem by asking, "Who is it that can explain it to me but God, who illumines my heart and searches out the dark corners thereof?" (2.8.16). The one who is now attempting to probe the depths of his soul knows that only the divine teacher can illuminate the darkness that results from his attempt to leap toward destruction by embracing the nothingness from which he has been created and to which he seeks to return.

The nothingness of creation and the nothingness of sin are not the same. The first is the metaphysical condition that makes creation *ex nihilo* possible. The second is the volitional condition that Augustine embraces when he leaps beyond the continuum of finite beings and attempts to return to the nothingness from which he comes. The locus of nonbeing in this second case is an act and not a content, and it is to be distinguished from the nothingness of creation *ex nihilo* by the fact that the direction of the act that typifies it is a radical inversion of the act of creation that brings the world into existence. In this case, as in so many others, the volitional orientation of the person rather than ontological considerations about its nature is the fundamental issue.

The absolute nonbeing to which the pear-stealing episode calls our attention cannot be characterized discursively or placed within a systematic framework as a categorial principle. This suggests that no dialectical relation between Being and Nonbeing makes the act in the orchard intelligible and that we cannot understand it as a structural element in a philosophical system. When we turn our attention from the episode to Augustine's relationship with his friends, we face a similar difficulty: on the one hand, both the episode and the companionship are nothing; on the other hand, there is something about adolescent friendship that makes stealing possible. How can we reconcile these claims without finding a third term that binds them together and without relativizing the absolute nonbeing of both the act and the companionship by giving them a place within a larger unity?

Augustine tries to evade this problem by suggesting that stealing the pears is an occasion for laughter that reaches into the hearts of himself and his companions, allows them to deceive the owners who do not know what they are doing and would have resented their actions if they had, and it permits him to derive pleasure from the fact that he does not engage in the act alone (2.9.17). Yet when he asks why companionship is essential, and when he suggests that it might be important only because no one laughs when he is alone, he replies that though this is usually the case, it is not always so. Indeed, individuals are sometimes overcome with laughter when they are alone if something very funny affects their senses or strikes their mind (2.9.17). Thus, laughter as a shared aesthetic phenomenon in response to the unethical dimension of a communal act of deception is not essential to it; and Augustine insists that he would never have engaged in it unless he had wished to embrace a gratuitous act of stealing with his friends.

At earlier stages of his account of the episode, Augustine suggests that the theft does not have a final or efficient cause in the ordinary sense of the terms. He also says that his reason for engaging in the act is negative, where the unlawfulness of the act is just as negative as the act itself. When he asks what he loves in the act in the sixteenth year of his age, where the shift from the earlier reference to the age of his body to the age of himself points to the predicament of the soul and the body together, he fastens once more on something negative, calling our attention to the trickery and the pale reflection of omnipotence that the act of stealing for its own sake displays. Yet in attempting to explain the *essence* of the theft, he turns away from causes, reasons, and negative imitations of God to something negative in principle: the orientation of the act away from God toward the nothingness into which he plunges.

Augustine drives toward the end of his analysis by claiming that the pear-stealing episode expresses his love for two things that are insubstantial: first, he loves the episode itself; second, he loves the companionship he shares in participating in it. The first is a negative act rather than a substance; the second is a community of friends that degenerates into a community of fallen creatures. In both cases, absolute nonbeing in its volitional guise surfaces as an inescapable dimension of the human situation. In the first instance, Augustine falls away from his origins as an individual; in the second, he falls away from them as a participant in a negative community. This suggests that the chasm into which he falls is not only volitional and performative, but also individual and communal.

The community in which Augustine participates is not negative from the outset anymore than are the pears on which he fastens his negative affections. Friendship defines the nature of an emerging individual, where for an adolescent, to be is to stand alongside others in a positive community. Augustine is being true to his friends when he says that he would not have stolen the pears without them. He is correct in considering the possibility that they are to blame for his behavior, and he is also accurate when he describes the delight he takes in the companionship of others. In both cases, he needs the recognition and support of his friends if his act is to have aesthetic, moral, and political significance.[92]

However, this way of formulating the issue focuses too exclusively on mutual recognition and social solidarity. The crucial point is not that Augustine needs recognition and support, but that the pear-stealing episode would have been impossible as a volitional act apart from the community in which it is embedded. Yet this raises a problem about how we can understand the role of the community in the theft without robbing Augustine and his companions of their individuality. This problem drives us beyond a dialectical attempt to understand the individual in terms of its role within the community to a negative community in which its members stand alone together.[93]

Though the pear-stealing episode begins in a community of friends, it unfolds as an act that Augustine and his friends commit alone, even though they act alone together. When he plucks the forbidden fruit, he becomes a member of "a lonely crowd";[94] and as his friends join him, they become lonely participants in a negative community as well. The act they share disrupts the bonds that bind them together and transcends aesthetic delight, ethical proscriptions, and political companionship in a process of spiritual degeneration. What begins as a community of friends ends as a community of mutual antagonism. In Augustine's words, the result of the theft is not friendship, but "unfriendly friendship" (2.9.17), where this kind of friendship is as negative as the "communal" act it presupposes. Unfriendly friendship seduces Augustine and his companions, where the trickster who plays such a decisive role in the Garden of Eden now appears in the orchard from which Augustine and his friends steal forbidden fruit. Before he steals the pears, Augustine enjoys the friendly friendship of his companions; but as the act unfolds, he and his comrades abandon the positive community to participate in a negative reflection of it.

At the deepest level, what connects Augustine with his companions is not aesthetic enjoyment, ethical defiance, or political solidarity, but the fact that they engage in the same negative act. As he understands the concept, a community is not a collection of individuals, a cluster of persons held together by a social contract, or a hierarchy of individuals bound together by a noble lie, but creatures that take delight in common objects of affection. In the biblical tradition, to be human is to be created in the image of God and to be placed beside other finite beings whose shared affections are oriented toward the one who brings them into existence. When God says, "Let us make man in our own image,"[95] he points to the positive interplay among the persons of the Trinity; and it is a common orientation toward this positive community that the lives of Augustine and his companions are intended to reflect.

In the pear-stealing episode, Augustine and his friends break the bond that binds them together by engaging in a communal act of lonely togetherness. The bond breaks when Augustine loves the theft alone; it reappears when every member of the group is oriented toward the same end; but it finally expresses itself only in an act of self-accentuation in which every member of the group participates. What begins as a community of friends bound together in playful interaction degenerates into a negative community of unfriendly friends because the object that binds them together is *nothing*. In this case, a community of wills becomes a community of willfulness where its members stand alone together as the negative act in which they participate comes to completion.

Augustine and his friends desire to do harm for fun and sport; and they want to steal from the owners of the vineyard, not for revenge, but to enjoy (*frui*) the act and the association with one another that arises out of a performative utterance. At the crucial moment, Augustine and his friends say, "Let's go, let's do it" (2.9.17). This evocative utterance expresses the intention of Augustine and his companions to act in unison. In chanting it together, every member of the group commits himself to the community they share. These words also issue quite naturally in the act, for there is no question in this case of a separation between intention and action. On this occasion, the intention and the action merge because language is not a verbal affair cut off from the action, but the performative act that initiates it.

In the biblical tradition, language is intended to bind us together into a community of finite freedom; but on this occasion, it becomes the vehicle through which Augustine and his friends masquerade as divinities. In saying, "Let's go, let's do it," they imitate God. Yet this utterance is a symptom of perverse imitation that inverts the original act of creation. In the first case, "Let there be light" generates a new world;[96] in the second, "Let's go; let's do it," refuses to let things be. The first utterance emerges from a trinitarian community and expresses the harmony the created order imitates;[97] the second emerges from a positive community of friends, but degenerates into its negative reflection. The first community reflects the act of creation that brings it into existence and that attempts to sustain it by commanding that we love our neighbors as ourselves. The second expresses the mutual loneliness of the fallen creatures into which it degenerates as they turn away from one another and turn back on themselves.

The performative utterance in which Augustine attempts to become divine reflects the violent gestures of infancy, the language of duplicity Satan uses to tempt Adam and Eve, and the transition from the (finite↑infinite) condition of created self-transcendence to the (finite↓infinite) predicament of fallen finitude. Augustine's wish to become divine expresses itself in the language that instigates the pear-stealing episode; and by acting in accord with his utterance, he plunges toward the *nihil* and embraces a negative community in which the bonds of friendship degenerate into chains of condemnation. When this occurs, the temporal, spatial, and eternal dimensions of his experience and the negative ways in which they express themselves point to the bottomless pit into which he continues to plunge until he finds God.

In attempting to describe and grapple with the pear-stealing episode, we must not override the presence of mystery in it. At the conclusion of the story, Augustine is correct in asking, "Who can unravel such a twisted and tangled knottiness?" (2.10.18) Sin can never find a place within a structural analysis or a dialectical articulation of the human situation; and as a consequence, Augustine does not want to look at it or to think about it. Instead, he wants to enter "into the joy of his Lord," where desire will no longer be misdirected, and where he will enjoy a satiety that can never be satiated. Nevertheless, his unrelenting narrative makes it clear that he understands the most important implications of the act that separates him and his adolescent companions from God. In depicting Augustine's final sentence about the theft as an inverted pyramid, we can see the author's picture of himself as he contracts into frozen isolation:

I fell away from you, O my God, and in my
youth I wandered too far from you
my true support. And I
became to myself a
wasteland.
(2.10.18)

2

The Philosophical Turn
Seven Stages of Experiential and
Reflective Development (Books III–IV)

Augustine continues to explore the relation between God and the soul and to develop a way of speaking that is appropriate to it by describing seven stages of experiential and reflective development, some of which make his separation from God more painful than before. These stages occur when he is between the ages of seventeen and twenty-seven and carry him through adolescence to the threshold of youthful maturity: he becomes a master in the School of Rhetoric at Carthage, embraces philosophy after reading a book of Cicero, and searches for a viable philosophical system by pursuing Manichaeism. In the process, he engages in speculation about astrology, responds to a personal tragedy, writes his first book, and masters Aristotle's *Categories* and the Liberal Arts.

In the first of these stages, Augustine falls in love, not with someone in particular, but with loving for its own sake; in the second, he falls in love with philosophy, not as it is reflected in a particular sect, but as it is embodied in the love of wisdom; and in the third, he embraces philosophical dualism as a way of giving determinate content to the wisdom he seeks. In this third stage, he comes face to face with the problem of fate and chance, responds to the death of his closest friend, attempts to place a theoretical veneer over the problem of death, and begins to wrestle with the problem of how language can be used to talk about God.

The temporal stages through which Augustine moves point to spatial contexts in which the interplay between the individual and the community emerges as a central theme. Having moved away from home, the young rhetorician lives with a group called "the Wreckers," where the unfriendly friendship that he experiences in the pear-stealing episode surfaces in a new form. Somewhat later, the men he encounters in the Manichaean sect also become his friends, where the pride he expresses in attempting to master philosophical dualism binds him to them. Finally, Augustine's relationship with his mother is the most important "community" in which he participates: in this context, he not only learns what friendship means, but also begins to move beyond space and time toward the positive relationship with God that Monica wants him to embrace.

The eternal dimension of experience manifests itself in a variety of ways in the spatiotemporal framework in which Augustine's life unfolds. First, the adolescent is not only searching for himself, but also searching for God; and a dream that his mother reports at the end of Book III points to the fact that he will find God eventually. Second, the spiritual disintegration that the pear-stealing episode epitomizes becomes even more pervasive as Augustine moves from stealing to loving, from loving to false images, from false images to philosophical dualism, and from philosophical dualism to deceiving innocent people. Finally, as the emerging philosopher struggles to find rest from his wanderings, the death of his friend causes him to see death wherever he looks; and as he flees from his birthplace, he is unable to find God by reflecting on the beautiful and the fitting or to frame a concept of God that is adequate to express divine transcendence. It is to these themes, and to the temporal, spatial, and eternal framework in which they emerge that we now turn.

LOVE, FALSE IMAGES, AND RHETORIC (3.1.1–3.3.6)

At the end of Book II, Augustine describes himself as an isolated wasteland; but this frozen land of destitution quickly becomes the inferno with which the account of his development continues in Book III. The young rhetorician comes to Carthage (*Karthago*), "where a caldron (*sartago*) of shameful loves seeth[es] and sound[s] about [him] on every side" (3.1.1). Carthage is the capitol of North Africa, and the splendor of the imperial city no doubt makes quite an impression on the young man from a small town who has never traveled more than a few miles from home. The city where he has come to study rhetoric is not only the political and academic capitol of North Africa, but also a context in which overt sexual expression flourishes. When he stands at the center of the city, Augustine sees pornography displayed in mosaics on the public buildings. Thus, he is not overstating the case by recalling that while he pursues his education in Carthage, a caldron of shameful loves seethes and bubbles all around him.[1]

Augustine tells us that he is not yet in love, but is in love with loving; and he says that from a hidden hunger, he hates himself for not loving something more substantial (3.1.1).[2] When he comes to the city where Dido lived, the love of stealing becomes the love of loving; and as a consequence, an isolated act of mischief is transformed into a pervasive condition that generalizes his predicament. If the love of stealing is a love of nothing, the love of loving is love for the deeper nothingness from which stealing for its own sake emerges. As Plato, Augustine, and Freud remind us, love is the root from which all our actions spring; and as a result, the love of loving is more fundamental than the love of stealing. Yet like the dangling gerund that expresses it, loving detached from determinate objects and from the creative ground from which it emerges floats in a vacuum that can never bound it, pointing to the fundamental predicament that permits Augustine to fall into a bottomless pit.

Loving for its own sake is an inversion of the restless heart to which Augustine refers on the first page of the text, and it is a negative reflection of the hidden love that will remain unsatisfied until it finds rest in God. From the standpoint of created innocence, the (finite⌐infinite) structure of consciousness is oriented toward God; and Augustine can find the fulfillment he seeks only when he comes to rest in him. Yet when he tries to become infinite in his own right, he falls away from God, seeking fulfillment in finite objects that attract him or attempting to come to rest in his own restlessness. The first six Books of the *Confessions* are the story of Augustine's failure to find happiness in either direction. Yet the author not only speaks for himself, but also speaks for us all by saying that the more empty he becomes, the more he despises what would bring fulfillment; and he points to a universal predicament by claiming that the more he moves away from God, the more his soul becomes "ulcered over" and "avid to be scratched by the things of sense." (3.1.1) In this context, bodily metaphors predicated of the soul are a way of binding the soul and the body together; and fornication is a symbol of our attempt to turn away from God by returning to the absolute nothingness from which the soul and the body are created.

As he continues to fall along the vertical axis of experience by accentuating the negative orientation of his soul, Augustine points to something positive by placing his passions in a human context. If something does not have a soul, it does not inspire his love; and stimulating interaction with other people is a persistent force that animates him. Yet he also turns away from the souls of those around him by insisting that loving and being loved are sweeter when he is able to possess the body of the person he loves (3.1.1). If bodily metaphors ascribed to the soul bring the soul and the body together, merely bodily ways of relating to another person separate these dimensions of our nature from one another.[3]

Augustine begins to lose contact with his soul and with the souls of other people when the fundamental thing that binds him to them is a bodily connection. The resulting separation between the soul and the body manifests itself in an obsession with sexuality; and the author expresses his preoccupation with it in a cluster of sexual metaphors: "I defiled the ... source of friendship by the filth of concupiscence, and its clear waters I befouled with the lust of hell." "I plunged headlong into love, whose captive I desired to be" (3.1.1). As he continues to fall away from God, the great rhetorician suggests that the healing waters of friendship in which he wants to bathe become an enveloping ocean of lust into which he plunges.

After Augustine finds joy in sexual fulfillment, troublesome ties begin to bind him that implicate both his soul and his body. As a result, he not only begins to drown in sexual addiction, but also flounders in the interpersonal entanglements of "jealousy, suspicion, fear, anger, and strife" (3.1.1). The predicament with which Augustine is struggling pervades his entire being; and as a consequence, he makes a transition from sins of the body to sins of the soul. The body is not sinful in itself, but becomes corrupt as it falls away from God; and the source of corruption is the soul that makes it possible for the entire person to fall into a chasm from which it is unable to escape on its own initiative.[4]

Soon after he comes to Carthage, Augustine becomes enraptured by the theater; and he tries to deal with the suffering that he experiences in relation to other people by projecting it on the stage. He is able to do this because the theater is filled with images of his own misery and because he can identify his own predicament with what he sees depicted there (3.2.2). On the other hand, he distances himself from the theater by insisting that he does not want the tragic events enacted there to happen to himself (3.2.2). As a consequence, his love for the theater becomes a counterfeit version of life and a counterfeit solution to the problems generated by his own misery.

The grief and vicarious suffering that a spectator loves to experience in the theater bring pleasure; but the more often this occurs, the less free the observer becomes from the passions that are simulated there (3.2.2).[5] In this way, counterfeit life in the theater makes an impact on the life of the spectator who is drawn toward it. Augustine tells us that if we suffer some of the things that we see in the theater, we are miserable; and he claims that if we grieve about the suffering of others, showing mercy is the appropriate response.[6] Yet he also says that in responding to unreal suffering on stage, we experience grief without mercy, where the more we grieve, the more we take delight in the actors who stimulate us (3.2.3).

Insofar as the images (*imago*) Augustine sees on stage are reflections of what really occurs, they are true rather than false. However, these same images are false because the actors to whom he responds need not experience the circumstances or the emotions that their imaginary (*imaginarius*) predicaments convey. The space between the actors and what they only seem to undergo generates a virtual place into which Augustine can flee from his own suffering; and within this context, he turns away from the anguish that distresses him by inverting the ordinary meaning of grief. In the real world, grief arises from suffering, and mercy is the appropriate response to it; in the theater, grief arises from fictions, and imaginary joy is often the consequence (3.2.3).

Augustine claims that we love to feel sorrow at the plight of other people because it makes mercy possible. Thus he says that friendship is the source of a positive connection among love, grief, and compassion. According to this way of understanding mercy, the love that friendship presupposes is the ground from which the grief that leads to compassion emerges (3.2.3). By contrast, Augustine tells us that when he becomes enamored of the theater, the impulse that makes friendship possible flows downward "into a torrent of boiling pitch" and "into . . . immense surges of loathsome lusts" (3.2.3). In this context, he experiences love and grief without compassion; and the jealous rage of the infant, the refusal of the child to learn what his instructors teach, the pear-stealing episode in which the adolescent falls away from God, and the transformation of stealing into loving for its own sake become the counterfeit existence that Augustine embraces as he continues to flee from God. In this precarious situation, the enjoyment that he can experience only in relation to God is inverted into "joy" in response to the imaginary suffering of others.

From his standpoint as the author of the text, Augustine wants to justify the grief that we experience in response to human suffering; but he also wants to make it clear that suffering is never lovable. In doing so, he transforms our love for sorrow by suggesting that we should love the sorrows of others even though they are not lovable. This means that we should not love them for our own satisfaction, but should love them with charity; for only in this way can we express the kind of love that does not simply satisfy our own needs (3.2.3).

In moving from one kind of love to the other, Augustine suggests that God is the ground of love because he manifests love and mercy without ever experiencing sorrow. As he formulates the point in addressing God directly,

> You love our souls with a purity of love more deep and wide than
> that we have for ourselves, and you are unalterably merciful, because
> you suffer no wound from sorrow. (3.2.3)

In the case of grief for actors on stage, we love grief and take delight in it without experiencing compassion; in the real world, we love grief in order to show mercy and can learn to transform love for sorrow into grief and charity for other people; and in God's case, love and mercy express themselves in a fashion that is free from grief altogether. Thus, the author's analysis of the contrast between counterfeit life in the theater that leads us away from God and life in the real world that makes access to God possible progresses from love and grief, to charity, grief, and mercy, to the charity and the mercy of God. This progression inverts the earlier inversion of the world into the counterfeit world of the theater, displacing the erotic love that we find in both places with the love of God that we have been created to imitate.

The images (*imagines*) that we encounter in the theater are the lowest level of the continuum of beings that God brings into existence; and to the extent that they are false, they point away from themselves to the *nihil* to which the pear-stealing episode calls our attention. By contrast, God is both the highest level of the continuum of Being and also beyond it, where divine love and mercy without grief manifest themselves to beings who can experience love and mercy only through the mediation of grief. Thus, love and grief without mercy that we find in the theater points to what is *beneath* the continuum of being; love, grief, and mercy that we find in the real world are *on* that same continuum; and love and mercy without grief that we can find only in God calls our attention to what is *beyond* the continuum altogether.

When he speaks about counterfeit compassion for actors that we see on stage, Augustine is functioning on an epistemic level that preserves an ontological distance between the center of his soul and fictional (*fictus*) contents of consciousness. In this context, he separates himself from the objects of knowledge, generating a space between the knower and the known that permits his soul to turn away from itself. Yet when Augustine speaks about compassion, he moves from knowing to willing, and by implication, turns toward suffering that touches him beneath the surface of his life. If knowing within a merely spectatorial context keeps us at a distance from the objects of knowledge, willing allows us to come into sympathetic contact with the suffering of other people in the real world. Finally, when Augustine claims that our deepest compassion for others can be expressed only when erotic love is transformed into charity, he shifts our attention from knowing and willing to being as the place where the most fundamental issues of life come to focus. Being points to the perfection of God from which grief and suffering are degenerations, calling our attention to the power through which Augustine's own suffering will finally be redeemed.

Augustine draws a distinction between the surface and the center of his existence by suggesting that fictions keep him at an emotional distance from himself. Though God and the soul are the central themes of the *Confessions*, the realities to which these themes call our attention intersect only when Augustine moves from the surface to the center of his life, finding not only himself, but finding God as well. Watching theatrical performances only scratches the surface of his everyday existence, apparently leaving him free from suffering that pierces him "deep down." However, Augustine also tells us that the "fingernails" that scrape his skin produce a diseased will that causes him to waste away (3.2.4). In the metaphor of the poisoned fingernail, the separation and unity between God and the soul that auditory metaphors presuppose collapses into the corruption that can be overcome only when Augustine listens to the voice of God. In this case, a bodily metaphor binds his soul and his body together, where the "I" that the fingernail scratches is not simply the soul, but the soul and the body that have turned away from God.[7]

Though God's mercy hovers over him from a distance, Augustine wears himself out by pursuing false images, by indulging in useless curiosity, and by permitting the sin of pride to drag him even deeper into the abyss where he is separated from God. As he says on more than one occasion, sensuality, curiosity, and pride are the most serious problems from which he suffers as he makes his torturous journey toward God (1.10.16), (1.19.30), (2.2.4), (2.6.13–14), (3.3.5), and (6.6.9).[8] Within this framework, he tells us that one day during the celebration of the mass, he arranges an affair that will produce the "fruit of death" (3.3.5).[9] The "death" to which he refers is manifest most clearly in the eventual birth of an illegitimate son (4.2.2). In this case, the enjoyment (*fructus*) he seeks becomes bitter fruit (*fructus*) that reflects his separation from God, rather than the joy (*fructus*) he can find only when he returns to God. Throughout this process, the one from whom he is estranged scourges him; but in spite of God's persistent attempts to reach him, Augustine continues to wander away from his creator by loving his own ways rather than God's (4.2.2).

At this stage of his narrative, Augustine points to the sins of his intellect in a brief account of his professional development. He tells us that his studies aim at distinction in the law courts and that he makes the transition from being a student to being a teacher by becoming a master in the School of Rhetoric. Nevertheless, a negative element taints what would otherwise be a positive achievement: the emerging rhetorician is "inflamed with arrogance"; and as he opens outward toward the larger world, he takes the first professional step in the fragmentation of his soul (3.3.6). Becoming a rhetorician in the tradition of the Second Sophistic ignores the problem of truth[10] and is a false resolution of the identity crisis with which he is struggling.[11] As the author of the text insists, rhetoric must not only be embraced, but must also be subordinated to truth before it can be used appropriately at later stages of his development (4.2.2).

At a number of places in the text, Augustine displays a curious tendency to emphasize his sins and then to insist that he could have been worse. He does this earlier when he says that in spite of his sins, he is an image of God (1.20.31); and he does it here when he claims that he is not a member of a gang of students called "The Wreckers" (3.3.6). The ambiguity of Augustine's attitude toward himself surfaces when he says that he is relatively sedate and asserts that he has no share "in the wreckings of 'the Wreckers,' " even though he lives with them and is ashamed that he is not as bad as they (3.3.6). In the pear-stealing episode, Augustine commits a negative act for its own sake with "unfriendly friends"; in this case, he distinguishes himself from friends who are even more unfriendly.

In contrasting himself with the Wreckers, Augustine is distinguishing between falling into the bottomless pit of the pear-stealing episode and congealing into a demon who has become a servant of evil for its own sake. In the first case, Augustine and his adolescent companions are oriented toward the absolute nonbeing they attempt to embrace; in the second case, the Wreckers are virtually identified with the *nihil* to which they have surrendered. This distinction between the negative direction in which Augustine is moving and the condition of absolute negativity he has not yet embraced prepares us for his later account of the death of his closest friend and of the years he squanders in unfriendly friendship with his Manichaean companions. In both cases, Augustine will come face to face with nonbeing in its most radical form.

Augustine's description of himself at this stage of his development suggests that he both is and is not on the lowest rung of creation. The sins of the body and the soul place him there; but when he evaluates his life in ethical terms, he claims that there are many individuals worse than he. Critics who object when Augustine speaks about himself as if he were the chief of sinners should not forget this passage. Nevertheless, the author implies throughout the text that from God's point of view, there are no distinctions among those who have fallen away from him. Though we make relative judgments at the horizontal level, sin is absolute along the vertical axis that expresses our relation to the ground of our existence. The moral dimension of Augustine's situation accounts for his attempts to justify himself, while the religious dimension explains the unequivocal character of his self-condemnation. The mature Augustine is more interested in religion than in ethics; and as a consequence, self-denunciation dominates the account of the disintegration he experiences as he falls away from God.

CICERO AND THE BIBLE (3.4.7–3.5.9)

Among unfriendly friends, and in an unstable period of his life, Augustine studies the textbooks of rhetoric, wanting to become eminent in a field in which he has already displayed considerable talent. Yet in the ordinary course of his professional education, he stumbles on a book of Cicero that leads in an unexpected direction. Cicero's *Hortensius* contains an exhortation to philosophy, and reading it changes the orientation of Augustine's life (3.4.7).

Though it might not be as inspiring as he suggests,[12] this book turns the young rhetorician's prayers toward God and gives him new hopes and new desires. Suddenly, every other hope becomes worthless; and with an incredible warmth in his heart, he begins to reverse the downward movement of his soul and to rise up so he might return to God (3.4.7).

A change of attitude about the most important questions is a delicate matter; and it often occurs in private, even though what occasions it is equally available to others. Cicero's book is part of the educational program of every student of rhetoric; but among the companions with whom he reads it, only Augustine cuts beneath the surface of its eloquence to embrace the content of the text (3.4.7). This transaction occurs along the vertical axis of experience, reverses the direction of the pear-stealing episode, changes the focus of Augustine's reflective orientation, and makes it possible for him to begin to return to his father.

The change of direction that Augustine undergoes occurs when he is nineteen: his father has been dead for two years, and his mother is paying for his education (3.4.7). This reference to the death of his father is significant because he devotes less than a sentence to it. By contrast, he spends eleven paragraphs in Book IX dwelling on the death of his mother (9.11.27–9.13.37). The death of Augustine's father means that the financial burden for his education shifts to his mother, but it also leaves an open space in which he can find a new father to replace the one who has died. Earlier, Monica says that she wants God to become Augustine's father rather than Patricius (1.11.17). Now the transition from one father to another begins to occur within the space generated by a book of eloquence that points beyond itself to the love of wisdom.

The most important dimension of Augustine's change of direction is the reason for it: what draws him to Cicero's book is not its style, but its substance (3.4.7). This is a serious matter for a rhetorician in the late Roman Empire: in that context, an education in rhetoric presupposes that what counts is the style and passion of a presentation rather than its truth.[13] Augustine's professional career depends on conveying this conviction to others, and he will continue to teach rhetoric with this presupposition in the background for nearly fourteen years. Even after his conversion, Augustine's language never loses its rhetorical flavor; and this dimension of his discourse continues to manifest itself in his use of antitheses, puns, plays on words, metaphors, analogies, and dialectical arguments to lead us to the heart of his spiritual intentions. Yet long before he writes the *Confessions*, the first step toward being able to do this is the glimpse of truth in Cicero that transcends the rhetorical tradition. For the first time, Augustine sees beyond images to something more fundamental that will transform his life.[14]

Cicero's book excites the erotic dimension of Augustine's soul that has surfaced already in more obvious ways. Now the saint and the confessor exclaims, "How I burned, O my God, how I burned with desire to fly away from earthly things and upwards to you!" (3.4.8). The adolescent attachment to earthly things has become a sexual addiction with which Augustine continues to struggle; and as a consequence, his sudden desire to return to God might seem to express a wish to repudiate the body and to embrace the one with whom he lives in perfect peace before his soul falls into the body. However, the problem is more complicated than this, requiring us to transpose the Neoplatonic emancipation of the soul from the body into the conversion of both the soul and the body that permits the entire person to return to God.[15]

As if to emphasize the bodily dimension of his conversion to the love of wisdom, Augustine tells us that Cicero's exhortation to embrace philosophy "inflames" him, stimulating him "to love, pursue, attain, catch hold of, and strongly embrace, not this or that sect, but wisdom itself, whatsoever it might be" (3.4.8). It is important to notice that the initial indeterminacy of wisdom is as significant as the passion it engenders. Augustine needs a new way of living more than a positive doctrine; and his significant insight in describing this stage of his development is that wisdom has its own richness, however difficult it might be to articulate. On the other hand, his initial commitment to the love of wisdom poses a critical problem because wisdom is so vague and indeterminate that many ways of thinking might be an instance of it. The wisdom that Augustine seeks as a result of reading Cicero's book is an abstract circle, the vagueness of which can scarcely counterbalance the concreteness of the existential predicament the pear-stealing episode, the love of loving, and the love of false images epitomize. Moving toward the love of wisdom opens a philosophical doorway into a new world, but Augustine moves through it without knowing where he is going. The pathway he follows in doing so issues in a painful journey from bondage to freedom that will last for fourteen years.

Augustine must learn to give the wisdom he seeks determinate content if it is to provide a framework within which his life and thought can develop. However, there is more than one way of doing this. The path most philosophers follow is to commit themselves to particular doctrines and to become defenders of a determinate philosophical method. Augustine does this initially when he embraces Manichaean dualism as a way of filling up the empty circle of abstract wisdom. The other path is to develop an open system that reflects the infinite richness of wisdom without leaving it in the abstract and indeterminate state in which we find it initially.[16] Augustine eventually chooses this second path, and it is his decision to do this that sets him apart from many other great thinkers in the Western tradition.

The only thing that checks Augustine's enthusiasm for Cicero's exhortation to embrace the love of wisdom is that the name of Christ is not mentioned in the book (3.4.8). Thus, the young rhetorician tries to pursue what is missing in the *Hortensius* by turning to the Bible. From his later perspective as the author of the *Confessions*, he sees something there that neither the proud can comprehend nor children can uncover. Rather, it is "lowly on one's entrance but lofty on further advance, and . . . veiled over in mysteries" (3.5.9). These phrases suggest that reading the Bible is like entering a cave, where one must first bend down at the entrance, but can then see a vast expanse opening out, where the richest and the deepest mysteries can be discovered. This is the first place in the text where the possibility of an allegorical interpretation of the Scriptures surfaces. Learning how to use this method of interpretation will be a decisive step in permitting Augustine to repudiate Manichaeism, and it will open up a way of reading the Bible in which understanding figurative discourse plays a crucial role. However, at the age of nineteen, the recent convert to the love of wisdom can scarcely be expected to understand the Scriptures in this way.

When Augustine first turns to the Bible, it appears unworthy to be compared with the dignity of Cicero: its style repels him, and even the sharpness of his intellect is not able to penetrate its hidden meaning. Later he realizes that the Scriptures are intended to encourage the growth of children and to sustain the mature readers that it permits them to become (3.5.9). However, having embraced the love of wisdom that eventually leads him back to God, the adolescent continues to be separated from his father because he is swollen with pride, refuses to become a child, and cuts himself off from the possibility of maturing into adulthood along a hermeneutical pathway (3.5.9).

There are two reasons why Augustine cannot understand the Bible when he is a young man. First, the version of the Scriptures that is available to him is a crude translation of the Greek text into the Latin vernacular.[17] Later, Augustine refuses to abandon this translation for Jerome's more nearly adequate version of the text in order not to upset his congregation.[18] However, at this stage of his life, the surface of the text is so repulsive to his sophisticated rhetorical consciousness that he is unable to read it. Second, the young rhetorician cannot distinguish between the surface and the center of the Bible; and as a consequence, he is unable to penetrate the spiritual meaning the letter of the text conceals. Simplicity and hidden depths permit the Bible to appeal to immature readers, on the one hand, and make it possible for more advanced readers to plunge beneath the literal meaning of the text on the other (3.5.9).

The inversions Augustine undergoes in one short paragraph establish the itinerary for a philosophical journey that spans fourteen years. First, he says that unlike his fellow students, he prefers the substance of Cicero to his style. Second, he refuses to commit himself to Cicero because the name of Christ is not in his book. Third, he claims that when he turns to the Bible to learn about Christ, its style repels him. Finally, his explanation for this response is that he cannot penetrate the substance of the text—a substance that differs radically from the substance of the book that turns him toward the love of wisdom (3.5.9).

What is the difference between the substance of Cicero's book and the substance of the Bible? The wisdom to which Cicero points is the culmination of an attempt to understand how the world hangs together. Since Cicero is both a Stoic and a Skeptic, he believes that the quest for wisdom can never reach theoretical completion. Philosophical wisdom consists in recognizing this and in attempting to lead an exemplary life in an uncertain world (3.4.7), (3.4.8).[19] By contrast, biblical wisdom is an expression of confidence in the power of God to bring deliverance to the fragmented soul. It does not ask us to understand the world, but to come to terms with ourselves; and it does not lead us to skeptical self-restraint or stoical resolve, but encourages us to embrace a transforming source of power that invades the world from beyond its natural limits.

How are we to distinguish between Augustine's commitment to philosophy as the love of wisdom and his need to become a child if he is to understand the hidden meaning a biblical text? Wisdom is the telos of a process of development that begins in childhood, moves through the stages of wonder, imagination, and analytical reflection, and finally reaches what transcends discursive explanation. On its theoretical side, self-transcendence culminates in an intellectual intuition of truth; and in practical terms, it demands a life of moderation in the face of theoretical uncertainties. By contrast, one must reverse the direction of philosophical eros and become a child again to find the hidden depths of a biblical text. A child understands figurative discourse naturally, and it is language of this kind that we must learn to understand again if we are to comprehend the meaning of the Bible. In understanding a biblical text, Augustine must learn to exercise his spiritual imagination. The imagination he needs does not have images as its content, but breaks beyond the surface simplicity of apparently crude and unlettered discourse to reveal hidden depths that are only accessible to allegorical interpretation.

Philosophy as Cicero represents it stands at the gateway of Augustine's reflective development, generating an open space that is abstract, vague, and indeterminate, but within which his religious and philosophical development can unfold. The wisdom to which the great Roman rhetorician points is indefinite enough to permit the natural development of consciousness to occur and to allow Augustine to understand the fundamental intentions of philosophical texts. Yet only when the pride that accompanies his turn toward philosophy collapses will he be able to move beyond Cicero and Plotinus to the text that undergirds the Christian tradition.

BECOMING A MANICHAEAN (3.6.10–3.12.21)

Augustine passes through the gateway that Cicero's book opens up; but in doing so, he makes a disastrous if predictable mistake. The wisdom to which Cicero points is too vague and indeterminate to satisfy him, and the version of the Bible that he reads is too crude and simplistic for him to penetrate beneath its surface. As a consequence, the nineteen-year-old convert moves away from traditional Christianity toward the Manichaean sect to develop his original attraction to philosophy. Though the love of wisdom is one thing and transforming it into a philosophical system is another, it is difficult for a young philosopher to suppress the desire to make the transition from one to the other. As a result, what begins as the love of wisdom becomes the desire for a comprehensive explanation of the world and one's place in it.

Manichaeism is a pseudo-Christian sect that originates in Persia; and though its cosmology offers a scientific explanation of the origin and nature of the universe, it also has a spiritual dimension.[20] The theoretical purpose of the sect is to allow its followers to understand the cosmos, but its more fundamental intention is to deliver them from the power of evil.[21] Augustine's adolescent struggle with sexuality and his participation in the pear-stealing episode make evil a pressing problem, and reading Cicero motivates him to respond to the attraction of abstract philosophical questions. Manichaeism attracts Augustine at both practical and theoretical levels, purporting to satisfy his religious and philosophical needs simultaneously.[22]

The Manichaean sect has two classes of members: one is an esoteric group that obeys the strict rules of an ascetic community; the other is a circle of auditors who follow at a distance. At this early stage of his development, Augustine is content to be an auditor because he cannot commit himself to the practical restrictions of an austere religious existence. Yet even though he remains outside the circle of the elect, he embraces the Manichaean solution to the problem of evil without reservation: good and evil are separate principles; the cosmos is a battleground between them; and the Manichaeans try to solve the problem of evil without placing the blame on those responsible for it. This allows its adherents to approach the moral dimension of life as if they were spectators, turning away from the problem of freedom and avoiding responsibility for their own actions (3.7.12), (5.10.18).

Augustine feels the opposition between good and evil acutely, but he does so within the vacuum of a love of wisdom that provides no moral guidance because it is abstract and theoretical. A philosophy that bifurcates the world attracts a young man in such a precarious position. The Manichaeans "solve" the problem of evil by describing the world as a cosmic conflict between two competing principles and by introducing a dyadic logic into the context of the love of wisdom for which Cicero's book has inflamed Augustine.

One of the easiest ways to respond to an indeterminate context is to make a theoretical distinction between two competing principles and to use the binary contrast that emerges from it to make an indeterminate situation clear, precise, and definite. Adolescents often go through an abstract logical stage in which dyadic thinking seems natural and preferable to the more difficult task of drawing subtle distinctions. In this respect, Augustine is no different from many other people at this stage of his development.

The young philosopher embraces a solution to the problem of good and evil that will prove to be inadequate, but it is important to notice that the dualism to which he commits himself in doing so reflects the positive and negative dimensions of his earlier experience. In infancy, original innocence stands alongside original sin; in childhood, natural exuberance stands opposed to burdensome restrictions; and in adolescence, the journey away from God is counterbalanced by the wish to go back home. Unfortunately, in restating the contrast between the positive and negative aspects of Augustine's experience, Manichaean dualism posits two principles that are at war with one another instead of liberating him from the bondage that the contrast between them imposes.

The bifurcated thinking of the Manichaeans is so impoverished from a philosophical point of view that an elaborate mythology is required to build a poetic element into a logic that is otherwise devoid of human significance. Yet when they use dyadic thinking to approach the problem of good and evil, the corresponding mythology becomes an outrageous description of the world that no one unimpoverished by a binary logic would ever embrace. The simplicity of the logic and the literalism of the language that make the Manichaean solution to the problem of evil so attractive carries with it a fanciful story about God and the world that attracts Augustine initially, but from which he turns away as he begins to think more profoundly about the most fundamental human questions.

The problem of evil that Augustine faces is both theoretical and practical; and by allowing him to choose between two classes of membership, the Manichaeans move beyond a theoretical dyad to a bifurcation in the religious cult they ask him to embrace. This bifurcation permits Augustine to make a choice between two ways of living, one of which is easier and more comfortable that the other. Dualities are appealing to Augustine because they allow him to bifurcate the world, permit him to bifurcate himself into theoretical and practical dimensions, and encourage him to drive this bifurcation into the center of his daily existence. Only later will he realize that life cannot be bifurcated, not only theoretically, or in the distinction between theory and practice, but also in the contrast between two ways of living, one of which demands everything, while the one he chooses to embrace demands very little.

At this stage of his life, Augustine is hungering for truth; and from his standpoint as the author of the *Confessions*, he identifies God with Truth itself. Yet from this same perspective, he also insists that the Manichaeans know nothing about God and that what they teach fails to nourish him (3.6.10). In doing so, he anticipates Descartes' distinction between what we experience in sleep and what we encounter when we are awake, insisting that though the first is like the second, we can derive no sustenance from it.[23] Augustine also prefigures the Cartesian claim that there is a form of error that is more serious than the contrast between waking and sleeping and that it manifests itself as a disparity between truth and falsehood for which only a deceiver could be responsible.[24] In this second case, he claims that the fantasies of the Manichaeans are not like the truth in any way, but are simply "fantastic and false" (3.6.10). If Descartes could have leaned over his shoulder, Augustine might even have said that Manichaean claims about God are as fantastic as the assertion that 2 + 2 = 5, where the evil genius is responsible for what fails to approximate the truth altogether.[25]

In developing his own point without introducing either mathematics or a deceiver of cosmic proportions, Augustine distinguishes between two kinds of image (*imago*): one is both like and unlike the object it represents (*phantasia*), while the other represents nothing at all (*phantasma*). Unlike images in the theater that are true and false at the same time, the images that fascinate the Manichaeans are false altogether, not only failing to exist, but also failing to correspond to what Augustine's inner voice teaches him. The distance between these two kinds of image is as great as Descartes' distinction between what we dream and what we might be deceived into believing at the mathematical level, where this second kind of deception is more radical than the first. Images (*phantasiae*) are products of the reproductive imagination and correspond more or less adequately to reality, while fantasies (*phantasmae*) are products of the productive imagination that do not correspond to anything at all. It is images of this second kind, and the radical deception to which they lead, that Augustine accuses the Manichaeans of trying to foist on him.

The mature Augustine rejects the Manichaean doctrine that God is to be identified with bodies in the heavens rather than with the creative source of existence, and he insists that even the heavenly bodies are not among God's most exalted works because his most important works are spiritual (3.6.10). This is Augustine's first reference to what he calls "the heaven of heaven," which is a crucial element in the cosmology that he elaborates in Books XII and XIII. However, the most important thing to notice is that in focusing on objects that do not exist rather than on images that correspond more or less well to reality, Augustine is no longer preparing the way for Descartes, but committing himself to a hierarchy of Being that spans the chasm between nothingness (*nihil*) and God.

This hierarchy does not bifurcate the world into *res extensa* and *res cogitans*, but places images, objects, the human soul, and God on an ontological continuum of increasing richness and reality. According to this view, images (*imagines*) of bodies are on the lowest level of the ladder of being; bodies are one rung higher; the soul understood as a spiritual principle that can cleave to God is higher still; and God himself is the eternal ground of changing things—the life of souls, the life of lives, having life in himself and never changing.

Though the continuity of the Neoplatonic hierarchy Augustine traces out is its most obvious feature, it is important to remember that God is not only to be found on the highest level of the ontological continuum, but is also to be distinguished radically from the beings he creates. God is the life of souls and the life of lives because he creates, orders and imposes standards on them; but he has life in himself because he is self-sufficient. This fact distinguishes God from the created order, not in degree, but in kind; and it generates a chasm between God and the world that an ontological continuum can never bridge. Unhappily, the Manichaean dualist uses this empty space to identify God with an object that does not exist, equating him with nonbeing (*nihil*) in an attempt to make him accessible to the senses.

The Manichaeans transform the love of wisdom into an account of the world that identifies God with a phantom; and as an avid adherent of their mythological constructions,[26] Augustine believes everything they say (3.6.10). In the counterfeit world of the theater, he knows that what he sees on stage is merely a fiction; but having become a philosophical dualist, he does not realize that the phantasms to which Manichaean doctrine points do not exist. At this stage of his life, Augustine suffers from a delusion that outstrips anything he has experienced before: he fails to understand that the wisdom he pursues cannot be found by using the senses rather than by turning to the intellect.

Augustine falls prey to Manichaean doctrine because his soul remains outside itself, not only allowing him to believe that God can be identified with objects that do not exist, but also cutting him off from the paradoxical fact that the one who is so far away is also closer to the soul than it is to itself (3.6.11). The dyadic logic of the Manichaeans, and the elaborate mythology that masks it, will never lead him to the place where he can find God. For this to occur, God must speak, the soul must respond, and Augustine must develop a figurative way of speaking that reaches beyond dyadic logic to make God accessible.

Augustine is attracted to the Manichaeans, not only because of the dyadic logic they presuppose, or because of the fanciful stories they construct, but also because they ask and try to answer questions that the other version of Christianity with which he is familiar apparently cannot answer. Augustine's only live options are traditional Christianity and Manichaeism, where the first seems to be founded exclusively on authority, and the second claims to be dependent on reason.[27] However fanciful and deceptive Manichaean cosmology may be, it is based on a logic that permits its adherents to cloak themselves in the garments of reason as opposed to what they regard as Christian superstition. One of the principle reasons that Augustine becomes a Manichaean convert is that the members of the sect, who are proud of their intellectual superiority, claim to accept the dictates of reason as they attack the simple and unsophisticated Christians around them.[28]

The Manichaeans do this by asking three questions that they believe orthodox Christians are unable to answer. First, "Whence comes evil?" (3.7.12). Second, "If God is to be understood as he is represented in the Old Testament, does he have a bodily shape, complete with hair and nails?" (3.7.12). Finally, "Are the Biblical patriarchs, who had many wives, killed men, and sacrificed animals, to be regarded as righteous; and if so, what kind of morality must those who defend the Biblical tradition be prepared to accept?" (3.7.12). The target of the first question is the biblical doctrine of creation: "How could God create the world without being responsible for evil; and if he is responsible for it, why would he be worthy of worship?" The other two questions raise critical problems about the Old Testament: the first ridicules an anthropomorphic concept of God, and the second scorns Hebrew morality when it is compared with the ascetic practices of the Manichaean elect.

Augustine's only comment about his understanding of the problem of evil at this relatively early stage of his life is that he does not know that it is a privation. Since his eyes cannot see beyond physical objects, and since his mind cannot transcend false images, he is unable to comprehend the claim that evil does not exist as a substance alongside God. Thus, he cannot grasp the fact that evil is a privation of goodness (3.7.12). When Augustine shifts his attention from the problem of evil to problems about the nature of God, a "metaphysics of presence" prevents him from making philosophical progress. The recent convert to Manichaeism cannot deal with a being who will prove to be both absent and present, and he does not know how to conceive of God as a spirit without any parts. He also says that when he is still an adolescent, he does not understand the relation between God and the soul and that he does not know what it means to say that God creates us in his own image (3.7.12).

It is easy to misunderstand Augustine's first point about evil as a privation. One might be tempted to claim that evil can be real, and hence a real problem, only if it is a substantial principle. As a consequence, we might be inclined to join the Manichaeans in acknowledging the reality of evil by accepting good and evil as competing principles. The resulting dualism explains the theoretical and moral attractiveness of Manichaean doctrine to an adolescent who is prepared to use the law of excluded middle as if it were a club. Should we wish to become more sophisticated than the Manichaeans, we might seek a solution to the problem of evil according to which it is a necessary but subordinate part of a larger good from which it has been abstracted. Augustine himself seems to adopt this solution to the problem at several stages of his philosophical development (7.13.19).[29] However, it is important to understand that the privation doctrine is more profound than either of these alternatives and that in his better moments, Augustine grasps this.

The dualist presupposes that evil is a substance by placing it alongside the good as a competing principle, and a holistic position does something worse by subordinating evil to goodness as a proper part of itself. By contrast, the Neoplatonic view that evil is a privation of goodness implies that evil is both a deprivation and a distortion of the good, where this implication does not make it less "real" than the dualist or the inclusivist suggest, but more so. According to Augustine, evil is real because it corrupts what is good (7.16.22); and it is a real problem because the corruption in question escapes our categorial nets.

It is important to draw a distinction between evil as a *deprivation* and a *distortion* of goodness and evil as an *absence* of goodness. Privation should be identified with the former rather than the latter; otherwise, one thing would be worse than another simply because it occupies a lower place on the onto-logical continuum than the other. More specifically, a being exhibits a privation because it is *less* than it is meant to be rather than because it is lower than another kind of being. Both Manichaeism and its holistic counterpart presuppose a logic of parts and wholes. The Manichaean bifurcates the universe by insisting on the validity of the law of excluded middle. This means that evil and goodness stand in opposition to one another and delimit the whole. By contrast, the dialectical position assumes that *p* includes not-*p* as a subordinate element, implying that evil is a finite part of an infinite good. The Manichaean position entails that God is finite and that he stands in contrast with evil, while the dialectical position entails that both evil and the world it infects are internal elements of the whole from which they must be distinguished. Both views are defective when we compare them with the privation doctrine.

To say that evil is a privation of goodness is to subordinate it to a higher principle, but evil stands in contrast with goodness by being a deprivation or distortion of it. As a consequence, Neoplatonists are committed to the view that the problem of evil is irresolvable if it is understood as a substantial principle. The dyadic logic of the Manichaeans and the part-whole logic of the dialectician cannot express the subtlety of the privation doctrine because deprivation and distortion are inaccessible to both ways of thinking. The problem of evil is like the problem of God. In the first case, we need the power to understand the distinction between distortion and intrinsic goodness; in the second, we need the ability to conceive of a spirit that is present and absent at the same time. As this early stage of his development, Augustine cannot understand either problem because both of them are inaccessible to a dyadic or holistic mentality.

Even the Neoplatonists obscure the philosophical power of their concept of privation by sometimes yielding to the temptation to identify the relative nonbeing (*non esse*) of matter with evil. In addition to the monistic strand in Neoplatonism that insists that everything emanates from the One, there is a dualistic tendency in their doctrine according to which evil becomes the second element in a dualism that splits the world in two.[30] If we embrace the dualistic tendency to which Neoplatonism sometimes gives way, evil is not relative to goodness because it is a deprivation or distortion of it, but because it stands over against the One as a substantial explanation for the presence of evil in the world.

To refine the Neoplatonic account of evil, Augustine must do two things. First, he needs to develop a doctrine of creation *ex nihilo* that allows him to move beyond the relative nonbeing (*non esse*) of Neoplatonism to the absolute nonbeing (*nihil*) from which the world has been brought into existence. Second, he needs to supplement the privation doctrine by indicating that absolute nonbeing can be reflected in a negative act of the will that issues in a radical separation from God.[31] On the other hand, evil must not be identified with nothingness (*nihil*), but only with the attempt of the creature to return to the nothingness from which it emerges. Otherwise, the nothingness from which God creates the world would be an evil principle that stands in contrast with him, regenerating a dualism at the very place where Christian cosmology escapes it. It is one of Augustine's fundamental insights that a cosmology of this kind can be developed to outflank the defects of its dualistic and dialectical competitors.

The one who eventually makes it possible for Augustine to deal with the problem of evil is not a body with nails and hair, but a spirit that can be everywhere at once, concentrating its power on a single soul that has chosen to fall away from it (3.7.12). At a later stage of his argument, Augustine defends the view that God is a being that can be both present and absent at once. However, even at this early stage of the *Confessions*, he is extraordinarily perceptive in pointing to the problem of the nature of God immediately after broaching the problem of evil. A certain absence characterizes both concepts; and this suggests that the problem of God and the problem of evil should always be considered together.

Though Augustine mentions both these themes when he confesses his initial bondage to Manichaean doctrine, he devotes most of his attention to practical problems about interpreting the Bible. In doing so, he responds to familiar critical questions about the morality of the biblical Patriarchs. The core of Augustine's answer to the Manichaean critique of the Old Testament is his insistence that the mores of different times and places are appropriate, even though the Law always remains the same (3.7.13). We must not judge the customs of the entire human race on the basis of our own, and some things that are lawful for men in the past are not lawful now. God commands one thing of them and another of us, even though the principles of justice never change.

The principles Augustine has in mind are not abstract standards that have independent existence and that can be modified or reinterpreted in particular circumstances. Rather, they are divine decrees that express an overarching plan for the universe, permitting particular customs to be appropriate in one epoch and inappropriate in another (3.7.13). Augustine alludes to the kind of framework he has in mind in his introduction to the *Confessions*, claiming that though God changes his works, he never alters his plan (1.4.4). The best way to understand Augustine's ethics is not to assimilate it to classical philosophy, but to grasp the fact that God's abiding principles are decrees that span the ages, permitting modifications that are appropriate to his plan in particular epochs and on particular occasions. Augustine's Christianity is not simply Platonism for the people, but a sophisticated account of the interplay between God's overarching plan and his willingness to carry it out by commands that are appropriate to particular times and places.

The general principles that express divine decrees are not only flexible on particular occasions, but also have a content that is determinate, even though this content always requires interpretation. For example, it is always right to embrace the Two Great Commandments, loving God with our whole being and loving our neighbors as ourselves. What this means remains open to question; but in pointing to the principle, Augustine turns to the center of the law and the prophets (3.7.13). The writer of the *Confessions* also makes objections to sins that are contrary to nature because they disrupt the fellowship between God and human beings, and he insists that we must not transgress what we agree to obey by convention (3.8.15). Even so, this way of formulating the matter leaves him sufficient logical space to insist that when God commands anything contrary to the customs of a nation, its citizens should obey him; for even kings have the right to make demands of this kind when they accord with the public interest (3.8.15).

Having confessed that he does not yet understand that evil is a privation of the Good, having admitted that he does not understand that God is a spirit rather than a man, and having dealt with Manichaean criticisms of Old Testament morality, Augustine returns to the problem of evil in a brief allusion to its origin. Earlier he hints at the point he wants to make by claiming, "I did not know that evil is only the privation of a good, even to the point of *complete nonentity* [my emphasis]" (3.7.12). He also amplifies this remark by suggesting that evil is a chain we forge for ourselves as we become prisoners of our negative volition (3.8.16).

According to Augustine, evil does not result from a condition that someone else forces on us, but emerges from acts of our own that generate a bondage of the will. The prisoner in Plato's cave wakes up to find himself in chains;[32] by contrast, the Augustinian prisoner fashions chains of his own that result from self-accentuation. The false freedom of pride reminds us of the pear-stealing episode, which expresses the temptation that always besets finite freedom. The finite being loses everything by craving something more, and he also loses himself by loving his own good more than God, "the common good of all" (3.8.16).

A loss of this kind depends on the will rather than the intellect, breaking beyond the continuum on which relative absence has an ontological and an epistemic place to an act of will that orients itself toward nonbeing (*nihil*) for its own sake. As I have suggested already, Augustine identifies evil, not only with the privation of goodness, but also with a negative act that attempts to return to the absolute nothingness out of which he has been created. Thus, he claims that through the arrogance of a false freedom, our willfulness can *lose everything* by craving something more.

Even in this bleak analysis of sin that threatens to separate us from God, there is a ray of hope; but to see it, we must turn away from considering willful acts of pride to focus on the sins that individuals commit while they are making progress in their journey toward God. In these cases, we condemn the transgressions, but commend the people who commit them. Augustine warns us not to condemn others too readily without knowing the pressures they face; and he reminds us that an action, the agent, and the circumstances of a situation are often so complex that we should adopt a sensitive and nuanced ethical contextualism with respect to them (3.9.17). He also claims in passing that people sometimes respond to special demands that God makes on them that are strange and unexpected, and he insists that we should not blame individuals in such cases when they obey them. Yet to be sure that we are not misled into believing that divine exceptions to customary norms occur more often than they do, he adds somewhat sarcastically, "Happy are they who know that it was you that gave the command" (3.9.17).

The author of the *Confessions* brings his criticism of Manichaean doctrine to a conclusion by plunging beneath the distinction between the sinner and the saint to a source of power that will finally set him free. Standing at the vertical axis that intersects the temporal and spatial dimensions of his experience, he writes,

"You put forth your hand from on high," and you drew my soul out
of that pit of darkness when before you my mother, your faithful

servant, wept more over me than mothers weep over their childrens'
dead bodies. (3.11.19)

In this passage, Augustine does not approach God for himself, but describes
his mother as his mediator. Working in the place that Monica's faith makes
accessible, the spirit of God begins to draw Augustine up from the bottomless
pit, where the tears on his mother's cheeks displace the fictitious tears of fig
trees that the Maintains attempt to redeem by ingesting their fruit.

Monica's attempt to rescue Augustine unfolds in four stages. First, God
responds to her tears and hears her prayers, not turning away, but stretching
forth his hand. In doing so, he breaks his silence and begins to speak to
Augustine through the mother who has been concerned about his salvation
since he was an infant. Second, God sends Monica a dream to console her
and to give her hope in which she sees herself standing on a wooden rule. A
young man approaches her with a smile on his face; and when he asks why
she is so sad, she answers that she is lamenting the death of her son. Then
he asks her to notice that Augustine is standing beside her on the same rule,
prompting the author of the *Confessions* to ask, "Whence was this, but that
your ears were inclined towards her heart?" (3.11.19).

The third stage of Monica's intercession involves a conversation with
Augustine about the content of her dream. When her son suggests that the
vision means she will someday be like him, she replies without hesitation:
"No; it was not said to me 'Where he is, there also are you' but 'Where you
are, there also is he'" (3.11.20). Monica's answer inverts the relation of superiority that the son tries to assert over his mother, even though he is
imprisoned by deception in so many ways, and though he is barely able to
respond to the truth that he hears on this occasion.[33]

The wooden rule about which Monica dreams measures what stands on it
and serves as a standard of value, but the cross of Christ to which it calls our
attention expresses the rule of faith that makes salvation possible and that
points to the pathway that we must follow if we are to overcome the infinite
self-accentuation that leads away from God. This path does not permit any
deviation; and it calls our attention to the words of Jesus in the Gospel of John:
"I am the way, the truth, and the life. No man comes to the Father except by
me."[34] Though it is not to be equated with a cluster of determinate principles,
the rule of Christ is both the *ratio* and the pathway to salvation, and it is this
central fact to which the dream about the wooden ruler calls our attention.

The final stage in Monica's attempt to intercede on her son's behalf
occurs when she receives an answer from God that is even more decisive than
her dream. She receives this answer when she tries to persuade a bishop to
talk with Augustine and to refute his errors, knowing that this bishop often
does this when he finds a person ready to respond. Yet on this occasion, the

bishop refuses to intervene. Instead, he advises Monica to leave Augustine alone and pray for him, predicting that he will discover his own error and renounce it on his own initiative. The bishop had been a Manichaean and had come to reject its tenants without argument from anyone else, and he is confident that Augustine will do the same thing (3.12.21).

As we might expect, the bishop's advice does not satisfy Monica; and she repeats her request, shedding copious tears and continuing to beg the bishop to talk with Augustine on her behalf. Finally, he exclaims in exasperation: " 'Go away from me now. As you live, it is impossible that the son of such tears should perish' " (3.12.21). Only then does a reversal of consciousness occur, allowing Monica to respond to the voice of the bishop as though it "sounded forth from heaven" (3.12.21). God no longer remains silent, but speaks to Monica in the words of a priest that point toward redemption; and she finds the answer she seeks when she responds to a voice that inverts the direction of her natural consciousness. Though she does not succeed in provoking the bishop to intervene, she anticipates Augustine's existential transformation, even though it will take nine years for the voice that speaks through the bishop to accomplish what it promises.

FRAGMENTATION, ILLEGITIMACY, AND ASTROLOGY (4.1.1–4.3.6)

Between the ages of nineteen and twenty-eight, Augustine is seduced and seduces others; and he is deceived and deceives those who follow him into trying to gratify insatiable desires that separate him from God. In doing so, he moves from stealing at the end of Book II, to loving at the beginning of Book III, to deceiving at the beginning of Book IV. These three conditions—stealing, loving, and deceiving—have a life of their own, directed not toward accomplishing determinate purposes, but toward negative activity for its own sake that reflects the bottomless pit into which Augustine continues to fall.

Stealing is more determinate than loving and occurs within a community of unfriendly friends; loving is a generalization of stealing and condemns Augustine to float in a vacuum of absolute negativity; and deceiving is a cognitive reflection of the discord he experiences when he turns away from God. Stealing for its own sake leads Augustine into an abyss; loving without focusing on determinate objects accelerates his fall away from God; and deceiving simply to deceive expresses the negative character of the "place" into which he is falling more clearly than any other way of living.

Augustine deceives his students openly by teaching the liberal arts, and he deceives them secretly in the guise of religion. In public, he is proud of himself, strives after fame, seeks theatrical applause, and enters poetical contests to win public acclaim; in private, he seeks purgation by carrying food to

Manichaean saints because he believes that they can transform it into angels and gods (4.1.1). The young rhetorician vacillates between public success and private superstition, permitting the existential opposition between the outer and the inner dimensions of his life to split him apart.

At this stage of his narrative, Augustine says three important things about himself. First, when he is separated from God, he is responsible for his own sins and is the leader of his own destruction. Second, when all is well with him, he is an infant, nourished by the milk that he receives from God. Finally, when he considers the conflict that arises between the negative and the positive dimensions of his life, the question emerges, "What manner of man is any man, since he is but a man?" (4.1.1) One commentator takes this strange and involuted sentence to imply that a man in the ordinary sense is not a man at all and that the true person is a disembodied soul that falls into the body when it turns away from God.[35]

A more reasonable interpretation of Augustine's question suggests itself in the statement that follows it, where he contrasts those who are strong and mighty, and who laugh at him, with those who are weak and needy, and who confess their sins (4.1.1). Is not the great rhetorician suggesting that in the eyes of God, even the strong and the mighty are weak and needy, and that those who try to stand over against their creator should remember that any man is nothing but a man? Three paragraphs later, he confirms this suggestion by claiming that a man is made of "flesh and blood, and of proud corruption," pointing not to the fall of the soul into the body, but to the disintegration of the entire person when it falls away from God (4.3.4). As the initiator of his own destruction, Augustine's soul leads his body astray; and the result in both instances is death—in the first case, the spiritual death of the soul, and in the second, the physical death of the body. Two deaths await the person who falls away from God; and as it moves toward them, the entire person orients itself toward the nothingness (*nihil*) out of which it has been created.

At this juncture, Augustine moves in a negative direction by making a fateful decision to become a teacher of rhetoric. A desire for money conquers him; he sells speaking skills to enable his students to conquer others in the courts; he teaches them tricks of speech to sway their audiences; and though he claims that they do not put their skills to use against innocent people, he knows that they will often use them to save the life of a guilty man (4.2.2). Again Augustine paints an ambiguous picture of himself: he is not as immoral as he might be, but not as good as he wishes he were; he is far away from God, but insists that he is made in God's image; and though he is stumbling on a slippery path, God sees him "sending out flashes of fidelity amid much smoke" (4.2.2). This is the first reference to the concept of faith in the text, where "flashes of fidelity" to his students are expressions of a positive dimension of the soul that has not been effaced by the fall.

Augustine continues to sketch an ambiguous picture of himself by referring to his mistress as a woman that he stumbles across in attempting to
gratify his passions, but by also insisting that he is faithful to her bed (4.2.2).
In doing so, he points once more to faith at work in him that will flourish
eventually into a more productive form. The relationship between Augustine
and his mistress teaches him the difference between marriage and "the com-
pact of a lustful love" (4.2.2). In the late Roman Empire, marriage is a legal
arrangement for having legitimate children, and a relationship with a mistress
is a context in which children are sometimes born against their parents' will.[36]
Yet Augustine insists that even children born in these circumstances compel
us to love them. He is no doubt thinking about the child his mistress bears
him; for though their son is illegitimate, they call him "Adeodatus," where the
name suggests that even the offspring of an illicit relationship can be a gift
from God.[37]

Augustine's attitudes toward marriage and his mistress raise serious questions: "Why does he tell us the name of his son, but never reveal the name of
his mistress?" "Does his failure to do so suggest that he regards her with contempt?" "Why is the distinction between marriage and having a mistress so stark
and unappealing, even to the pagan audience to which he sometimes addresses
himself?" "And does the saint and the confessor intend for us to conclude that
marriage is simply a contract for having children and that a man in such circumstances is justified in directing all his passion toward his mistress?"

At least one answer to these questions emerges if we consider Augustine's
cultural situation. In Augustine's world, where marriage is a contract,[38] a man
usually reserves his passion for his mistress. Augustine's mistress comes from
a lower social class than he; and in a cultural context where having a name
is having a place within society, she quite naturally remains nameless. Augustine might even be trying to spare the woman, who is still alive when he
writes the *Confessions*, the embarrassment that might result from revealing her
name.[39] However this may be, the parents of a child born out of wedlock face
innumerable difficulties in Roman society because Roman law forbids a man
to marry his mistress. Thus, Augustine is merely stating the obvious when he
says that grappling with these problems teaches him the difference between
a lawful marriage and a lustful love.[40]

At this stage of his life, Augustine continues to turn away from God by
consulting astrologers about his destiny. Astrologers attract the Manichaean
convert because they say that the cause of sin is not in him, but in the stars,
permitting God and the heavens to bear the blame for sin while its adherents
remain blameless (4.3.4). Astrology also appeals to Augustine because it is
"scientific." The Latin word for astrologer is *mathematicus*, pointing to the
pseudo-mathematical dimension of astrological procedures. The astrologer's
belief in the importance of fate in human affairs also fascinates Augustine

because it meshes perfectly with the literalism of Manichaean doctrine. What could be more straightforward than a doctrine that explains human actions by invoking a scientific principle that seems to be so clearly intelligible? Fate stands in contrast with chance; the relation between them mirrors the Manichaean distinction between good and evil; and in both cases, a binary opposition results that is easy for the literalistic mentality to invoke and manipulate.

A wise man who is skilled and famous in medicine and who had once placed a crown on Augustine's head when he had won a rhetorical contest tries to rescue him from his commitment to astrology. The doctor reminds the young rhetorician that he already has a career and that he is embracing astrology by his own free will rather than from necessity. These remarks point from fate to freedom, and they challenge Augustine to move beyond the opposition between chance and necessity. Yet when he asks the physician to explain why the predictions of the astrologers are often so accurate, the doctor embraces the astrologer's opposition between chance and necessity by responding that the force of chance, diffused through the whole order of nature, brings these things about (4.3.5).

If the physician had stopped there, he would not have been superior to the astrologers. Simply embracing one pole of a binary opposition is not an appropriate way to refute a person who embraces its contrary. Yet the wise man plunges deeper, claiming that when one opens a book by accident, "a verse often appears that is wonderfully appropriate to the business at hand" (4.3.5). The physician tells Augustine that a person sometimes arrives at answers to his deepest questions by a higher instinct without knowing what goes on in his own mind, where the answers he seeks emerge from his soul, "not by art but by chance" (4.3.5).

This episode is important, not only because it allows Augustine to move beyond chance and necessity to a higher instinct that sometimes guides him, but also because it prepares the way for the account of his Christian conversion. In the situation before us, a wise man tells him that when a person picks up a book and reads a passage selected at random, a higher instinct sometimes guides him to the answer he seeks; in a garden in Milan, he picks up a book in response to a voice that speaks from beyond the garden wall, where what he reads transforms his life. In the first episode, a physician tries to heal Augustine by pointing to a higher instinct within his soul; in the second, the passage he reads points to a physician who can heal his fragmented heart. In both cases, freedom stands in contrast with bondage, but only in the second do we find a source of power that makes it possible for Augustine to make the transition from one to the other.

Later, Augustine faces the problem of freedom and bondage directly; but at the moment, neither the doctor nor his friend, Nebridius, can persuade him to turn away from astrology. The authority of the astrologers continues to influence him, and he has no proof that their predictions come from chance rather than from stargazing (4.3.6). In these respects, Augustine is a curious mixture of conflicting elements: on the one hand, he places his trust in the authority of the astrologers with whom he is fascinated; on the other hand, he refuses to reject astrology because their is no compelling proof that it is mistaken. In this interplay between authority and reason, he has faith in the predictions of the astrologers, where nothing will turn him away from them but a proof that their achievements rest on chance rather than necessity. At a later stage of his development, Augustine will find the evidence he needs to turn away from astrology; and when he does this, he will bring faith and reason together by responding to a voice that transcends fate and chance, freedom and necessity, habit and a higher instinct, and that finally sets him free.

THE DEATH OF A FRIEND (4.4.7–4.12.19)

When Augustine begins to teach rhetoric, he has a friend who is about the same age as he, and who is studying the same subjects. They had known one another since childhood, had gone to the same school, had played games together, but had not been as close then as they have now become. Indeed, Augustine says that they never become friends in the richest sense because true friendship can exist only among those who love God (4.4.7). In making this claim, the theologian contrasts the kind of friendship that emerges from playing games with the kind that presupposes charity, insisting that only the second can be regarded as friendship in the genuine sense. At this juncture, Augustine draws a distinction between the game of life and the life of love, suggesting that the first must be replaced by the second if we are ever to become what we are meant to be.

Augustine's friendship with his childhood companion is not the "unfriendly friendship" of the pear-stealing episode or of his association with "the Wreckers," but it is also not the kind of friendship that he will find in the Christian community. Their friendship falls somewhere in between these poles, and perhaps calling it "philosophical friendship" is the most accurate way to describe it. Friendship like this presupposes an interest in common problems and a commitment to philosophical conversation that allows these issues to be explored in friendly dialectical interchange. Augustine and his childhood acquaintance are both students of rhetoric, and they become friends because they devote themselves to common intellectual pursuits within the community of scholars to which they have both committed themselves.

Within this context, Augustine tells us that he turns his friend away from Christianity and that they wander off together into Manichaean dualism. We must remember that however absurd this sect might appear to contemporary readers, it is a sophisticated philosophical doctrine for its fourth century adherents. With this fact in mind, it is easy to understand how two young intellectuals could become enthralled by Manichaean doctrine as they pursue their quest for wisdom. It is also important to notice that philosophical friendship always has an erotic dimension and that Augustine acknowledges this fact when he says that in childhood, his companion is "not such a friend as he [becomes] later on" (4.4.7). Indeed, Augustine tells us that he and his friend become inseparable; and he even says that he could not exist without him.

Friends are important to Augustine from the beginning to the end of life. The temporal modulations of his personal development presuppose a communal dimension of his life that begins with his nurses and ends in a monastery. At every stage of his journey, Augustine's friends sustain him; and he makes it clear that he could not have lived without them.[41] However, the premature death of his closest companion their friendship; and it brings the philosophical conversations that sustain it to an end only one year after they had begun.

The unexpected loss of his friend brings Augustine face to face with the problem of death. This is the first time since the pear-stealing episode and since his reference to the problem of evil that he confronts an issue for which there is no theoretical resolution. Indeed, the death of his friend deepens his predicament by bringing him face to face with an existential negation that allows absolute nonbeing to express itself in human form. If nonbeing cannot be spoken about coherently from a systematic point of view because it violates the law of excluded middle,[42] its human face is even more intolerable because it forces us to confront the ultimate limit of human existence. This limit cannot be dealt with adequately by using a binary logic. As a consequence, even though the death of his friend is the most painful moment of Augustine's life until the death of his mother, it becomes a positive step in leading him back to God because it suggests that Manichaean dualism is inadequate.

A few days before his death, a priest baptizes Augustine's friend while he lies unconscious in a death sweat; but this does not worry the Manichaean convert because he assumes that his companion will retain what he has taken from him rather than what a stranger does to his body. Yet much to his dismay, he finds that matters turn out differently. When his friend regains consciousness, Augustine jests about his baptism, believing that his companion will ridicule what someone has done to him while he is unconscious. Yet the friend recoils from Augustine as if he were an enemy and insists that he not make jokes about his conversion (4.4.8).

Though his friend's response perplexes Augustine, he conceals his feelings about it until the friend recovers. However, the young man never regains consciousness; and when the fever returns a few days later, he dies (4.4.8).

The salvation of Augustine's companion is vertical rather than spatial or temporal, and it has more to do with his relation to God than with his affection for Augustine. As the saint expresses the point, God snatches him away "from my madness," so he might preserve him "for my consolation" (4.4.8). Yet for the sinner who has not yet become a saint, the "recovery" of his friend is a tragedy. As a consequence, the interplay between original innocence and original sin, the interaction between the positive volition of his nurses and the negative volition of his willfulness, and the disparity between his educational achievement and the pride that motivates it become the radical contrast between friendship and death.

Augustine sees death everywhere he looks; his native town becomes a torture room; he is unhappy even in his father's house; and all the joy that he has experienced with his friend returns to torment him. In the vacuum created by the death of his closest companion, and in the face of the radical nothingness to which the threat of dying calls his attention, the young rhetorician becomes a riddle to himself; and "being toward death" becomes "being toward nothingness" to which the threat of death gives him access.[43] When Augustine tells himself to hope in God, he is unable to do so; for the friend he has lost is real, while the deity to which he turns is a phantom. Since the threat of death cannot be overcome by the impotence of a fictitious god, Augustine tells us that only tears are sweet to him and that they take the place of his friend in his heart (4.4.9).

Augustine is finally facing problems from which he has fled for years. His hopes for a meaningful life have been predicated on his desire for success, on his association with the Manichaean sect, and on his commitment to a circle of friends; but when he loses his closest companion, the adolescent who has been proud in public and superstitious in private finally asks himself who he is. Yet when he turns inward, he does not know how to talk to himself; and when he asks himself why he is so sad, he does not know the answer. Augustine is finally alone; and having nothing to guide him but a growing awareness of the difference between phantasms and reality, he makes the most realistic response available: the young philosopher allows the tears that roll down his cheeks to take the place of his friend in his heart (4.4.9).

As the days pass, time begins to heal Augustine's wounds. When he is a boy, time passes through him as if he were an empty container; now the passage of time comes closer to the center of his soul by alleviating his suffering (4.8.13). Yet before he turns away from the pain produced by the death of his closest friend, he gives a profound analysis of tears, friendship, transience, and transformation. These existential and philosophical reflections occupy Augustine for ten paragraphs, permitting him to articulate the richness of the space within which friendship flourishes and to call our attention to the devastating consequences of its inevitable dissolution.

The author of the text asks God to put the ear of his heart to His mouth and to tell him why tears are so sweet to those who are in misery. The one who has lost his closest companion has no hope that his friend will come back to life, and he does not seek this in his tears. Rather, he grieves and weeps because he is miserable and because he has lost his greatest joy. This leaves the young man with only one hypothesis to explain his misery, but the question in which he formulates it expresses penetrating psychological insight: "Is weeping itself a bitter thing, and does it give us pleasure because of distaste for things in which we once took joy?" (4.5.10).

The greatest psychologist of the Middle Ages is keenly aware that pleasure sometimes comes from pain, but he also knows that there is a deeper source of pleasure that will bring peace to his soul and that the key to finding it is to address God from the center of his being. Augustine uses his favorite auditory metaphor when he says, "Put the ear of my heart to thy mouth" (4.5.10). The ear of the heart and the mouth of God stand over against one another. Yet wholeness can emerge out of separation only when the ear and the mouth come into contact with one another, not only allowing God to answer Augustine's questions, but also allowing Him to transform his fragmented soul.

Augustine tells us that a strange feeling comes over him as he contemplates the death of his friend. He finds it wearisome to live, but is afraid to die; and what he hates and fears most is not the death of his friend, but the *sting of death* that has robbed him of his closest companion (4.6.11). At this stage of his life, Augustine is a narcissist, more concerned about his own wretchedness than about the death of the friend that calls the threat of death to his attention. In a moment of existential anxiety, he even imagines that death will become omnivorous and that it will annihilate everything (4.6.11). Thus, the death of his friend is not simply a spatial and a temporal episode, or an occasion for him to indulge his narcissism, but a moment in which Augustine faces the threat of absolute nonbeing in its most serious form. Here Augustine encounters an opposition between friendship and dying that cannot be dealt with in merely theoretical terms because the second term threatens to swallow up the first.

Augustine does not know how to love men as he ought to love them; and as a consequence, he frets, sighs, weeps, torments himself, and cannot find rest. He drags his "pierced and bloodied soul" with him and can "find no place where [he] might put it down" (4.7.12). This sentence is important, not only because it expresses existential anguish, but also because it flies in the face of so many interpretations of Augustine's intentions. Who is the "he" who is carrying his bloody soul about and is unable to find a place to lay it down? If it is the body, the body is acting on the soul, contrary to the usual interpretation of Augustine's account of the relation between them. Yet if it is the person of whom both the soul and the body are dimensions, this suggests that though the soul may be the highest part of the individual, the person himself is not the soul, but the soul and the body together. This certainly seems to be Augustine's opinion, since he says on more than one occasion that a person is a composite of a soul and a body (e.g., 5.1.1), that this composite has been created in the image of God (3.7.12), and that we cannot help loving our own bodies.[44]

The reference to the pierced and bleeding soul that Augustine carries about presupposes the complex semantics that he has been presupposing, suggesting that the soul and the body are bound together and held apart in such a way that Augustine is able to refer to each of them in terms of the other. In the passage before us, he emphasizes their unity more than their separation by saying that he tries to put his soul to rest in pleasant groves, games and singing, sweet-scented spots, rich banquets, pleasures of the bed, and books and poems (4.7.12). However important the soul may be in Augustine's metaphysics, passages of this kind suggest that he never loses sight of the intimate relation between the soul and the body, and of the need to bring them both to rest in relation to the One who has brought them into existence.

The isolated wasteland of Book II, and the bubbling inferno of Book III, now give way to the unrelenting anxiety of Book IV, placing Augustine in between the bottomless pit toward which he has fallen and the resting place that he longs to embrace. Yet this middle ground is as puzzling as the abyss toward which he is oriented, and he expresses this fact by using paradoxical language. Augustine asks where he can fly from his own heart, and he wonders how he can fly away from himself without losing himself altogether (4.7.12). Presumably, the one who flies away would try to follow himself, illustrating the paradoxical fact that a person can be present and absent at the same time.

Once more, we must abandon literal discourse for a more flexible way of speaking, noting that separation from God and separation from one's self are states of consciousness in which unity and separation are intertwined. When Augustine says that he cannot find either God or himself, he means it, but not in the sense that there is a place in either case to which he might return. To the contrary, separation from one's self is self-separation; and separation from God is separation and unity that has not yet been transmuted into a community of finding, knowing, loving, and praising that will transform the person altogether.

Three significant factors define Augustine's predicament. First, his heart is breaking, and he is no longer able to find rest in phantasms. Second, when he tries to find relief in a fictional god, his grief comes hurtling down through a vacuum and crashes in on him. Finally, he is neither able to live with himself nor to flee from the sadness of his heart. At the deepest level, he does not have a problem to solve, either theoretically or practically, but has become a problem to himself[45] that can never be dealt with by seeking a merely geographical resolution. Yet in response to his predicament, Augustine tries to do the very thing that he knows he cannot do: he flees Thagaste to Carthage in order to run away from himself, allowing his native town to stand proxy for himself while he runs away to the bubbling caldron where he has lost his soul once before.[46]

Augustine makes an interesting remark at this stage about the nature of time in a passage that anticipates Proust:

> Time does not take time off, nor does it turn without purpose through our senses: it works wondrous effects in our minds. See how it came and went from day to day, and by coming and going, it planted in me other hopes and other memories, and little by little they filled me up again with my former sources of delight. (4.8.13)

This remark suggests that time is linear, but that it is not continuous. Augustine expresses the linear dimension by maintaining that time passes from day to day, but he also points to discontinuity by saying that it "works wondrous effects in our minds." Time juxtaposes ideas and memories from earlier times and places, and it often rearranges their order. This differs from his earlier experiences of time as passing through an empty container or as a dynamic medium that heals his grief. Now time becomes a principle of association that collects dispersed ideas and memories into the unity of the present moment. This new concept of time becomes a precondition that allows Augustine to write the *Confessions* as an interplay between recollection and reconstruction. Because time is linear, recollection is possible; because it is discontinuous, reconstruction is necessary.

Little by little, Augustine begins to remember earlier pleasures that remove the sting from his present experience. Yet before he turns away from it, he reiterates the cause of his predicament: the death of his friend devastates him because he loves a finite being as if he will never die. This infinite attachment to something finite echoes one of Augustine's earlier definitions of sin, and it reminds us of the fact that Augustine will never find the freedom he seeks until his infinite longing finds an infinite content that will bring him to rest.

This (finite↑infinite) being, who becomes a (finite↓infinite) being by refusing to accept his limitations, can only find rest by embracing his finitude and by using it as a vehicle for expressing the infinite richness that he has been created to reflect. Thus Augustine needs to move beyond the fall to conversion and fulfillment. Yet for the moment, he continues to seek rest in finite attachments, suggesting that what revives him is the consolation of other friends, with whom he keeps on loving the things he loves instead of

God. Augustine has itching ears, and the fable that suggests that he can find satisfaction in finite things does not die as quickly as his closest friend (4.8.13). What are the things that Augustine loves in the friends who comprise the community within which he develops? He loves "to talk and to laugh with them; to do friendly acts of service for one another; to read well-written books together; sometimes to tell jokes and sometimes to be serious" (4.8.13). When he disagrees with them, he does so without rancor, as he might do with himself. Sometimes teaching, sometimes being taught, he longs for his friends to return when they are absent, and he welcomes them home with joy. Tokens of friendship emerge spontaneously from those who love him and whom he loves in return. Finally, Augustine says that the love they express "by way of countenance, tongue, eyes, and a thousand pleasing gestures were like fuel to set our minds ablaze, and to make but one out of many" (4.8.13).

It is important to notice that this reference to unity does not blur the differences between Augustine and his friends by presupposing a world-soul of which they are parts.[47] Rather, the unity in question points to the possibility of a *community*, where its members are bound together by an orientation toward a common object of affection. In this case, the ontological concept of *containment* is replaced by the existential concept of *orientation*, where the orientation of the soul is more fundamental than a place in the heaven of heaven from which it has descended.

What is the source of our sorrow when a community like the one Augustine describes is fragmented by the death of a friend? Those who live feel death because they identify themselves so fully with the friend they have lost that there is scarcely any psychological space between them. Yet Augustine tells us that friendship with others is a lie when it is compared with friendship with God. He also suggests that the presence of life in our friends becomes the absence of death when they depart, and that the absence of sorrow when they are present becomes the presence of tears at their parting (4.8.13). Augustine believes that only God can satisfy our restless longing; and as a consequence, he insists that the remedy for our predicament is to love both our friends and our enemies in God. No one loses God but those who turn away from him; but when we do so, a question arises about where we can go. Earlier Augustine insists that we cannot run away from ourselves (4.7.12). Now he extends this claim to God by suggesting that we can never find a place that is beyond the reach of our creator (4.9.14). In this way, he sounds the theme that allows him to deal with the relation between transience and transformation.

The key to transformation is to learn to love all things in God. Yet what does it mean to love our friends and enemies in God, and what does it mean to suggest that we lose no one dear to us if all are dear to us in him? To be in God is to be oriented toward the "place" where those who live and die can find rest. Yet how can we love our *friends* if we love them *in God*, and how can we prevent loving them *in* him from collapsing into loving him *instead of* them?[48] The problems these questions raise point to some of the most subtle dimensions of the relation between God and the soul, and Augustine struggles to deal with them as he undertakes his meditation on transience and transformation.

The first step he takes is to pray that God will cause his face to shine on him and save him, insisting that when he turns to anyone but God, sorrows entangle him. This is so even if he surrounds himself with beautiful things that capture his attention. Beautiful creatures come from God; but because they are transient, it is inappropriate to seek lasting satisfaction in them. We are tempted to embrace them because they grow toward perfection; but when they are perfect, "they grow old and die, and even though all things do not grow old, . . . all die" (4.10.15). In fact, "the more quickly they grow so that they may be, so much the faster do they hasten toward ceasing to be." "This is the law of their being" according to which things are born, grow, decay, and die (4.10.15). Another way to formulate the point is to say that finite things are parts within a larger whole and that one part must die to make room for another. This cyclical law of nature obtains for things that do not exist all at once, and it is impossible to come to rest in them because they do not abide (4.10.15).

As he does so often, Augustine illustrates his point about finitude and transience with an auditory example. When we utter a sentence, it is not complete until one word passes away so that others may follow it. In the same way, nature is a dynamic totality in which beings not only change from one state to another, but also come to be and pass away according to the law of their development (4.10.15). Finite things are good; we should praise God for them; and it is appropriate for us to adopt a positive attitude toward nature because God has created it. Yet if we try to come to rest in finite things, they rend our souls because these things must die.

In the face of death, Augustine asks us to return to God through conversion and to commit whatever we have to him; and he promises that if we do so, we will lose nothing in return. If we return to our "dwelling place," everything in our souls that has decayed will flourish again; God will heal our diseases; and he will restore and bind around us all that flows and fades away as we fall away from him (4.11.16). When this occurs, the soul that drags us down will stand fast with us and will abide before God who never passes away.

Augustine urges us to quit following the flesh so the flesh can follow the soul that has been converted (4.11.17). These are scarcely the words of a man who believes that the soul has fallen into the body from which it needs to be liberated, but point instead to the transformation of the entire person. The wholeness that Augustine seeks is not achieved in the conversion of the soul, but in a life oriented toward God in which we stand before him as embodied beings. When we stand there, the dynamism involved in the positive relation between God and the world continues; for the one who creates us wants us to love him, to return to him, and to abide with him in the restless reciprocity of perfect love.

In speaking about finitude, transience, and our need for transformation, Augustine presupposes a distinction between created and fallen existence that needs to be made explicit. When he claims that nature is a domain in which things come to be and pass away and that the law of nature leads from birth and growth to decay and death, he is speaking about a created rather than a fallen region of finite things. Things that are created after their own kind are born and die according to nature, and this would have been so even if Adam had never fallen. By contrast, human beings are created in the image of God; and in this case, death results from sin rather than from the law of nature. Natural death and human death must therefore be distinguished. In the first case, death is part of a created being's natural existence; in the second, physical death would have never occurred apart from sin.[49]

When Augustine says that we can never find lasting satisfaction in finite things, this does not imply that there is something negative about them as they are in themselves. However, it does suggest that things that come to be and pass away will always disappoint us if we try to come to rest in them. Augustine believes that created beings should be used (*uti*) rather than enjoyed (*frui*), where their use is to serve as vehicles to bring us into relation with God.[50] When this order is observed, our orientation toward nature is what it is intended to be; and if we had never deviated from it, both the fall and the death that results from it would have never occurred.[51] The human being is created to orient itself toward God and to use created things as symbols to make this orientation possible.[52] Yet when we turn away from God and refuse to use them in this way, we first turn toward things instead of God, and then turn toward the nothingness from which these things are brought into existence. In both cases, sin separates us from God; and spiritual and physical death are the natural consequences.

When Augustine speaks about his grief in response to the death of his friend, and when he calls our attention to his need for transformation, he is presupposing the fallen condition that results from sin. The death of his friend is not simply a natural phenomenon, but is the consequence of sin; and his inconsolable grief in response to it results from sin as well. When Augustine orients himself toward his friend as if he would never die, he is responding to him as if he were infinite rather than finite; and when this occurs, sin is the inevitable result. Formulated in somewhat different terms, Augustine's relationship with his friend is idolatrous; for in pursuing it, he seeks to derive ultimate satisfaction from one of God's creatures rather than from God himself.

Augustine's response to the death of his friend presupposes four spatiotemporal levels that it is important to distinguish. First, the unfallen world is not only a collection of finite beings that come to be and pass away, but also a realm of (*finite*-infinite) beings who have been created in the image of God. Since human beings are finite, we are subject to change; but since finitude and fallenness are not the same, and since human death results from sin rather than from natural causes, we are not subject to death. Instead, we exist as (finite↑infinite) beings in an undistorted spatiotemporal matrix where we cleave to God in unbroken devotion. Second, when we fall away from God, we become (finite↓infinite) creatures; and as a consequence, we plunge into a fallen spatiotemporal context where we become subject, not only to change, but also to death. It is this fateful transition from finitude to fallenness that leads Augustine to reflect on his need for transformation and on his quest for fulfillment.[53] In doing so, he claims that conversion can overcome fallenness and the death that results from it, pointing to a converted spatiotemporal context that is appropriate to the transformed beings who live in it. The conversion of human beings presupposes the conversion of time, where time becomes an ecstatic context that permits us to reach for God. Finally, Augustine suggests that when we return to God, we will be able to express our infinite dimension without losing ourselves in finite things. In this case, conversion becomes fulfillment; and a new spatiotemporal framework will emerge in which we can cling without distortion to the one who has brought us into existence.[54]

There are three ways to describe the relation of these four levels of human existence to one another. First, we can regard the move from creation and the fall to conversion and fulfillment as a progression, where all four of these stages occur in an order of temporal succession. In this case, we can construct a narrative that begins with the first stage of Augustine's journey and leads to all the others. Second, we can understand the first two stages of this journey as ways of pointing to original innocence and original sin in every individual, where these dimensions are simultaneous rather than successive, where original innocence is the first word about the human situation and original sin is the second, and where conversion and fulfillment are temporal moments in which the fall away from God is overcome. In this case, the narrative about the first two stages is a way of symbolizing permanent truths about the human situation; and the narrative about conversion and fulfillment points to possibilities that can be actualized in our own individual situations. Finally, the progression in question can be understood from temporal and nontemporal points of view simultaneously. In this case, the narrative about the transition from creation and the fall to conversion and fulfillment is both temporal and typological at once, where the view that Augustine will finally adumbrate can be understood most adequately in these terms (10.20.29).

With the transition from creation and the fall to conversion and fulfillment in view, we should now be able to understand a puzzling passage that Augustine places at the center of his reflections on transience and transformation. In this passage, he says,

> If fleshly sense had been capable of comprehending the whole, and had not, for your punishment, been restricted to but a part of the universe, you would wish that whatever exists at present would pass away, so that all things might bring you the greater pleasure. For by that same fleshly sense, you hear what we speak, and you do not want the syllable to stand steady; you want them to fly away, so that others may succeed them and you may hear the whole statement. So it is always with all things out of which some one being is constituted, and the parts out of which it is fashioned do not exist all at once. All things together bring us more delight, if they can all be sensed at once, than do their single parts. But far better than such things is he who has made all things, and he is our God, and he does not depart, for there is none to succeed him. (4.11.17)

Augustine's reference to "fleshly sense" calls our attention to the kind of sensations we have by using the body, where according to Augustine's epistemology, the soul uses the body to make sensible contact with the world.[55] Yet this passage also makes it clear that embodied existence must be distinguished from fallen existence by suggesting that embodied beings would have been able to comprehend the entire universe by means of the senses if sensation had not been restricted to a part of it as a punishment for sin. If we take this passage seriously, a distinction emerges between created and fallen existence, where created existence involves an embodied consciousness of the universe as a whole, and where fallen existence is restricted to consciousness of only part of the universe because of its sin. However, even if this distinction between created and fallen beings obtains, there would still be a difference between consciousness of the entire universe and God's own way of knowing. If we had not fallen away from God, and were consciousness of the universe as a whole at any temporal moment, we would still wish for things to pass away so we might be conscious of the whole, not only spatially, but temporally as well. By contrast, God knows everything all at once because he has made all things and is not subject to temporal succession (4.11.17).

The unfallen Adam, whose existence Augustine presupposes in what he says about the nature of sensation, achieves stability in space and time, not only because he can know the entire universe at any temporal moment, but also because he clings to God with unwavering commitment. Doing this is necessary, since otherwise, Adam would fall from created to fragmented

temporality in which he would become estranged from God. Augustine believes that this has occurred, and that it occurs in the life of every individual.
Yet contrary to what many interpreters suggest,[56] he does not believe that
spatiotemporal existence is inherently negative, but that it becomes so as a
result of the fall.[57] As a consequence, Augustine longs for conversion and
fulfillment that will bring him into the kind of relation with God that he
enjoyed "before" the fall. In addition, he suggests that we need to bring the
natural order back into a positive relation with the Creator from whom both
nature and the human realm have fallen away.

Augustine moves in this direction by saying that we should praise God
for natural objects, but that we should also turn our love for them back
toward their creator (4.12.18). He also claims that we must learn to love other
human beings in God: in themselves, they are not only mutable, but will also
cease to exist because they fall away from him; in him, they have a place to
stand that does not pass away. Thus Augustine says once more that we should
love all things in God (4.12.18). Loving things in God does not mean that
we lose our identity, but that we love finite things as creatures that God has
brought into existence and has declared to be good. In loving creatures, we
are able to love God and the created order simultaneously; for the things he
creates display both *finite* and *infinite* dimensions as essential aspects of their
nature, not only allowing them to be determinate objects of affection, but also
to point beyond themselves to the ground that sustains them.

The answer to the question about how we can love our friends in God
without loving God instead of them is that loving others is to love their finite
and infinite dimensions, the first of which points to *them*, and the second of
which points *beyond* them.[58] The *imago dei* that binds us to God allows us to
love all things in him, for the imprint of God on our natures points beyond
us to the source that has brought us into existence. As Augustine formulates
the point, we ought to love *God*, and to love our friends *in* God, because he
has created the world and is not far away from us (4.12.18).

Augustine reminds us that God did not create the things that he has
made and then go away, for "they are from him and in him." The one who
creates and sustains us is "within our very hearts, but our hearts have strayed
away from him." Thus, we must return to our hearts and "cling to him who
made [us]"; for if we "stand fast with him, [we] will in truth stand fast," and
if we "rest in him, [we] will in truth have rest" (4.12.18). At this point,
Augustine has the Trinity in view, suggesting that we are made *by* the Father,
come *from* the Son, and return to him *in* the Spirit that binds us together.
He urges us to continue to seek what we seek, but not where we seek it; and
he implores us to understand that what we seek only expresses itself in the
richness of God that every finite being reflects (4.12.18).

To rest in our creator is to share the Sabbath rest of God after the creation, where this moment of rest is neither static, nor structural, nor an expression of an ontology of part and whole. Rather, it is the dynamic activity of love in which God wants his creatures to participate after they move from creation and the fall to conversion and fulfillment. To love all things in God is first to love *God*; then to love all creatures *in relation to* the love that creates them; and finally, to redeem the death of our friends by bringing the fallen world back *into relation with* its sustaining ground. Loving things in God allows our souls to seek the one who creates and sustains us; but it also becomes the occasion on which we can join the rest of creation in being oriented toward God and in responding with love to the grace that makes fulfillment possible.[59]

The love that Augustine has in mind is illustrated best by the incarnation and ascension of Christ. Christ comes to earth and overcomes our death with the abundance of his life, and he calls us to join him in the "secret place" from which he has descended (4.12.19). In this case, the concept of place points directly to God; for Augustine is clear that the Father and the Son are one, and that they are bound together in the divine life they share with one another in the Holy Spirit. Thus, when he asks us to join him in the "secret place" from which he comes, he is asking us to join him in God.

There is a radical difference between the way in which the Son is related to the Father and the way in which other human beings can be related to Him. In the case of Christ, to be in God points to ontological identity, where the Father and the Son are both divine and eternal and have the same nature. In our case, to be in God is to be related to him in a positive orientation that we enjoy in creation, from which we are averted by falling away from him, to which we can return by being converted, and where we can be fulfilled when we embrace the restless rest of dynamic interaction.

Augustine believes that Christ makes this transformation and fulfillment possible by entering a virgin's womb and by joining our flesh to him so it will not always remain mortal (4.12.19). Prior to the fall, our flesh is finite but immortal; for it has not yet experienced the "sting of death" that is a necessary consequence of the sin of pride. Yet even after the fall, redemption is possible because Christ "espouses" his sinless nature to ours and allows us to participate in the redeeming power of God that sets us free from what Paul describes as "the body of this death."[60] This is the reason that we can redeem the transience of death by loving things in God, but also the reason why we cannot interpret the redemption Augustine embraces in Neoplatonic terms.

The body is a positive part of creation, and the redemption of it is integral to the transformation of the soul. The embodied Christ enters the world in sinless flesh, and it is this fact that allows him to be the "second

Adam" who can bring salvation to the first. The body of Adam in Paradise is sinless at the outset, becomes part of the sinful nature of the "first Adam" because he rebels against God, and requires redemption and fulfillment by an embodied being who can return him to his original state. To make this possible, Christ emerges from the place where he is born and runs through the world, crying out "by words and deeds, by death and life, by descent and ascension" for us to return to him (4.12.19). Yet he could scarcely do this if the "second Adam" were a soul that had fallen into a body whose negative significance it longs to escape. Words, deeds, death, life, descent, and ascension are meaningless apart from the embodied being in and through whom they speak to our fragmented condition; and they fall on deaf ears unless the sinless body through which they express themselves addresses both a body and a soul that can listen.

Augustine suggests once more that our return to God does not take us to a disembodied place that simply transcends us. The one who calls us

departed from our eyes, so that we might return into our hearts and find him there. He departed, but lo, he is here. He would not stay long with us, and yet he does not leave us. He departed from here, where he has never departed, for "the world was made by him" and "he was in the world," and he "came into this world to save sinners." (4.12.19)

Finally, Augustine addresses his readers directly:

"O you sons of men, how long will you be dull of heart?" Even now, after the descent of life to you, do you not wish to ascend and to live? But how can you ascend when you have set yourselves up high and have placed your mouth against heaven? Descend, so that you may ascend, so that you may ascend to God. For you have fallen by ascending against God. Tell this to those souls, so that they may weep in the valley of tears, and thus you will carry them along with you to God. For it is of his spirit that you tell them this, if you speak while burning with the fire of love. (4.12.19)

Once more love becomes the central theme. Loving all things in God not only means loving God, but also loving the self-transcendence of our friends by loving them in relation to God. And when they have fallen away from God, it means trying to bring them back to God by speaking with the fire of love.

THE BEAUTIFUL AND THE FITTING (4.13.20–4.15.27)

Though the mature Augustine understands what it means to love all things in God, the adolescent who loses his dearest friend does not. Instead, he loves the beautiful things that surround him without allowing them to call his attention to the creative source that brings them into existence. Thus he says to his adolescent companions, " 'Do we love anything except what is beautiful? What then is the beautiful? [And] what is beauty?' " (4.13.20) Though he asks these questions five years after the death of his friend, asking them at this stage of the *Confessions* becomes a rhetorical way of turning away from the place where the loss of beautiful things occurs to a domain where he can cover over the existential anxiety that continues to pervade his life with a theoretical veneer. This drives a wedge between experience and reflection, allowing the philosopher to shift his attention from the flux of experience to the reflective level where he can try to bring stability to it.

Introducing this theoretical topic is an ingenious way of juxtaposing the experience he has just recounted with theoretical issues that have a bearing on it. Doing so permits Augustine to continue his narrative by turning his attention away from experience to the nature of beauty as a philosophical problem. When he does this, he draws an important distinction between two kinds of beauty: first, objects are beautiful in themselves because they form a whole; second, they are beautiful in relation to other things because they harmonize with them (4.13.20). Thus, the twenty-seven-year-old author distinguishes between intrinsic beauty and the beauty that arises from mutual fittingness, writing his first book on the topic of the beautiful and the fitting.

Augustine says that he remembers very little about this book, claiming that he has somehow mislaid it. Nevertheless, he gives a lengthy account, not only of the content of the book, but also of his decision to dedicate it to an orator that he has never met (4.14.21). Augustine loves this orator because of his status and reputation as a rhetorician and because of some of the remarks the man has made that please him, but he loves him even more because he pleases others. The young professor is surprised that a Syrian should become such a powerful Latin orator; and this fact no doubt impresses him because he is a provincial rhetorician himself, who wants Roman society to accept him. Yet instead of pursing this point directly, he turns away again from what troubles him to ask a theoretical question: "Does our love for another person come into our hearts from the mouth of one who praises him, or is there a deeper reason for it?" (4.14.21). Finally, he points to the reason when he says that one catches the spark of love from one who loves.

Augustine distinguishes his love for the orator from his admiration for famous men in other professions. In doing so, he tells us that he loves the

Syrian orator as he wants his listeners to love him, where in both cases love is a response to rhetorical power. However, he also claims that he does not want an audience to praise and love him as they love an actor, even though he loves certain actors as well. In fact, he says that he would prefer that spectators would ignore or even hate him rather than love him in this way.

This seemingly innocent distinction between love for the orator and admiration for an actor puzzles Augustine and prompts him to interrupt the temporal flow of his narrative to ask why we sometimes love traits in other people that we would despise in ourselves. Though it is understandable that we might love a horse without wanting to change places with it, how could a rhetorician love an actor without wanting to imitate his success on stage? In this second case, we not only belong to the same genus, but also to the same species; and the unity of the species would seem to require that if we love certain characteristics in another, we should be happy to have them exemplified in ourselves.

One way to outflank this argument is to claim that the traits we admire in another person are ones that we might prefer not to embody. This is so because in addition to the unity of the species, there is a certain unity to be found in a way of life that one individual embraces and another rejects. Yet if we admire this other way of living, why would we not want to imitate it? And how can the unity of life as an actor or an orator override the natural unity of the species that binds us together?

In response to this problem, Augustine drives beneath the unity of the species, concludes that an individual has hidden depths, and insists that it is impossible to fathom the affections and movements of the heart (4.14.22). In doing so, he points beyond the genus and the species to the uniqueness of the individual that makes it possible for our preferences to override the ontological structures under which we are subsumed. Plotinus prepares the way for this maneuver by suggesting that there is an individual form corresponding to every individual, from which it would follow that individuals can be distinguished from one another, not only *qua* species, but also *qua* individual.[61] Thus, one individual who is a rhetorician might admire an actor of the same species without wanting to imitate him in his own case.[62]

Yet Augustine moves beyond Plotinus by suggesting that our preferences rather than our individual forms override the unity of the species, pointing in this way to the priority of the will in his thinking. As Augustine understands the issue, the human being is a "mighty deep," not because it has an individual form, but because the thoughts and intents of the heart serve to individuate it. Again, Augustine suggests that individuation depends on the will rather than on the intelligible structures we exemplify, and it is this fact that sets him apart from his Neoplatonic predecessors. However, his point is not to try to solve a paradox, but to call our attention to the infinite richness of the human being as it is embodied and reflected in the will. The key to under-standing Augustine's anthropology, and his claim that man has hidden depths, is to grasp the fact that freedom rather than necessity defines our uniqueness and that the most serious problem we face is to plumb the mystery of the freedom of the will as we attempt to come face to face with ourselves.

The orator whom the young Augustine admires is the kind of man he wants to be, for he is sensitive to the comparison between a successful for-eigner and a Latin provincial from a small town in North Africa. Yet the author of the text is preoccupied primarily with the contrast between the pride of his youth and the stability of God, concentrating his attention on two concepts of love. The rhetorician loves the Syrian orator because others praise him; and if the appraisals had been different, he would not have loved him, even though his qualities would have been the same. Thus, even as a young man, Augustine stands in between incompatible concepts of love: the first is love for others that depends on unstable opinions and resembles the "blasting" voices of the Manichaeans that have led him astray; the second is love for abiding characteristics that do not fluctuate in proportion to the appraisals they evoke in others (4.14.23).

By drawing this distinction, Augustine is beginning to turn away from merely rhetorical uses of language to the stability of truth that can be identified with Truth itself, and which the rhetoric he is attempting to develop in the *Confessions* can express. Indeed, he has a glimpse of the distinction between opinion and truth when he admires his own book, though no one else joins him in doing so. As an adolescent approaching youthful maturity, he stands alone in assessing the value of his work (4.14.23); but his willingness to do this brings him one step closer to the authenticity that will permit him to stand alone before God and to subject his heart to divine scrutiny.

When Augustine writes his first book, he does not understand that the reason things are beautiful is that God has created them, focusing instead on finite things as they exist in themselves (4.15.24). Having characterized the beautiful as what is attractive in itself, and having defined the fitting as what is beautiful in relation to other things, he turns his attention to the nature of the mind, though false opinions about the nature of a spiritual substance prevent him from grasping the truth. Indeed, the force of truth dazzles his eyes; and he turns his soul away from incorporeal substance to lines, colors, and expanding quantities (4.15.24). Since these elements are more abstract than phantasms or physical objects, they have a place on the divided line[63] between the physical and the spiritual realms; but since Augustine cannot perceive them in his mind, he concludes that he cannot perceive the mind itself (4.15.24). At this stage of his life, he has not understood that he must learn to "see" in a different sense, and that the kind of vision appropriate at one level of reality is inappropriate for achieving insight at another.

Augustine tries to move along the philosophical pathway that his reading of Cicero's book has opened up by distinguishing the unity of virtue from the discord of vice and by claiming that this unity consists in the rational soul, the nature of truth, and the highest good (4.15.24). Yet as we might expect from someone who has not yet learned the discipline of the cave,[64] it is here that his analysis veers away from Truth in the most obvious way. Augustine commits himself to the view that the soul is part of the supreme unity, and he imagines that disunity is a substance and that evil is an entity (4.15.24). In doing so, he continues to follow the Manichaeans in placing evil in a binary contrast with goodness; and he accepts the logical consequence that evil exists independently of God. The rhetorician calls the first principle a Monad and the second a Dyad, where the Monad is "a soul without sex," and the Dyad is a monster that expresses its radical negativity in deeds of violence, passion, and lust (4.15.24).

When he writes the *Confessions*, Augustine is clear about the fact that the soul is the source of the human predicament. In acts of violence, the violent impulse is to blame; in acts of passion, the affection of the soul that gives rise to it is at fault; and when we express false opinions, our error arises, not from a negative principle that displays ontological independence, but from a distortion of the rational part of the soul that derives its goodness from the creative source that brings it into existence (4.15.25). Yet at this earlier stage of his life, Augustine does not know that if he is to move beyond his predicament, he must be enlightened by the light of Truth (4.15.25). He also does not know that the source of sin is the negative orientation of the soul, where the soul leads us to participate in sins of the flesh and in deeds of shame. In the first instance, there are determinate reasons for our actions; in the second, shame is the goal toward which the soul and the body fall away as they attempt to embrace the nonbeing (*nihil*) from which they emerge.

As Augustine continues to wander away from his creator at both the existential and the reflective levels, God thrusts him back on himself so he can begin to experience the spiritual death that arises from the fact that God resists the proud. Indeed, what could be more proud than for Augustine to think that God must be mutable like him rather than to admit that he, who is clearly mutable, is not divine (4.15.26). As a consequence, he continues to walk toward things that are not, oriented toward the nonbeing out of which he is created and to which he is attempting to return. Once more, a distinction between the mutability that he refuses to embrace and the mortality that he inherits emerges as an important, but implicit distinction. The mutability that distinguishes Augustine from God is finite and good, while the mortality into which he sinks is a distortion, resulting from the pride that fails to acknowledge the difference between the creator and the finite beings that he brings into existence. As he will discover when he embraces Neoplatonism and moves beyond it to Christianity, mortality can be overcome only through conversion, which will permit him to stand before God and to find the fulfillment he seeks.

In describing his first book it is interesting to notice that he uses a surprising number of auditory metaphors. In *The Beautiful and the Fitting*, he not only analyzes the sensory images that clamor in "[his] heart's ears," but also "[strains] those ears" to hear the "interior melody" of truth, pondering on the problem of beauty, and longing to stay and listen to God, rejoicing greatly at " 'the bridegroom's Voice' " (4.15.27). However, the mature Augustine tells us that when he writes the book, he cannot hear the voice of God because the clamor of his errors takes him outside himself, and that he cannot respond to God because the weight of his pride causes him to sink into the bottomless pit into which he falls at the end of Book II. Augustine expresses the predicament in which he participates at an earlier stage of his development by exclaiming, "You did not give to my hearing joy and gladness, nor did my bones rejoice, for they had not yet been humbled" (4.15.27). The voice Augustine needs to hear must speak to his soul to redeem it from destruction, but he suggests that it must also revive the dry bones of his body so he can stand before God as an individual who has been transformed altogether.

CATEGORIES, TRANSCENDENTALS, AND THE LIBERAL ARTS (4.16.28–4.16.31)

Augustine concludes the account of these stages of his experiential and reflective development by interrupting the temporal flow of his narrative once more, and he does this by recalling an episode that occurs seven years before he writes his first book. When he is scarcely twenty, he reads a Latin translation of Aristotle's *Categories*, regarding the very title of the book as almost divine. Yet Augustine reads and understands it by himself; and when he discusses the text with others, he finds that they can scarcely understand it even with assistance. To him, Aristotle speaks plainly enough about the category of substance and about the categories that are subordinated to it; but to others, he scarcely speaks at all (4.16.28).

Once again a curious ambiguity emerges in Augustine's description of himself: he is proud of his accomplishments as a student and does not hide this fact from his readers, but he also uses his achievements to point directly to his defects. Thus, he claims that however valuable the study of Aristotle's *Categories* may be, his interpretation of the book hinders his religious and philosophical development. The young man imagines that whatever exists can be subsumed under the categories, and this mistake leads him to try to understand God as an instance of the categories rather than as identical with the transcendentals (4.16.29).[65] The author of the *Confessions* tries to rectify this earlier mistake by claiming that God's magnitude and beauty do not exist in him as their subject, but that he is to be identified with them (4.16.29).

This claim is important because it points to the kind of language that Augustine needs to use in describing God. Since God is identical with the transcendentals, the philosopher must stretch ordinary uses of language to speak about him. All these uses of language presuppose that God transcends the ontological continuum and the subject-predicate framework of the Aristotelian categories, pointing beyond them both to the creative source of existence that can never be captured in a categorial net. However, just as Augustine tries to infinitize the finite by describing the beautiful and the fitting as if they were divine, he is now tempted to finitize the infinite by using ordinary discourse to speak about God. And just as the only remedy for the first problem is to recognize that the creator of the beautiful and the fitting is infinite, while they are not, the solution to the second problem is to recognize that ordinary discourse has figurative uses that preserve the infinite richness of the one to whom they point.

Having indulged in a moment of pride, the saint continues to criticize himself by focusing on his mastery of the liberal arts: he wonders what it profits him to read and understand so many books, while he flounders in slavery to sexual addiction (4.16.30). Indeed, even the books in which he delights pose a problem because he does not know the source of truth and certainty from which they originate. Augustine has his back toward the light and his face toward the books on which it falls, permitting them to be illuminated while his face remains in darkness (4.16.30). Yet even though the young man remains in darkness, the author of the text continues to point to what is positive about his earlier self by claiming that he not only masters Aristotle's *Categories*, but also understands rhetoric, logic, geometry, music, and arithmetic without any difficulty and without the instruction of others. Indeed, the brilliant adolescent comprehends both the trivium and the quadrivium without the intellectual difficulties that he observes in his classmates (4.16.30).

Augustine also fastens his attention on another fact about himself that is even more important: his abilities do not serve for his profit but for his loss, since he tries to bring a large part of himself *under his own power* (4.16.30). Indeed, his earlier criticisms of himself are trivial in comparison with this one. In this passage, he does not juxtapose his natural abilities with his spiritual failures, but blames himself for his overriding desire for autonomy, and by implication, for not understanding his extraordinary talents as gifts from God (4.16.30). Thus, he brings us back to the theme of God and the soul by implying that he needs to thank God for the abilities that He has given him, and by suggesting that the price he pays for not doing so is slavery to an abortive quest for self-control.

Augustine must choose a master; and in the final analysis, the only viable candidates are God and the soul. To choose God is to bring one's soul into a vertical relation with the grace that sustains it; to choose oneself is to join the Prodigal Son on a journey into a far country that separates us from our highest good. Augustine's evaluation of his intelligence in comparison with others is realistic, but he misses the mark by trying to bring his extraordinary talents under his control. This compulsive desire for self-mastery stands opposed to the willingness to open himself to a source of power that stands beyond him, and it is Augustine's persistent failure to do this that continues to separate him from God.

The young rhetorician also blasphemes God, and in the process, he "bays like a hound" against him (4.16.31). Barking like the Manichaean he is, he places a burden on those around him, who are more like birds in a nest than the dogs that pursue them at the bottom of the tree (4.16.31). Thus, Augustine the saint, looking back on Augustine the sinner, moves beyond the "garden" in which he is created, the abyss into which he falls, the journey he takes into an unknown country, and the wasteland he becomes by identifying himself with the birds in the nest of the church:

> O Lord our God, under the shadow of your wings let us hope, and do you protect and carry us. You will carry us, as little ones you will carry us, and even up to our gray hairs will you carry us. For since you are our strength, then it is strength indeed; but when it is our own, then it is but weakness. With you our good lives forever, and because we have turned away from you, we have become perverted. Now let us return, O Lord, so that we be not overturned, for with you our good, which is yourself, lives beyond all decay. And we do not fear lest there be no place to return to, although we rushed headlong from it, for while we were far from you, our mansion, your eternity, fell not in ruin. (4.16.31)

It is instructive to notice that the "birds" God carries and protects are embodied individuals in space and time, who begin in infancy, and who move from there through the other stages of life until they finally acquire the gray hairs of old age. In addition, though Augustine seeks stability by bringing us to rest in God rather than in ourselves, the goal that he has in mind is life *with* God in which we do not dissolve in him, but preserve our individual integrity by standing over against him. When he urges us to return to God so we might not be overturned like "the Wreckers," and when he assures us that our home has not fallen away in our absence, he does not have a place in mind in the ontological sense, but is focusing instead on a positive *orientation* toward God that will reverse the effects of our fallen condition.[66] By pointing in this direction, he is challenging us once more to embrace the ground of our existence with the whole of our being.

3

Manichaeism, Skepticism,
and Christianity (Books V–VI)

As our account of the temporal, spatial, and eternal dimensions of Augustine's development continues to unfold, the relation between God and the soul and the language that permits us to speak about it are once again our central themes. This chapter focuses on the first of these themes by beginning with the presence and absence of God and by concluding with Augustine's conviction that God will lead him home and set him free. In between, the language of God and the soul allows us to place a spiritual and linguistic framework around our description of Augustine's life in Carthage, Rome, and Milan.

Within this framework, Augustine searches for a stable identity by moving through a series of personal, spiritual, and reflective stages that his encounter with Cicero's *Hortensius* initiates. In reflecting on these stages, he calls our attention to the temporal and the spatial dimensions of his journey toward God; but he also emphasizes the eternal dimension of his life in the three cities in which his quest for wholeness unfolds. When he writes the *Confessions*, Augustine is keenly aware of the fact that his journeys from one city to another not only occur in space and time, but also point to vertical transitions within his soul that lead him toward God.

In this chapter, the vertical axis of Augustine's development comes to focus on the opposition between Manichaeism and Christianity; and the author of the text retraces the steps through which he moves from one way of living toward the other. His flight from Carthage to Rome is motivated by the young philosopher's loss of confidence in the Manichaean picture of nature and its fanciful descriptions of the history and the structure of the cosmos. Somewhat later, a transition from Rome to Milan becomes the occasion for him to repudiate dualism, to embrace Academic Skepticism, and to reexamine his rejection of the Catholic faith.

The interpersonal dimension of Augustine's life becomes increasingly important as he moves from one city to another, mobilizing the communal aspect of his experience and the interplay between the outer and the inner worlds between which he is suspended. Three dominant personalities have a decisive impact on him: Faustus, a celebrated Manichaean teacher; Monica, the mother who pursues him relentlessly from one stage of his life to another; and Ambrose, the Bishop of Milan who makes the Christian faith accessible to him. As Augustine moves from Faustus to Ambrose against the background of the constant influence of his mother, he makes progress in his journey toward God that expresses itself in the temporal and spatial aspects of his life.

Two expressions of the temporal and spatial dimensions of Augustine's experience point to the resting place in God that he longs to enter: first, he suffers from temporal, spatial, and eternal hysteria as he begins to move toward pivotal experiences that will transform his life; second, he discovers the crucial role of friendship in helping him carry the almost unbearable burden of the fear of dying that haunts him at almost every stage of his journey. Augustine could not live without his friends, and he gives a moving account of how he loves them as he tries to cope with an attack of anxiety that almost overwhelms him. The interplay between fragmentation and friendship is a theme that binds the reflective and the personal dimensions of Augustine's life together; and though turmoil disorders his feelings and disturbs his intellect, the friends with whom he surrounds himself sustain him as he begins to catch a glimpse of the end of his journey.

The Presence and Absence of God (5.1.1–5.2.2)

Augustine begins this stage of his narrative by asking God to accept the sacrifice of his confessions from the hand of his tongue and to heal his bones so he will be able to praise him (5.1.1). Both these requests are important: the first reminds us that speaking and hearing remain at the center of the *Confessions,* and both the first and the second suggest that the deliverance Augustine seeks involves not only his soul, but his body as well. In asking God to accept the sacrifice of his tongue, and in claiming that his bones cry out for redemption, Augustine uses figurative discourse to bind the soul and the body together, where both dimensions of his nature participate in the quest for transformation that he continues to pursue.

Augustine's remarks about the meaning of confession are an even more important aspect of his introductory comments. He tells us that since no one can hide from God's probing presence, the primary purpose of the act of confession is not to inform God about what goes on within us, but to praise and love him by confessing our sins (5.1.1). Confessing makes praising possible; praising makes loving possible; and taken together, these acts reverse the downward spiral that begins with stealing for its own sake, becomes loving as an end in itself, and issues in deception that leads Augustine's friends and students astray. The triad of stealing, loving, and deceiving that originates and characterizes Augustine's life in the wasteland can be overcome only when confessing, praising, and loving take their place.

In the description of confession that leads from confessing to praising and from praising to loving, Augustine begins with the *body*, moves from there to the *person*, and concludes by exhorting his *soul* to praise and love the one who bestows his mercies on him. In this way, he not only binds the soul and the body together, but also holds them apart, allowing their unity and separation to reflect the continuity and the discontinuity that confession presupposes. Since Augustine is separated from God, confession is necessary; but since the grace of God sustains him, confession is possible as a way of crossing the chasm between them.

Augustine's complex semantics not only allows him to unify and separate the soul and the body, but also permits him to do justice to the intricate interplay between God and the soul. He does this by mobilizing the ideas of identity and difference that make the concepts of creation, fall, conversion, and fulfillment intelligible. In the first case, God and the soul are different in kind, but are bound together by an imagistic relation; in the second, the soul is radically separated from God, but continues to exist as an image of God that is never effaced; in the third, the soul reverses its negative orientation toward God, but continues to stand over against God as a being in its own right; and in the fourth, the soul returns to God, but is able to preserve its integrity when it reaches the goal it seeks. In all these cases, unity and separation interplay with one another as a way of binding God and the soul together, but also as a way of holding them apart.

Augustine claims that the whole creation points beyond itself to the source that brings it into existence: souls praise God directly, and animals and corporeal things praise him indirectly through those who meditate on them. Thus, the soul arouses itself from its weariness, separates itself from the body, rests on the things that God has made, and moves toward the one who creates it to find rest from its wanderings (5.1.1). Yet the salvation and fulfillment that Augustine seeks do not pertain to the soul alone: in his ascent toward his origins, the body follows the soul;[1] and when they reach the end of their journey, the entire person stands before God as an embodied being (5.1.1).[2]

Augustine's reflections about the presence and absence of God occur immediately after his brief remarks about the nature of confession, and they are the first step in preparing his readers for the final stage of his journey toward God. At this juncture, he warns us that if we try to flee from God, God will see us in the shadows that we cast by running away from him (5.2.2). Thus, light and darkness are added to the collection of metaphors that Augustine uses to characterize his existential journey. This journey begins in a garden, moves across an ocean, leads to a wasteland, and finally reaches dry land where a nest can be constructed. From there, Augustine invites us to fly on wings that carry us into the presence of God, where the soul can be enlightened by the source of its existence, and where both the soul and the body can be rescued from the abyss into which they have fallen.

Augustine tells us that though the created order is beautiful, turning away from God in order to lose ourselves in it is misguided because it is not as beautiful as the one who brings it into existence. He also says that it is impossible for those who flee from God to injure him or to challenge his authority, since the justice of God is perfect from the highest heavens to the lowest depths (5.2.2). Here Augustine anticipates the cosmology that he will develop at a later stage in the *Confessions*, where God is not only the ruler of the visible heaven and the visible earth, but also the creator and sustainer of the spiritual heaven (12.2.2), and the one who can reverse our orientation toward the chasm into which we have fallen.

If we try to wander away from God, we forget that he is everywhere and that he is present even when we try to separate ourselves from him. God is both present and absent because he is present all at once in places that are separated from one another (5.2.2). As a consequence, the omnipresence of God, and the concept of "place" it presupposes, explodes the concept of place in the ordinary sense. Augustine's conception of God's omnipresence also undermines the suggestion that he understands the fall of the soul in terms of a literalistic conception of a spiritual heaven from which it turns away. Rather, as he suggests on so many occasions, he is concerned primarily about the negative *orientation* of the soul that leads it away from the creative ground of its existence (2.6.14), (6.16.26), (8.5.10).

The paradoxes involved in the concept of the omnipresence of God become inescapable when we notice the asymmetry involved in the fact that even though we have forsaken God, he has not forsaken us (5.2.2). In this context, absence falls on the side of the creature, presence on the side of the creator, and omnipresence on both sides, pointing to the characteristic of God that makes it possible for us to find him, even though we sometimes forsake the one who never leaves us alone. If God were present, we could avoid him by absenting ourselves; if he were absent, we would not need to flee; but since he is both present and absent at once, we are frustrated when we try to run away from the one who is with us and beyond us simultaneously.

Augustine's only hope for redemption is to turn back from his wanderings to seek the creator who has never abandoned him. If he does this, he will move from a fallen to a converted spatiotemporal matrix,[3] finding that the one who is both present and absent at once is the God of his heart. Yet at this stage of his life, the sinner stands opposed to the saint, turning away from God to pursue a path of his own. Indeed, Augustine is even absent from himself; and when he asks, "Where was I when I sought you?" he answers, "You were before me, but I had departed from myself, and I could not find myself, much less you" (5.2.2). Before his journey toward God reaches its culmination, Augustine will come to himself by allowing the presence and the absence of God to expand his intellect, to mobilize his will, and to re-create his being. Yet for the present, he will continue to wander, making it necessary for God to approach him in subliminal stages.

THE FAILURE OF FAUSTUS (5.3.3–5.7.13)

Against the background of the presence and absence of God, Augustine begins to focus on the interplay among the personal, the spiritual, and the reflective dimensions of his experience. The discussion of his meeting with Faustus, a famous Manichaean Bishop, is the first indication of this; and the young philosopher emphasizes the importance of his encounter with the celebrated Manichaean by saying that it occurs in his twenty-ninth year (5.3.3). Making the date of his meeting with Faustus explicit indicates that it is a temporal turning point for Augustine; but as we shall soon discover, the episode also has profound implications for the spatial and eternal dimensions of his development.

Faustus comes to Carthage and entangles many of his listeners in the snare of his eloquence. However, Augustine distinguishes himself from the other auditors by claiming that even though he finds the flowing language of Faustus fascinating, he is able to distinguish rhetoric from the truth of the things that he is longing to grasp (5.3.3). The focus of Augustine's attention is the content of Faustus's teaching rather than its form; and though he is anxious to meet the celebrated rhetorician, he is more interested in his reputation for learning than in the power of his public presentations.

Before he describes his meeting with Faustus, the young professor of rhetoric places it within a broader philosophical context. Augustine has read and memorized many of the injunctions of the philosophers of nature; and having compared them with the fables of the Manichaeans, he is convinced that the probability lies on the side of the philosophers. The natural philosophers give an adequate picture of the cosmos by numbering the stars and the sands, mapping out the constellations, and tracing the course of the planets. They are also able to predict eclipses of the sun and the moon many years in advance; and the principles accordingly to which they do so can be written down and used to make predictions in the future, much to the amazement of those who do not understand such matters. Yet Augustine criticizes the philosophers for failing to seek and worship the creator of the world they try to understand, and he repudiates the pride at the heart of their enterprise that causes them to fall away from God and to suffer an eclipse of God's light (5.3.4).

Pride is not primarily a problem of the intellect, but a defect of the will; and it is the willful rather than the intellectual attempt to turn away from God that troubles Augustine most. He expresses his point in three analogies, saying that the pride of the philosophers is like the birds of the air, that their curiosity is like the fishes in the sea, and that their carnal indulgence is like the beasts in the field (5.3.4). In making these comparisons, Augustine points to three classes of sin with which he is preoccupied on a number of occasions, arranging them in a descending order of significance (10.30.41). Yet these analogies are important, not only because they descend from birds, to fish, to beasts, but also because introducing them provides an illustration of one of the most important kinds of figurative language that Augustine uses.

What is distinctive about the similarities in this case is that spiritual conditions are compared with corporeal entities rather than the other way about. This use of analogy does not point away from the physical world to a domain of disembodied entities, but gives intangible characteristics physical significance by attaching them to the existential context in which they express themselves. In doing so, they discourage us from turning away from our embodied existence to a domain in which the separation of the soul from the body becomes the focus of our attention.

The philosophers that Augustine criticizes do not realize that God creates the world through a dynamic Word, nor do they understand that his nature transcends the scope of mathematical calculation that they have brought to bear on astronomical phenomena. They also have no knowledge of the incarnation, failing to understand that they must first descend from themselves if the are to ascend to God. As a consequence, those who have lifted themselves up to the heavens fall back to earth and are darkened over.[4] Though they say many true things about creation, they do not seek the creator; and even if they find him, they do not honor him as God. Instead, they are blinded by perversity, changing truth into a lie by worshiping idols rather than the one who is to be identified with Truth itself (5.3.5). Along the vertical access of experience, truth consists in being true to the creative source of existence; and the philosophers to whom Augustine is referring fail to do this when they try to understand the creator as if he were a creature. In this case, the familiar correspondence theory of truth[5] gives way to a concept of truth that presupposes a contrast between creator and creature, where "truth" means "being true" to God rather than transforming God into a lie that leads both us and others astray.

The author of the *Confessions* insists that no one pleases God simply because he understands the laws that govern the natural world. If a person knows these things and does not know God, he is unhappy; but if this same person knows God, he is content, even though he does not understand the order of nature. In fact, Augustine claims that one who knows both God and nature is no happier because of his knowledge of the natural order (5.4.7). Augustine believes that nature is a symbol for the One who brings it into existence; and he concludes that a person who knows this is better off than one who can measure the heavens and can number the stars, but who turns away from God.

The crucial Augustinian distinction between use and enjoyment underlies this claim. As on so many other occasions, Augustine suggests that only God is a proper object of enjoyment and that everything else is to be used as an instrument for this more important end.[6] This does not mean that knowledge of the natural order is unimportant, but that its value can be appreciated only when we bring it into relation with God. Since God creates whatever exists, knowledge of the created order is valuable; but its ultimate value derives from the extent to which it gives us access to the creator. As Augustine understands the issue, inquiry into the nature of things is valuable, not as an end in itself, but as a path that leads to God; and it is only as we follow this pathway that we can prevent our inquiries from becoming idle curiosity.

However serious his criticism of the philosophers may be, Augustine reserves his most sustained attack for the founder of the Manichaean sect. The author of the *Confessions* criticizes the founder of the sect that entangles him for four defects in his knowledge and character: first, he has a limited knowledge of the natural order, but writes about it as if he were an authority; second, he has no knowledge of heavenly things, but writes about them as if he does; third, he professes what he claims to know rather than confessing the extent to which he is separated from God; finally, he not only speaks falsely about nature, but also deceives his hearers about more important ethical and spiritual matters (5.5.8-9). The first two criticisms focus on the intellectual failures of Mani, while the final pair point to the crucial distinction between a profession of knowledge and a confession of sin.

The distinction between profession and confession is important because its first prong enables the intellect to turn away from God, while the second permits the will to return to the sustaining ground of its existence. Augustine's chief complaint against the founder of Manichaean doctrine is that his preference for profession rather than confession leads him not only to speak

falsely about nature, but also to deceive his hearers about even more important issues (5.5.9). The pride of Mani outstrips the pride of the philosophers
because he tries to persuade his readers that the Holy Spirit is present in him
with absolute authority.[7] Yet when he makes elementary blunders about astronomical phenomena, the pious presumption of his identification of himself
with the third person of the Trinity becomes evident.

Though the mature Augustine rejects the teachings of the founder of the
Manichean sect, he is unable to decide at this stage of his life whether the
phenomena that the natural philosophers explain can also be explained by
appealing to the writings of the Manichaeans. Yet even if they could, it would
remain an open question whether the theories of the Manichaeans are true
(5.5.9). Augustine makes an important distinction at this juncture between
consistency and truth, refusing to move from the capacity of a theory to
explain the same phenomena as another to the truth of that theory considered
in itself. More specifically, he rejects the claim that because Manichaean
doctrine might be consistent with another theory we have good reason to
accept, we are justified in believing it to be true. Augustine will accept only
positive evidence for a philosophical position; and in trying to find it, he will
not be content with logical considerations alone.

The young philosopher also exhibits another tendency that continues to
play a crucial role in his thinking: in explaining his willingness to embrace
Manichaean doctrine at an earlier stage of his development, the saint informs
us that the sinner places his faith in the authority of its author (5.5.9). This
remark about authority has two purposes: first, it prepares us for Augustine's
appeal to the authority of the Bible in cases where reason is not sufficient to
decide an issue; second, it allows Augustine to silence the voice of his later
opinions and return to the narrative present. In doing so, he makes a rhetorical transition from his mature criticism of Manichaean doctrine to his youthful enthusiasm about the appearance of Faustus.

Augustine tells us that he has been waiting to meet the Manichaean
Bishop for almost nine years. When members of the Manichaean sect are
unable to answer his questions, they always refer to the coming of Faustus,
promising Augustine that he can deal with his difficulties. Yet when Faustus
arrives, Augustine finds that though he is gracious and pleasant in conversation, he speaks about the same things that the other Manichaeans teach,
where the only discernable difference is that he does so more fluently and in
a more agreeable style (5.6.10). Thus, Augustine shifts once more to the voice
of the saint appraising the condition of the sinner, complaining that his ears
are already full of dualistic nonsense and that he is no longer prepared to
equate wisdom with the eloquence of rhetoric.

One reason for this shift in narrative perspective is to permit Augustine
to introduce two influences in his life that will ultimately undermine the

authority of Manichaean doctrine. First, he mentions the skeptics who hold truth in suspension and refuse to accept doctrines that are presented in an elegant and copious style (5.6.10). This reference is important, for it prepares us for the emergence of skepticism as a principle of negation that turns Augustine away from the outrageous constructions of Manichaean cosmology. Second, he mentions God, who has already begun to teach him in ways that surpass his understanding (5.6.10). This second reference is more important than the first because it points to the source of redemption that will not only lead him beyond Manichaeism, but also beyond skepticism and Neoplatonism as doctrines that transform his intellect without redeeming his will.

God has already begun to teach Augustine an important lesson about the positive relation between rhetoric and truth: though it is appropriate to distinguish truth from the ornamental language rhetoricians use, it is equally important not to be suspicious when a speaker expresses the truth in smooth and flowing language (5.6.10). In relating the story of his life, Augustine embraces the power of rhetoric; but unlike the tendency to which he succumbs as a young rhetorician, the saint and the writer attempt to subordinate his eloquent manner of speaking to the truth.[8]

By this time, Augustine has learned several crucial facts about the relation between rhetoric and truth: first, God is the teacher of truth who speaks to him with an inner voice; second, an utterance is not true simply because it is eloquent rather than clear and simple; third, we should not suppose that a statement is false because someone utters it with "stammering lips"; fourth, an assertion is not true simply because the utterance is straightforward; finally, we should not infer that an utterance is false because the language in which it is expressed is either brilliant or clever. Augustine concludes that wisdom and folly are like wholesome and unwholesome food, where "both kinds of food can be served on rich dishes or on peasant ware" (5.6.10).

The philosopher who has just distinguished between positive and negative uses of rhetoric now makes another rhetorical shift to the narrative present by claiming that the action, the enthusiasm, and the eloquence of Faustus delight him. Despite his earlier reservations, Augustine not only joins others in praising him, but also exceeds them; and the only remnant of the distinction he has drawn between eloquence and truth is his objection that Faustus will not allow him to ask questions about the issues that trouble him (5.6.11). Yet this is a serious defect from a philosophical point of view, since an inquiry that has truth as its object can proceed successfully only by asking and answering questions. Asking skeptical questions is appropriate in this case because the Manichaeans give theoretical explanations of the cosmos, inviting one to inquire about whether their assertions can withstand the test of critical scrutiny.[9]

When Augustine finally talks with Faustus in private, he discovers something even more disturbing: Faustus knows nothing about the liberal arts except grammar (5.6.11), which implies that the other parts of the trivium and quadrivium do not fall within his preview. This means that he has no knowledge of logic or rhetoric and that he is totally ignorant of arithmetic, geometry, music, and astronomy.[10] Faustus has read only some of Cicero's orations, a few books of Seneca and some of the poets, and a few of the writings of his own sect (5.6.11). Thus, he is trapped on the lowest level of the divided line that Augustine has begun to climb, and he is totally inadequate to deal with the theoretical problems that the young philosopher raises.

When Faustus is unable to demonstrate that the fables of the Manichaeans about astronomical phenomena are as good as the mathematical explanations Augustine has read elsewhere, the young philosopher begins to doubt the truth of Manichaean doctrine for the first time. Yet when the Manichaean Bishop confesses that he has no knowledge of such things, Augustine finds something positive in the charming and eloquent man that he has waited so long to meet: though Faustus lacks a proper orientation toward God, his willingness to acknowledge his own ignorance indicates that he is not altogether false to himself. Augustine is attracted to Faustus all the more because of this, concluding that his humility is a finer thing than the acquisition of the knowledge that he wishes to obtain from discussing mathematical questions with him (5.7.12).

Augustine's confidence that he can make progress in Manichaeism comes to an end because of the failure of Faustus to deal with his perplexities. He begins to despair of learning anything from the rest of their teachers and concludes that he must find an alternative to Manichaean doctrine if he is to develop the quest for wisdom that begins when he reads Cicero's *Hortensius* (5.7.13). The young philosopher has put his faith in phantasms and in the dyadic logic for which they generate the mythology; and when this fanciful picture of the universe and the logic it expresses begin to collapse, his hopes for redemption by pursuing philosophical dualism begin to collapse as well.

The failure of Manichaeism not only results from the fact that it is a tissue of fabrications, but also from its failure to permit the soul to develop toward maturity through a dynamic series of stages. The radical dualism of Manichaean doctrine poses an abstract opposition that forces Augustine to vacillate between opposing principles instead of providing an open space through which he can move from one stage of life to another.[11] Philosophical dualism also fails to provide the linguistic flexibility that Augustine needs to speak about the relation between God and the soul, where figurative language points to a dimension of human experience that literal discourse can never articulate.

As Augustine's life continues to unfold, he becomes increasingly aware of the fact that he needs a way of thinking that will enable him to bind the temporal, special, and eternal dimensions of his experience and reflection together. Yet he does not find it until he embraces faith seeking understanding and stands in the middle ground between God and the soul to which faith gives him access. Augustine needs to express self-transcendence in the space this middle ground provides, and he needs to learn a polymorphous way of speaking by standing between the poles that define dyadic ways of thinking.

Since Augustine's primary problem is practical rather than theoretical, he does not separate himself from his Manichaean companions altogether, deciding to rest content with them until something more desirable emerges (5.7.13). For the moment, Augustine's relationship with Faustus also remains ambiguous: the Manichaean Bishop for whom he has waited so long does not know anything, causing him to turn away from Manichaean doctrine; but the man he meets is so gracious and unassuming that Augustine responds to him in human terms. This points to an ambiguity along the vertical axis of experience, where the incompetence of Faustus is counterbalanced by authenticity.

The ambiguity between the ignorance and the attractiveness of Faustus leads Augustine to ask one of the most important questions a philosopher can ever raise: How can I embrace the truth toward which philosophical reflection is oriented, and at the same time, how can I remain embedded in the human realm in which my longing for truth originates? This is the most significant existential and reflective problem that Augustine faces as he develops toward maturity, and it is this question that he must struggle to answer as his journey toward God begins to reach its culmination.

Augustine concludes the recollection of his meeting with Faustus by pointing toward the freedom that will emerge from it eventually. In doing so, he praises both the providence of God and the mediation of his mother, both of which allow him to bridge the chasm between the truth he seeks and his fragmented existential situation. Finally, Augustine tells us that without understanding what he is doing, the Manichaean teacher begins "to loosen the snare" in which the young rhetorician has been captured for more than nine years (5.7.13).

Augustine begins to move from bondage to liberation, not only because of the misguided teaching of Faustus, but also because the hands of God do not desert him, and because the blood of his mother's heart mingles with her tears in a "daily sacrifice" for the soul of her son (5.7.13). Again, figurative discourse becomes a central element in Augustine's enterprise: a bodily predicate ascribed to God binds God and Augustine's body together; the reference to Augustine's soul points to the irreducible difference between God and the soul and between the soul and the body; and the reference to the blood, the heart, and the tears of his mother are ways of indicating that her entire being is oriented toward the salvation of her son, both soul and body together.

THE FLIGHT TO ROME (5.8.14–5.12.22)

After the failure of Faustus, Augustine decides to leave Carthage and to go to Rome to advance his career as a teacher of rhetoric. From the perspective of the author of the text, his reasons for doing this involve an interplay between horizontal and vertical dimensions that point beyond space and time to eternity. The writer insists that the providence of God is near at hand to lift him up, even though the protagonist of the drama is unable to recognize God's presence at this early stage of his development (5.8.14).

Augustine says that he does not want to go to Rome to receive richer fees from the students or to achieve higher dignity in his profession, though he admits that these considerations affect his decision. His principal reason for moving to Italy is that the students there are better disciplined than the ones in Carthage. At Carthage, students who are not enrolled in his classes burst in and disrupt the discipline that he has established for the good of his pupils, where by contrast, he has heard that the students in Rome are more serious and sophisticated. The young rhetorician is delighted to go where his friends assure him that the situation is different; but from the perspective of the saint assessing the geographical transitions of the sinner, he is leaving "true misery" in Carthage to seek "false felicity" in Rome (5.8.14).

Augustine tells us that though God knows the fundamental reason for his move from North Africa to Italy, He does not disclose it to him or to his mother. Monica grieves about Augustine's departure, follows him down to the sea, clasps him tightly, begs him not to go, and says that if he must, she wants to go with him. This scene is obviously intended to remind us of Virgil's account of the tragedy of Dido and Aeneas, who abandons the Carthaginian Queen on the shore of North Africa to pursue his destiny as the founder of the Roman Empire.[12]

The analogies between these two situations are almost too many to mention, and they have been canvassed thoroughly in the vast secondary literature about the *Confessions*.[13] Yet at least three of these analogies are crucial elements in our own attempt to understand Augustine's journey toward God. First, women close to Aeneas and Augustine try to bind the two heroes to themselves rather than permit the separation necessary for accomplishing a world historical task. In the case of Aeneas, this involves the founding of a secular empire; in the case of Augustine, it involves the establishment of Christianity as the dominant theological force in Western Civilization. Second, both Aeneas and Augustine are brutal in abandoning the women who love them, shaking off attachment to a lover and a mother to sublimate it toward a higher end. Aeneas abandons the bed of Dido to return to the ocean that will lead him eventually to a new world; and Augustine abandons the solicitations of his mother to advance his career in rhetoric. Finally, the abandonment of Dido permits Aeneas to found a city from the ashes of one that has been destroyed and to erect a greater empire than the city of Troy could have ever been. By analogy, the abandonment of his mother permits Augustine to transform the secular city Aeneas builds into a prototype of "a city not made with hands, whose builder and maker is God."

Augustine accomplishes these purposes, not as a young man who flees from North Africa to Rome, but as the writer of a book that helps lay the foundation of Christendom. In a similar way, it is not so much Aeneas who founds Rome, but the poet who glorifies him who is the founder of the Roman Empire as an abiding force in Western history. Yet whatever can be said about Aeneas, Virgil, or the author of the *Confessions*, and about the numerous comparisons between them, the young Augustine does not understand his deepest motivations when he deceives his mother on the shore of North Africa. In describing himself at this crucial moment in his life, he says simply, "Thus I lied to my mother—to such a mother!—and slipped away from her" (5.8.15).

In addition to the literary interpretation of Augustine's departure for Italy, it is not surprising that psychoanalytic commentators find special significance in the radical separation of Augustine from his mother.[14] Instead of patiently explaining the reasons for his departure and fabricating a plausible excuse about why she could not follow him to Rome, Augustine leaves his mother behind by wrenching himself from her grasp and by lying about what he intends to do. In this desperate situation, the rational and the nonrational dimensions of Augustine split apart; and the two sides of his consciousness pull him in opposite directions. On the one hand, it would have been reasonable for him to invent a credible explanation for his behavior; on the other hand, his emotional turmoil pulls him away from his mother to seek independence in a strange country.

The tension between Augustine and his mother reminds us of other crucial dyads that pervade the *Confessions*. Friendship and death, education and pride, nurses and willfulness, and origins and dependency are oppositions from which Augustine has been unable to escape at earlier stages of his development; and as he tries to free himself from the tension between himself and his mother, the discord this opposition produces tears his soul apart. What motivates Augustine to flee from Carthage is not only the desire to improve his professional situation, but also the wish to escape from his mother's obsessive demands that he follow a spiritual pathway that he has not chosen for himself. As a consequence, the decision to go to Rome is pervaded by anxiety that separates Augustine from himself; and his journey is contaminated by a negative dimension that prevents the young philosopher and rhetorician from coming to himself.

If we adopt a psychoanalytic approach to the text, Augustine's behavior is not a transaction between God and the soul, but a struggle between a gifted child and an overprotective mother, the outcome of which can be appraised persuasively in psychological terms. According to accounts of this kind, the adolescent transfers the protection he receives from his mother to the sustenance he receives from God, imagining himself as a child who still seeks nourishment from the breast of its mother.[15] Yet the most striking fact about this analysis is the extent to which Augustine anticipates it: he does not need a psychoanalyst to inform him about the psychological dimension of his relationship with his mother. After all, it is Augustine who says, "I lied to my mother—to such a mother!"

Augustine moves from a psychological to a spiritual interpretation of his deception of his mother by developing a cluster of metaphors to describe his escape from North Africa. The young man sets out on his journey at night; Monica sheds tears to prevent him from sailing; the wind fills his sails; and the shore on which he and his mother have been standing recedes from sight. The next morning, his mother is there, standing on the land, filling the ears of God with "complaints and groans" that even the one to whom she appeals disregards (5.8.15). Yet in this case, God turns away, not to express indifference, but to use Augustine's desire for earthly advancement as a way of hastening the satisfaction of his deeper longing for spiritual fulfillment. The author tells us that God preserves the young rhetorician from the waters of the sea to keep him safe for the waters of God's grace (5.8.15), so the rivers of his mother's tears that water the wasteland he has become can be dried up by the mercy of God.

Though the author of the *Confessions* refuses to reduce the work of providence to the relationship between himself and his mother, he is also critical of his mother, suggesting that the earthly part of her love for him requires purgation. The great psychologist is aware of the fact that his mother's love for him is abnormal; and he reveals this candidly, not only by recounting Monica's reactions to his departure, but also by telling us that Monica loves to have him close to her, even more than most mothers (5.8.15). Monica attempts to cancel the interplay between presence and absence that characterizes healthy relationships and to substitute a way of being present that almost smothers her son, making it necessary for Augustine to separate himself from her. If it is true that Augustine can move toward God only in the open space generated by the interplay between presence and absence, it is equally true that he can find himself only by balancing the presence of the person closest to him with an equally important period of absence.

On the other hand, Augustine refuses to subordinate the theological interpretation of the relationship between himself and his mother to a psychological framework by informing us that after Monica's accusations of trickery and cruelty, she continues to pray for him (5.8.15). The underlying message of the text is that the tears of Monica for the founder of the Western theological tradition are richer than the tears of Dido for the founder of Rome; that his mother is stronger than the Queen of Carthage because she goes back home instead of plunging a dagger into her heart; that the prayers of Monica are deeper than the emotional maladjustment of both herself and her son; and that the intercession of the one he leaves behind are indispensable in helping Augustine find a place of rest in God.

Though Augustine has a sufficient measure of self-transcendence to see beyond his psychological situation, the unconscious dimension of his predicament asserts itself when he arrives in Rome. After he finally reaches land, he suffers a serious illness from which he almost fails to recover (5.9.16). Though the place where he lives in Rome suggests that the disease from which he suffers is malaria, the psychologist can easily discern a connection between Augustine's physical condition and the emotional turmoil that the separation from his mother engenders. The escape from Monica, which rips his soul apart, makes him more susceptible than usual to a physical illness that almost takes his life (5.9.16).[16]

Augustine ignores the psychological dimension of his situation by focusing on its spiritual significance, insisting that his illness almost casts him into hell, and claiming that it weighs him down more deeply than the sickness of his body. What distresses him most are the sins that he has committed against God, himself, and others that go beyond the bondage of original sin that leads to spiritual death. Yet even his description of the sin that he inherits does not focus on genetic transmission, but upon the fact that he, like every other person, dies "in Adam," and that the only remedy for his predicament is to be made alive "in Christ" (5.9.16).[17]

As a way of elaborating this position, we should notice that Augustine does not formulate the problem of sin and redemption in exclusively spatiotemporal terms. Instead, he claims that sin occurs because we stand alongside the fallen Adam at the intersection of space, time, and eternity and that we can be delivered from destruction only by standing with Christ at the place where space and time are redeemed. Thus, when the author of the *Confessions* contemplates dying, he does not emphasize the fact that sin is transmitted by genetic succession,[18] but points to the battle between the first and the second Adam for the destiny of his soul. This battle is waged at the place where creation, fall, conversion, and fulfillment meet; and the life and death of every human being can be understood within the framework generated by these fundamental conceptions.

At this stage of his development, Augustine still embraces the Manichaean belief that the body is evil, not only rejecting the incarnation, but also failing to understand the triumph of the grace of Christ over Adam's sin. From Augustine's Manichaean perspective, the crucifixion of Jesus is the death of a phantom that is unable to heal his illness. Yet the saint looking back upon the sinner concludes that the death of his soul is just as real as the death of the body of Jesus seems to be unreal, and that the life of his soul is as unreal as the death of the flesh of Jesus is real (5.9.16). This suggests that belief in the bodily death of a person whose soul has not fallen into the body is necessary if Augustine's body is to join his soul in standing before God.

At this decisive moment in her son's development, Augustine's mother reenters the scene. Yet she does so, not by rushing to his side to close the psychological distance between them, but by praying that God will bring about the transformation she seeks. In this respect, she is not only superior to Dido, but also helps her son become superior to the author of the *Aeneid* by writing a book that "converts" the text on which the Roman Empire is founded. Monica and the son for whom she sheds so many tears transcend the polytheism of Aeneas and Virgil because they are sustained by an omnipresent God who is present and absent at once. Thus, Augustine tells us that though Monica is still in Carthage and knows nothing about his illness, she continues to pray for him; and he claims that God, who is everywhere, hears her where she is and takes pity on her son so far away in Rome.

Augustine says that God heals his body and that his reason for doing so is to make it possible for him to heal his fragmented heart. Yet when he returns to the narrative present, the confessor tells us that he begins to associate with Manichaean saints in Rome (5.10.18). This is an important transition because it brings the sinner into relation with the inner circle of the Manichaean elect. However, this stage in Augustine's development is curious, since Manichaean saints are ascetics who despise the body and identify the flesh with evil. Augustine's subsequent behavior makes it clear that even though he identifies himself with the Manichaean elect, he has no intention of giving up the pleasures of the body. It is also difficult to understand why Augustine continues to commit himself to the Manichaeans after his negative experience with Faustus. From a psychological point of view, perhaps he is still running away from his mother by plunging more deeply into the sect that she despises.

Augustine's own explanation for his decision to remain a Manichaean focuses on what he still regards as the practical value of the Manichaean solution to the problem of evil. Even though he has become dissatisfied with their fanciful picture of the cosmos, and though he has become disenchanted by the failure of Faustus to answer his skeptical questions, the Manichaean explanation of the problem of evil continues to attract him. Augustine believes that when sin occurs, it does not result from his own agency, but from the activity of an evil principle working within him. As a consequence, he is able to distance himself from his own actions and to excuse himself from taking moral responsibility for them (5.10.18).

From his standpoint as the author of the text, Augustine admits that he is to blame for his sin because his own actions divide him against himself. Eventually, Augustine realizes that the literal discourse in which he characterizes the conflict between good and evil within his soul must be transcended by a figurative way of speaking about the war of his soul with itself. Yet at this stage of his development, the sinner displaces his guilt on an alien force that he distinguishes from the center of his soul; and he remains in bondage to philosophical dualism as a way of rationalizing his behavior.

Augustine embraces the Manichaean view that the self is a spectator and that a person is not to blame for the evil that often thrusts itself on him as he takes action in the world. He also follows the Manichaeans in believing that evil is a problem a person *has*, failing to notice the more fundamental fact that *the person himself is the problem*.[19] As Augustine will understand eventually, this person is not a battleground between two competing principles, but an individual that has become divided against itself by its own actions. According to this second view, the flesh and the spirit are at war with one another; and sin occurs when the soul turns away from God to follow a path of its own (8.5.11).

Even though Augustine continues to communicate with the Manichaean saints, he despairs of ever finding the truth by pursing philosophical dualism and begins to hold more loosely to the tenants of the sect with which he had resolved to remain content. In fact, he is now inclined to believe that the Academic skeptics are wiser than the rest in claiming that everything is doubtful and that truth is beyond the reach of human beings. Augustine is drawn to skepticism, not only because he is inclined to believe its doctrine, but also because critical questions have been left unresolved by his earlier encounter with Faustus. Thus, his growing skepticism about his earlier convictions leads him to restrain the man with whom he is living from believing the fables with which the Manichaean books are filled (5.10.19).

Though the young Augustine understands skepticism as an exclusively negative principle that sweeps positive doctrines away (5.10.19), (5.14.25), the author of the *Confessions* believes that skeptical questions are an essential step in framing an adequate account of his reflective development (5.10.19). In this respect, his project is like the task of Hegel's *Phenomenology*, where skepticism is not a roadblock in the path of inquiry, but a moving principle that makes the quest for wisdom possible.[20] In fact, both the similarities and the differences between Augustine's and Hegel's philosophical projects are important ways of giving us access to what is distinctive about Augustine's approach to the role of negation in human experience.

In the *Phenomenology*, Hegel's inquiry is philosophical rather than personal. Among other things, this means that his protagonist is not an individual, but the natural consciousness as it moves from stage to stage in its dialectical development. Skepticism about immediate experience drives consciousness to seek refuge in perception; difficulties about perception move it to understanding; and questions at this level propel it through the various stages of Reason toward the richer development of Spirit. In the process, Hegel invites his readers to identify themselves with the development of consciousness as it moves from stage to stage. In addition, he challenges us to incorporate the truth of earlier stages of our development in subsequent stages of our quest for wisdom, laying aside the defects of those earlier points of view as we move from one stage of consciousness to the next.[21] This does not mean that negativity is transcended in these later stages of development, but only that it manifests itself in new forms.

Though Augustine's *Confessions* focuses on certain details of his experiential and reflective development rather than on the natural development of consciousness, there is something universal about his procedure that reminds us of Hegel. Augustine is not simply writing about himself, but also telling the story of the return of the fallen individual to God; and as a consequence, his development from childhood faith, through the reading of Cicero's *Hortensius*, to Manichaeism, Skepticism, Neoplatonism, and Christianity trace out an intellectual pattern that is not peculiar to himself.[22] Indeed, this might lead us to believe that Augustine is the prototype of the natural consciousness, and that the kinship between the author of the *Confessions* and the architect of the *Phenomenology of Spirit* is closer than we might have assumed originally.

Despite their similarities, Augustine stands in contrast with Hegel because he is less concerned than the dialectical thinker to preserve the truth of earlier stages of his life in later stages of his development. This difference with Hegel rests on the role and power of negation in human experience. Because he understands nonbeing as the negation of a prior affirmation, Hegel attempts to hold the stages of experience together rather than allowing them to fall apart into patterns of behavior, some of which must be rejected altogether. The crucial difference between the two thinkers is that Hegel wants our natural consciousness to move from stage to stage and to preserve both the positive and the negative elements of what is essential in each stage until it reaches dialectical satisfaction,[23] while Augustine wants us to reject ways of living that are *essential expressions* of our fallen predicament and that are *incompatible with* our ultimate transformation.[24]

Despite the fact that he is more radical than Hegel about the problem of discontinuity, Augustine admits that as a young man, he does not understand the skepticism of the Academics to which Hegel's concept of determinate negation calls our attention. The young philosopher only grasps the negative part of their teaching, failing to appreciate their view that probability is the guide of life (5.10.19).[25] Augustine also tells us that he does not become a Skeptic at this juncture. Instead, he remains on more friendly terms with the Manichaeans than with any other group, claiming that "close association" with members of the sect makes him slow to seek another path (5.10.19).

Augustine's need for friendship is a crucial consideration in his hesitation to abandon the Manichaeans, but there are also two philosophical reasons for his reluctance to do so. First, he has no hope of finding truth in the Catholic Church from which the Manichaeans have turned him away; for he is convinced that the Church embraces the ridiculous opinion that God has a human form. Second, he does not know how to conceive of God as anything but a bright extended body; for he continues to believe that if something does not have bodily extension, it does not exist. As a way of summarizing this aspect of his predicament, Augustine concludes that his failure to be able to conceive of anything other than a physical substance is "the greatest and almost the sole cause of [his] inevitable error" (5.10.19).

One of the consequences of Augustine's materialism is that he believes that evil is a substance that possesses "its own foul and hideous mass, either gross, . . . or thin and subtle" (5.10.20). Since he believes that God would never create anything evil, he postulates two masses that are in opposition to one another, where both of them are infinite, and where the evil mass is smaller than the good one. Yet because these two masses stand in contrast with one another, Augustine is forced to admit that God is also finite insofar as the evil mass conditions the positive principle with which he is identified. The young man would rather believe that God is finite than believe that he is responsible for the creation of evil (5.10.20).

Augustine also believes that Christ emerges from the shining substance of God, and the close metaphysical connection between the father and the son leads him to reject the incarnation. At this stage of his development, he is unable to believe that such a nature could be born without being mingled with the flesh; and he cannot see how it could be joined to the flesh without being contaminated by it. Thus he concludes: "I feared to believe that he was born in the flesh, lest I be forced to believe that he had been defiled by the flesh" (5.10.20). The point Augustine expresses here is negative; but in drawing the distinction between being *born* in the flesh and being *contaminated* by it, he implies that he does not regard the body as evil in its own right. Indeed, when Augustine finally embraces the incarnation, it will become clear that he has laid this misconception aside altogether.

Augustine also tells us that as a young man, he does not believe that it is possible to defend the scriptures against the objections that the Manichaeans bring against them (5.11.21). As we have seen in the previous chapter, he develops a defense of this kind in the replies he makes to Manichaean changes against Christianity that pertain to the problem of evil, the nature of God, and the morality of the Old Testament patriarchs. For the moment, he can only register his earlier discomfort at the inadequacy of Manichaean replies to a certain scholar who defends the Scriptures, expressing his incredulity about Manichaean claims that the New Testament has been corrupted by Jewish authors who have tried to insert the teachings of the law into the heart of the gospel (5.11.21).

Even though he has so many doubts about the integrity of the Manichaeans, Augustine remains in bondage to their dualistic picture of the world and to the two principles that he has been constrained to postulate to explain the problem of evil. He pictures these principles as a heavy load on his back, under which he gasps for the pure, clean air of truth that he is unable to breathe (5.11.21). Panting under the load of so much spiritual and philosophical uncertainty, he also tells us that he begins to teach rhetoric in Rome and that his first step is to invite a few friends into his home. However, he soon learns that the students in Rome are not what he had expected. Many of them conspire with one another and transfer to another teacher to avoid paying Augustine's fees, prompting him to hate them and to accuse them of fornication against God. Augustine admits that his hatred is not what it ought to have been because it focuses on his own suffering rather than on his students' need for transformation (5.12.22). Yet in chiding himself for this, he is able to bring the account of this stage of his life to a close by speaking with the voice of the confessor, by emphasizing God's love for those who have wandered away from him, and by calling our attention once more to God's willingness to welcome those who go back home.

AMBROSE AND THE CHRISTIAN FAITH (5.13.23–6.5.8)

As he begins this crucial stage of his journey toward God, officials from Milan ask for a teacher of rhetoric; Augustine applies for the position; and his Manichaean friends recommend that the prefect of Rome give him the appointment. The prefect is a Manichaean and a gifted orator; and when he hears Augustine speak, he decides to recommend him to Milan, not only because of his obvious talents, but also because he will be an able representative of the Manichaean sect at the seat of the Emperors.[26] The prefect, Augustine, and his friends believe that the move to Milan will advance his career, not realizing that the providential purpose of his journey is to free him from Manichaean entanglements. After he has understood this deeper purpose, the author of the text expresses it in one of the most memorable lines of the book: "I came to Milan, to Ambrose, the bishop" (5.13.23).

In Ambrose, Augustine meets a rhetorician whose way of speaking he wants to assess, but he also finds a teacher who can give him a sophisticated understanding of the Christian faith. At a personal level, Ambrose receives Augustine as a father and welcomes him as a bishop; and the young professor begins to love him, not as a teacher of truth, but as a friendly man (5.13.23). The prodigal son is finally coming home, and Ambrose is a symbol of the one who is waiting to receive him.

At first Augustine has no interest in the message conveyed by the sermons of Ambrose, only wanting to determine whether the eloquence of the preacher matches his reputation. Thus, he listens to his words intently, but is contemptuous of the subject matter. Augustine is delighted with the eloquence of Ambrose's discourse, though it is "less lively and entertaining" than the style of Faustus. Yet with respect to substantive issues, there is no comparison between the two orators: Faustus wanders around in Manichaean deceptions, while Ambrose points to the pathway that leads to liberation. As he looks back on this stage of his life, the writer confesses that he is still far away from home; but he adds, "Little by little I was drawing closer to you, although I did not know it" (5.13.23).

The power of Augustine's unconscious is nowhere more evident than in his response to the preaching of Ambrose. Along with the eloquence he prizes, the ideas of Ambrose come into his mind; and as he listens to his sermons, he cannot separate their form from their content. When Faustus speaks about phantasms, the young philosopher can make the distinction between form and content without any difficulty; but when Ambrose speaks about the Bible, Augustine not only acknowledges how skillfully he preaches, but gradually begins to realize how truly he speaks (5.14.24). In the case of phantasms, form and content diverge; in the case of truth, they merge. In this second instance, truth and rhetoric are compatible; and this fact makes it possible for Augustine to find the truth he is seeking, to find a way of speaking that is compatible with it, and to write a book that responds to the needs of both the will and the intellect.

Part of the reason for Augustine's responsiveness to Ambrose is that his ideas seem to be defensible. Augustine is beginning to realize that the Catholic faith can be defended against the criticisms of the Manichaeans, and this realization is confirmed when he discovers the power of the allegorical interpretation of scripture. Ambrose explains the Old Testament in figurative language, permitting Augustine to recognize the fact that Manichean objections to the Law and the Prophets that had disturbed him for years can be overcome. As we have seen, the Manicheans reject the Old Testament because of its primitive concept of God and because it contains bloodthirsty and morally repugnant passages. However, after he listens to Ambrose, Augustine begins to realize that passages can be freed from absurdity if they are interpreted allegorically (5.4.24).

Ambrose is a student of Philo and Origen, and he applies their method of interpretation to the exposition of Scripture. Indeed, he is not only saturated with Alexandrian philosophy, but also blends it with Neoplatonism to give it an even richer philosophical expression.[27] However, Ambrose's primary purpose is not to read philosophical doctrines into the passages he considers, but to protect the Bible from criticism by interpreting it on three levels: the first is literal, the second is moral, and the third is spiritual. In his sermons, Ambrose gives a straightforward reading of a biblical text; then he examines its practical implications; and on this basis, he attempts to give his listeners access to the hidden meaning that the surface of the text conceals. In the judgment of Ambrose, this third level is the most important because it frees Old Testament passages from absurdity and points to a living connection between the symbols of the Old Testament and the pivotal icons of the Christian community.[28]

For example, Ambrose uses allegory to interpret Noah's drunkenness, Abraham's adultery, Job's curse, and David's dancing before God. In one instance, he reasons as follows:

> Isaac means laughter; laughter is the sign of joy; the fount of joy is Christ; Isaac, therefore, is the figure of Christ. But if Isaac represents Christ, then Rebecca must represent the Church or the devout soul. Thus the story of Isaac and Rebecca illustrates phases of the relationship between Christ and the Church, the Savior and the soul, the Spouse and the bride.[29]

It is tempting to believe that this method of biblical interpretation can permit the one who employs it to read the text as he pleases. However, this is not the case; for the most important point to notice is that Ambrose employs the hermeneutical tools of the Alexandrians and the Neoplatonists to defend the Old Testament Scriptures from charges of self-contradiction.

Though Augustine is influenced decisively by this method of interpretation, there are crucial differences between the way he uses it in his own exegesis of Scripture and the way of reading a biblical text that he learns from Ambrose. First, on at least some occasions, Augustine replaces the three levels of interpretation that Ambrose distinguishes with four—historical, aetiological, analogical, and allegorical. Second, he combines the first two to give a literal reading of the text and uses the third and fourth to give a figurative reading.[30] Third, whereas Ambrose correlates biblical names with philosophical abstractions, Augustine often reverses the order, moving from abstractions to the concrete contexts in which they are embedded. Finally, when Ambrose uses allegorical discourse to connect the Old and the New Testaments, he equates biblical names with abstract entities, while Augustine relates embodied beings mentioned in the Old Testament to concrete individuals who come into existence at a later stage of history.

For example, in the *Utility of Believing*, which is written at least five years before the *Confessions*, Augustine compares the three days and nights the prophet Jonah spends in the belly of the whale with the three days and nights Jesus spends in "the heart of the earth."[31] It is one thing to equate Isaac with laughter and Rebecca with a devout soul and quite another to compare the three days and nights Jonah spends in the belly of the whale with the time Jesus spends in the bowels of the earth. Though the first way of speaking might raise our intellectual vision to the heavens, the second tries to reach our hearts by bringing Jonah and Jesus into a direct correlation with our existential situation.[32]

Despite the success of Ambrose in leading Augustine toward a new way of understanding the Bible, the skepticism by which he is tempted earlier is still at work, preventing him from embracing the Christian faith without reservation. Augustine will not become a Christian simply because the faith Ambrose defends can answer objections; and as a consequence, he remains suspended between Manichaean fables and the Christian faith, which seem to be equal in their power to reply to objections. The sermons of Ambrose motivate Augustine to wonder whether he can prove that the Manichaeans are guilty of falsehood; and he concludes that if "[he] were only able to conceive a spiritual substance, all those stratagems would be foiled and cast out of [his] mind" (5.14.25). But this he cannot do until he finds a new way of speaking that is even more subtle than the allegorical mode of interpretation that he learns from Ambrose.

Nevertheless, Augustine finally decides that the natural philosophers hold the more probable views about the structure of the world; and since he cannot see how he can remain in a sect to which he prefers the philosophers, he decides that he must abandon the Manichaeans (5.14.25). This decision is important, not only because it frees him from Manichaean doctrine, but also because it prefigures a transformation of the will that is necessary if Augustine is to come to himself as a transformed being. The young philosopher does not repudiate the Manichaeans because he has demonstrated that their teachings are false; rather, he *resolves* to turn away from them to embrace a more probable view of the structure of the universe. This decision is as much volitional as it is intellectual, allowing him to reject a dualistic picture of the world without already possessing intellectual certainty about the alternatives before him.

Having decided to repudiate the Manichaeans, Augustine makes another decision, this time with respect to the natural philosophers that he has begun to prefer in contrast with them. In this case, he refuses "to commit the cure of [his] soul to the philosophers because they were without the saving name of Christ"; and he decides to renew his childhood commitment to the Catholic Church, which his parents had commended to him, waiting until something certain appears to illuminate his path (5.14.25). In the meantime, his decision to turn away from the natural philosophers and to turn toward the Church repeats the pattern he has followed already in his response to Cicero's *Hortensius*. In that case, he cannot embrace the book because the name of Christ is not in it; in this case, he is unable to commit himself to the teachings of the natural philosophers for the same reason (5.14.25).

Augustine's incapacity to conceive of a spiritual substance is an important obstacle to finding certainty. Among other things, it prevents him from rejecting a materialistic conception of God to embrace the God of his heart. The concreteness of substance is a central element in the Manichaean position; and even though he has turned away from Manichaeaism, Augustine cannot understand how an immaterial entity can provide the stability he seeks. What he needs is a spiritual substance that is both stable and sufficiently rich to address the human spirit. In the language of Hegel's *Phenomenology*, he must transform substance into subject if he is to find the kind of stability that can heal his fragmented heart.

The concept of a spiritual substance mobilizes material and spiritual dimensions simultaneously, but Augustine has not yet developed a way of speaking that is sophisticated enough to express the concept in question. As a consequence, his inability to bind the concepts of substance and subject together becomes a barrier that hinders his religious and philosophical development. Yet even here he has begun to realize the significance of the problem of spiritual substance and to struggle with it. Bypassing the natural philosophers to continue as a catechumen of the Catholic Church is the first stage in resolving this problem; and in moving from one context to the other, he begins to turn away from nature to the realm where spirit and substance meet.

At this stage of his narrative, Augustine tells us that his psychological situation is becoming increasingly more complicated: his mother has joined him in Milan, having endured the perils of an ocean journey to follow him over land and sea. In fact, she is still her indomitable self, having lost none of the confidence that has always characterized her relation to her gifted son. During the ocean voyage, she even imitates the Apostle Paul by comforting the experienced sailors when they face the storms at sea;[33] and she promises them a safe arrival at the port because God has assured her of it in a vision (6.1.1).

When Monica finds Augustine, her son is still in despair about ever finding the truth. Yet when he tells her that he is not a Manichaean any longer, he marvels that she does not leap for joy, not realizing that God has already reassured her about this aspect of his predicament. Though Augustine has not yet found the truth, he has at least been rescued from falsehood; and Monica is confident that having turned away from the Manichaeans, her son will eventually become a Christian (6.1.1). The quiet confidence that Monica displays also exhibits the wisdom that her son needs to embrace, for the domineering mother finally gives her vacillating son enough space to make his own decisions. In the meantime, she pours out her prayers and tears in private, appeals to the fountain of God's mercy so he will enlighten Augustine's darkness, and hurries to the church to listen to the sermons of Ambrose that flow from his mouth like a "fountain of water" (6.1.1).

Monica knows that the words of Ambrose have brought her son to his wavering state of agitation, and she is convinced that having listened to them, Augustine will pass from sickness to health and from death to life. What she does not know is that this will occur only after he passes through "that paroxysm which doctors call the crisis" (6.1.1). In mentioning a crisis, the master rhetorician is preparing the attentive reader for his eventual conversion, where he will find the rest he has been seeking by returning to the house of his father.

If Augustine is to become a Christian, he must pass through a crisis that will touch his will as well as his intellect, and that will redeem both his soul and his body from the abyss into which he has fallen. Faith seeking understanding is more than belief in the truth of propositions; for in addition to its intellectual dimension, it requires commitment to a way of living in which Augustine renounces his pride and embraces the God of his heart. For faith of this kind to grip the soul, in this or any other situation, an existential crisis is necessary.

Augustine has not yet begun to pray that God will help him, but is intent on asking questions and on engaging in disputation (6.3.3). To this extent, he is still involved in the kind of theoretical activity that had characterized his earlier days as a Manichaean convert. At this stage of his development, Augustine still does not realize that faith precedes understanding, that belief directs the heart toward truth, that his existential predicament can be overcome only by the transformation of the will, and that the bondage of the will prevents him from understanding the nature of God. As a consequence, he continues to fall short of a conversion that not only transforms his intellect, but that liberates his will as well.

The author underscores the distinction between the theoretical and the affective dimensions of his soul by claiming that though his experience with Ambrose is positive at the intellectual level, it is puzzling from an interpersonal point of view. Though Ambrose appears to be happy because so many powerful individuals honor him, the young catechumen regards the celibacy of the Bishop as a painful burden. Augustine simply cannot believe that a man can be happy by committing himself to a way of living that does not include sexual satisfaction (6.3.3). For his part, Ambrose does not understand the young man's seething passions, nor does he grasp the extent to which he is still floundering in the abyss that separates him from God (6.3.3).

Augustine complains that Ambrose does not understand his intellectual frustrations, will never talk with him for an extended period, and will not allow him to ask the questions that have been troubling him so long. Crowds prevent Augustine from hearing and speaking to him; and when Ambrose is not dealing with them, he is either caring for his body or improving his mind. As a consequence, Augustine cannot find the intellectual satisfaction he seeks by making contact with Ambrose (6.3.3).

For example, when Augustine and his friends go to Ambrose's study, they observe him reading attentively. In one of the most well-known passages in the text, Augustine expresses amazement at this by claiming, "When he read, his eyes moved down the pages and his heart sought out their meaning, while his voice and tongue remained silent" (6.3.3). Many scholars have commented on these sentences: some maintain that silent reading is rarely if ever present in antiquity; others claim that Augustine is a provincial who speaks when he reads and has no experience with a sophisticated scholar like Ambrose; and still others point out that Augustine is a rhetorician who associates the use of language almost exclusively with speaking.[34] Yet all these explanations fail to grasp the deeper significance of Augustine's account of the behavior of Ambrose with respect to speech and silence.

Augustine suggests that Ambrose reads in silence to prevent distraction and to avoid conversation with others. He also speculates that if the author that Ambrose is reading expresses himself vaguely, a student who hears him reading aloud might ask him to explain the passage, preventing him from reading as much as he wishes without interruption. Finally, Augustine says that perhaps the correct explanation for the silent reading of Ambrose is the understandable desire to preserve his voice, which is weakened very easily (6.3.3).

These points are important, not only as explanations of the phenomenon at hand, but also as ways of understanding the behavior of Ambrose from a vertical point of view. The eyes of Ambrose move along the page in the silence of intellectual absorption, where absorption of this kind points to the possibility of the contemplation of God. After his conversion, Augustine himself embraces this possibility, turning to the exposition of the Bible with which Ambrose is often preoccupied. However, prior to the conversion of Augustine, Ambrose needs to use his voice to reach the young man's heart. Indeed, if Augustine is to be converted, the stillness of his intellect (*animus*) as it comes to rest on the written word presupposes that his will has already embraced the dynamic word that speaks in the text. In this case, speech is prior to silence, where as in so many other cases, order is everything.

Augustine complains that he cannot ask the questions that trouble him unless Ambrose can deal with them briefly. The gifted student needs a teacher to give him his full attention, but Ambrose is never able to do this. Augustine must be content with hearing Ambrose preach to his parishioners at a distance; but even in this relatively impersonal context, the young man is persuaded that the crafty fables of the Manichaeans can be refuted. Though Augustine is frustrated because he is unable to speak with Ambrose in private, the Neoplatonic bishop convinces the Catholic catechumen that it is possible to unravel the knots that the dualists have tied around his probing intellect (6.3.4).

Before we turn to what Augustine learns from Ambrose, we should notice the contrast between Faustus and the Christian bishop. Though each appears at a different juncture in Augustine's spatial and temporal development, the vertical difference between them is even more instructive. Faustus is pleasant and friendly, though it soon becomes clear that he does not have the truth. Ambrose seems to possess the truth, but refrains from addressing his pupil directly. Faustus speaks, but has nothing to say; Ambrose has something to say, but refuses to speak. As a consequence, Augustine's principal problem is how to bring the spirit of Faustus and the knowledge of Ambrose together. In more systematic terms, Augustine must learn how to unite two senses of the Word, one of which points to the act of speaking and the other of which calls our attention to the content spoken. Faustus uses the rhetorical dimension of language to address Augustine's heart, while Ambrose gives an intelligible account of the Old Testament by using an allegorical method of interpretation. As a consequence, Augustine needs to ask how it is possible for two such different ways of speaking to be held together.

Augustine admires Faustus because of his willingness to communicate without presuming to know more than he does. By contrast, his regard for Ambrose rests on the Bishop's use of a method of interpretation that satisfies the intellect. Yet neither Faustus nor Ambrose are able to bring the structural and the dynamic dimensions of language together. If Augustine is to overcome the defects of his two acquaintances, the same Word that makes the Bible intelligible must address him directly; and his own discourse must allow the allegorical use of language that is appropriate to biblical interpretation to be related to the language that speaks directly to the heart.

Though Ambrose does not deal with Augustine adequately in private, his public sermons answer some of his student's questions and stimulate his theological reflections. As a result of listening to Ambrose, Augustine becomes clearer about Catholic doctrine, about the interpretation of the Old

Testament, about the relation between faith and reason, and about the value of religious authority. For example, he learns that creation in the image of God does not imply that God has a human form and that by claiming for so long that it does, he has been barking at a phantasm. Augustine still does not understand the nature of a spiritual substance, but at least he has begun to realize that the version of *imago dei* that he has been attacking is a fiction. The Church holds that God is both high and near, secret and present, everywhere and nowhere and that he does not have a corporeal form. Nevertheless, he creates us in his own image, allowing us to dwell in space "from head and foot" (6.3.4).

This reference to the body suggests that the doctrine of the image of God is compatible with the view that a person is a composite, created with both a soul and a body. Otherwise, Augustine would have scarcely claimed that the image of God is "embedded" in space and that it has both "head" and "feet." If the head is a metaphorical way of pointing to the soul, the feet point metaphorically to the body; and taken together, both are necessary elements in the analogical relation between God and the creatures that he has chosen to make in his own image.

The "space" in which the image of God is to be found has more than one ontological and linguistic layer. Insofar as the image remains intact, it occupies an unfallen spatiotemporal region in which it participates in the original innocence of Adam in the garden. Insofar as the image is distorted, it is part of the intractable existential medium through which Augustine moves in his tortuous journey toward God. And insofar as it is restored to its original condition, it is a converted and a resurrected version of the soul and the body that fall away from God and that are finally able to go back home.

To say that we continue to participate in Adam's original innocence is simply to claim that the individuals that God has brought into existence are good. Indeed, Augustine points to his own goodness when he tells us in Book I that "it was good for them [Augustine's nurses] that my good come from them" and, addressing God, says, "you have given to the infant life and a body . . . and, for its complete good and perfection . . . endowed with all the powers of a living being" (1.6.7), (1.7.12). It is this dimension of goodness, which is never effaced, that justifies the claim that we continue to occupy an unfallen spatiotemporal context alongside Adam in the garden. In an analogous way, the spatiotemporal matrix in which we are embedded displays different sides of itself as we move from creation to the fall, from the fall to conversion, and from conversion to fulfillment. This suggests that in addition to an unfallen spatiotemporal region, we need to acknowledge a fallen, a converted, and a fulfilled dimension of space and time that reflects these different aspects of our existential situation.

At this stage of his development, Augustine begins to wonder what he can believe with certainty; and he is ashamed that he has accepted so many Manichaean uncertainties as if they were certain. Even now he does not know that these fables are false, but at least he is certain that they are uncertain. And though he does not know that the Catholic Church teaches the truth, he knows that it does not teach what he had thought. Thus, he claims that even though he has not discovered the truth of the Catholic faith, he is in the process of "being refuted and converted" (6.4.5). Augustine rejoices that the Church does not embrace a doctrine that presses God into space or declares that he has the shape of a human body, though he is unable once more to determine the truth of the doctrine they defend (6.4.5).

Part of the reason for Augustine's delight in discovering that the Church does not teach that God has a body is his negative assessment of the human body at this stage of his development. The Manichaeans have convinced him that the body is evil; and as a consequence, he is happy to learn that the Church does not teach that God exists in human form (6.4.5). Only later will he discover that the whole creation is good, including both the soul and the body. The reason that the Church holds that God does not have a body is not that the body is evil, but that it is finite. As he continues to move toward the truth, Augustine has not yet distinguished between finitude and fallenness— a distinction that he must draw if he is to be able to deal with the problem of evil. Finitude allows the body and the soul to stand in contrast with God, while fallenness accounts for the evil of both the soul and the body when they stand opposed to him.

The second thing that Augustine learns from Ambrose is the value of allegorical interpretation, which permits him to reconsider the Christian Faith as a viable alternative to dualism. Allegorical interpretation allows him to use figurative discourse in dealing with theological questions and makes it possible for him to make the transition from a literal to a richer kind of language that transcends Manichaean dualism. Ambrose often says, " 'The letter kills, but the spirit quickens,' " where following this maxim permits Augustine to move closer to Christianity by overcoming his bondage to a literal interpretation of the Bible (6.4.6). Yet even though he has no difficulty in understanding what Ambrose says, he still does not know that what he says is true. In fact, he holds himself back from making assent to what he hears because he fears that he might fall headlong into falsity. Augustine wants to be just as certain about what he cannot see as he is about the truths of mathematics; but at this stage of his journey, he is unable to find the certainty he seeks (6.4.6).

Augustine realizes that if he could have believed, he could have been saved; but he adds, "just as a man who has had trouble with a poor physician fears to entrust himself to a good one, so it was with my soul's health" (6.4.6). Like the philosopher Hegel mentions who transforms a fear of error into a fear of the truth,[35] Augustine is afraid to commit himself to a new way of living after his disappointing experiences with the Manichaeans. From his later perspective as the author of the text, Augustine knows that he could never have been healed without believing; but because he is afraid to believe what is false, he *refuses to be cured*, resisting the hands of God who has applied "the remedies of faith" to "the diseases of the world" (6.4.6). In this case, medical terminology points to the essence of the matter; for faith seeking understanding is not belief without evidence, but an act of the will that renounces its pride and accepts the transformation of the soul. "Salvation" means "healing," where the transition from faith to understanding is mediated by healing, and where this way of speaking suggests that a "moral conversion" is a necessary if Augustine is to return to the father from whom he has turned away.

Augustine says that from this moment on, he prefers Catholic teaching. However, this does not mean that he has decided to become a Christian, but only that Christianity is superior to Manichaeism in its attitude toward the problem of religious authority. The young philosopher comes to the conclusion that it is more reasonable for the Church to command that he believe certain doctrines that it cannot demonstrate than for the Manichaeans to promise certain knowledge, and then force him to believe many things that are absurd *because* they cannot demonstrate them (6.5.7).

In elaborating his early views about authority, Augustine recalls how many things he believes, even though he has never seen them nor been present when they occur. For example, many events in human history, facts about places and cities where he has never been, and much of the information that he knows about his friends and about other men and women fall into this category. He also tells us that he believes many things on the testimony of others, including his belief about which two people are his parents; and he claims that for similar reasons, we should believe the Scriptures that God has established with authority among the nations (6.5.7).

When someone asks, " 'How do you know that these are the books of the one and most truthful God, dispensed by his spirit to the human race?,' " Augustine responds in four ways (6.5.7). First, he claims that hostile and slanderous questions from philosophers who contradict one another will never convince him that God does not exist and that he is not in control of human affairs, even though he does not understand the nature of God or know the pathway that leads back to him. Second, he commits himself to the view that since unaided reason is too weak to find the truth, God has chosen to reveal his will in the Bible, which he has given great authority throughout the world. Third, he believes that he can understand puzzling passages in the

Bible through the kind of spiritual interpretation that he has learned from Ambrose. Finally, he claims that Scripture is worthy of belief because it is visible to all, and because it safeguards "the dignity of [its] hidden truth within a deeper meaning" (6.5.8).

This final claim is important, not only in itself, but also because it contrasts so radically with Augustine's earlier attitude toward the Bible. After he reads Cicero's *Hortensius*, Augustine turns toward Scripture in his search for wisdom; but he quickly turns away from it because of the simplicity of its content and the inelegance of its style. Yet having learned about Ambrose's approach to the Bible, the rhetorician finally realizes that one can read the text on more than one level: its plainness and simplicity of style appeal to children, while its hidden depths and secret wisdom require the closest attention of the most thoughtful reader (6.5.8). Allegorical interpretation opens up the center of the text beneath the surface, forcing Augustine and his friends to use all their powers to interpret it. Thus, the Bible not only requires the reader to bend over in humility as he enters the gateway of the text, but also opens up the richness of a magnificent temple, where narrow pathways lead into a Holy of Holies that is veiled in mystery when one approaches it for the first time.

Augustine concludes his reflections on biblical interpretation by expressing the ambiguities of his heart and by declaring his confidence in God:

> I thought over these things, and you were present to me. I uttered sighs, and you gave ear to me. I wavered back and forth, and you guided me. I wandered in the broad way of the world, and you did not forsake me. (6.5.8)

As Augustine reflects on his predicament, God remains with him; and as he sighs, God listens. Despite his vacillations, Augustine begins to come to himself because God guides him; and even though he roams this way and that, the creative ground of his existence does not desert him, permitting him to continue the journey that leads back to the house of his father.

Augustine begins his journey toward God with an interplay between original innocence and original sin; but he quickly undertakes a downward journey that expresses itself in the jealous outburst of the infant and in the refusal of the child to learn what his instructors teach. The adolescent then moves toward the radical negativity of the pear-stealing episode; and this same kind of negation manifests itself in the love of false images and in loving and deceiving for its own sake. Reading Cicero's *Hortensius* allows Augustine to reverse this negative direction for the first time, but he quickly falls into Manichaean dualism as a way of giving determinate content to the wisdom he seeks. Dualism reinstates the duality with which his journey begins, but it is unable to liberate him from the conflict between positive and negative elements that define his experiential and reflective situation. The death of his closest friend accentuates his existential predicament, causing him to see death wherever he looks; and both the failure of Faustus to answer his questions and the failure of Ambrose to reach his heart leave him uncertain about how to find the salvation he seeks. However, what he learns from Ambrose leads him to prefer Christian doctrine and prepares him to undergo the pivotal experiences that will set him free.

FRAGMENTATION AND FRIENDSHIP (6.6.9–6.16.26)

Augustine now returns to the personal dimension of his struggle to find a stable identity and points to the fragmented spirit in which he pursues it by confessing, "I looked with longing at honors, wealth, and marriage; and you laughed at me" (6.6.9). In permitting these ambitions to dominate his life, the young man endures a series of hardships that tear his soul apart; but from his later perspective as the author of the *Confessions*, Augustine gives a positive interpretation of their significance (6.6.9). As he continues to trace out a path of his own, God is seeking him; and as he tries to find fulfillment in finite contexts, the one who creates him will not permit him to find satisfaction in anything less than Himself.

Augustine says that God is irritating the nerves of his wounded soul so it will forsake everything finite, be converted, and cleave to Him without vacillation (6.6.9). This reference to the nerves of the soul ties it to the body metaphorically, while the conversion of the entire person allows it to cling to God by means of the soul (*animus*). Once more, though the soul is higher than the body, the true man is not the soul, but the soul and the body understood as a composite, where metaphors bind the soul and the body together and analogies hold them apart. When he falls away from God, Augustine's soul (*anima*) takes the body with it, requiring a radical reversal of orientation if both the soul and the body are to return to the ground of their existence. This crucial fact suggests that the unity and separation of the soul and the body is not only linguistic, but also ontological, and that Augustine's rhetorical use of language is more than an ornamental accretion on a literal way of speaking. In this and so many other cases, his figurative use of language points to the fact that creation, fall, conversion, and fulfillment pertain not only to the soul, but to the body as well.

As Augustine prepares to make an oration in praise of the Emperor, the seriousness of his predicament finally dawns on him when he catches a glimpse of a beggar who is already drunk in the morning, but is also "making jokes and feeling high" (6.6.9). When he sees the man who is so far beneath him in social, economic, and professional terms, he sighs to his friends that their ambitions are dragging them down and that he is afraid that they will never find the happiness the even the beggar enjoys (6.6.9). With the few coins passers-by have given him, he has found a momentary version of the happiness Augustine and his companions have been struggling to find for many years (6.6.9).

The Bishop admits that the beggar has not found genuine happiness; but he is also aware that in all his ambitions, he is seeking a happiness that is still more elusive. The beggar is joyous and Augustine is anxious; and the man who is drunk is free from care, in contrast with the rhetorician who is on his way to glorify the emperor, filled with apprehension. Though Augustine does not want to change places with the beggar, he realizes that he ought not to prefer himself to the other man. The professor gets no pleasure from his learning, but simply seeks to please others by exhibiting it; and he does not wish to instruct the students who depend on him, but only to please the ears of an audience who knows he is lying. Thus, however confused the young rhetorician may be when he sees the beggar drunk in the street, the author concludes that God is seeking him in order to break "his bones" and to discipline him (6.6.9).

Augustine knows that the beggar is rejoicing in his drunkenness, while the young rhetorician is longing for glory; but he also knows that the glory he seeks is false because it does not bring rest. Augustine acknowledges the fact that the beggar has not found joy, but he also confesses that neither has he. Augustine realizes that the beggar will recover from his drunkenness that same night, while he has slept with his "drunkenness" for "many nights" and will continue to do so in the future (6.6.10). It makes a difference where a man finds his joy; but at the same time, the beggar has transcended Augustine's professional persona: he is not only steeped in his mirth, but has gotten his wine by giving good wishes to those who have tossed him coins, while the rhetorician is not only torn to pieces by his cares, but is pursuing his professional ambitions by lying about the virtues of the Emperor (6.6.10).

Augustine's companions agree with his assessment of his situation; but instead of finding joy in the companionship he shares with them, the rhetorician becomes even more distraught. When things do not go well, he frets and compounds the difficulty; and when prosperity comes, it flies away before he can grasp it. Yet at least Augustine does not isolate himself from his friends; and they continue to sustain him, especially Alypius and Nebridius. In this case, the theoretical incompetence of Faustus, the silence of Ambrose, and the tears of Monica are supplemented by conversations that Augustine has with his closest companions.

The author's introduction of his friends at this stage of his narrative reflects his abiding awareness of the importance of the spatial dimension of his experience and of the crucial role the interplay between the individual and the community continues to play in his development. In describing his friends, Augustine points to traits of character that allow his relationships with them to play a significant role in his development. For example, he speaks in some detail about Alypius, describing his temperament (6.7.11–6.10.16), and contrasting it with the temperament of Nebridius (6.10.17), his other frequent companion.

Alypius is born in the same town as Augustine; his parents are of the highest rank; and the father of Alypius helps finance Augustine's education. The wealthy young man, who is a bit younger than Augustine and who has been his pupil at both Tagaste and Carthage, respects his teacher because he appears to be "well disposed toward him and to be a learned man," while Augustine admires Alypius "because of his great natural virtue" (6.7.11). In these brief characterizations, we get the first hint of the difference between Augustine and his friend: Alypius is less erotic than Augustine, while Augustine attributes the difference between himself and his pupil to an inborn love of virtue.

Alypius has a weakness that confirms this assessment, though it might appear to contradict it. The circus is especially attractive to him, and he has both a blind and a persistent passion for it. However, this vicarious passion allows him to adopt the standpoint of a spectator, not only at the games he enjoys, but also in the religious companions with whom he chooses to associate. The passivity that reflects the character of Alypius predisposes him to become involved with Augustine in the Manichaean sect, loving its members' outward display of ascetic discipline that he believes is genuine (6.7.12). In this respect, Alypius stands in contrast with his more gifted companion, whose commitment to the Manichaeans derives from too much eros rather than too little. Unlike Alypius, Augustine is captivated by the dualistic sect, not because of their pretenses toward asceticism, but because their doctrine of evil frees him from blame for indulging the desires by which he has been enslaved since early adolescence.

The sublimated passion of Alypius continues to plague him when he moves to Rome to study law. One sunny afternoon, some of his acquaintances and fellow students compel him to witness a gladiatorial contest against his will. Alypius protests that though his body is present, he will not give his eyes and mind to the spectacle. Thus, he tries to be absent though present, overcoming both the insistence of his friends and the attractions of the competition by a stoical exercise in self-control. Alypius keeps his eyes closed and tries to master his emotions during the frenzy; but as the author of the text exclaims, "Would that he had been able to close his ears as well!" (6.8.13). When one of the participants falls in the fight, a cry from the audience stirs him so strongly that he opens his eyes; and as a consequence, a deeper wound strikes his soul than the wound to the body of the victim (6.8.13).

Augustine describes the transformation of the virtuous Alypius into a bloodthirsty maniac:

> As he saw the blood, he drank in savageness at the same time. He did not turn away, but fixed his sight on it, and drank in madness without knowing it. He took delight in that evil struggle, and he became drunk on blood and pleasure. He was no longer the man who entered there, but only one of the crowd that he had joined, and a true comrade of those who brought him there. What more shall I say? He looked, he shouted, he took fire, he bore away with himself a madness that should arouse him to return, not only with those who had drawn him there, but even before them, and dragging along others as well. (6.8.13)

This scene is important for at least two reasons. First, Alypius is still transforming his natural eros into a spectatorial form by watching a gladiatorial contest rather that engaging more directly in erotic activity. To be sure, Alypius's behavior is active in its own right: he shouts, becomes agitated, participates fully in the madness of the spectacle, and resolves to come again, dragging others with him to enjoy the bloody contest. Nevertheless, this expression of the erotic consciousness is still a sublimation, distinguishing him from his more famous friend. Second, there is an auditory dimension to the episode. Alypius covers his eyes; and if it had not been for the shouts of the spectators, he could have avoided looking at the spectacle. The primacy of hearing that stands at the center of Augustine's enterprise surfaces even in this unexpected place, suggesting once more that speaking and hearing are more important than seeing in his quest to understand himself.

When Augustine shifts his attention to the description of his other friend, Nebridius, it soon becomes evident that he is very different from Alypius. Nebridius comes to Milan to live with Augustine and to undertake a common search for truth. He leaves his family estate in Carthage, abandoning his house and his mother, who refuses to follow him to Milan. Like Augustine, he sighs and wavers, though he also joins him in pursuing philosophy, prompting the author to describe him as "a subtle critic of the most difficult questions" (6.10.17). This single remark helps us understand the difference between Alypius and Nebridius and the significance of Augustine's later comment that Nebridius is not present at his Christian conversion (8.6.14, 8.12.29–30). As we shall observe in another book, what will be required on that occasion is not acute analysis, but a volitional response to the transforming power of God.

As his journey toward God begins to reach its culmination, Augustine responds to his predicament with temporal, spatial, and eternal hysteria, noticing that eleven years have passed since he began his quest for wisdom and his attempt to find satisfaction in philosophical friendship. He is now nearly thirty, but is still enjoying the fleeting pleasures of the present moment. The fragmented rhetorician exclaims, " 'Tomorrow I will find it! Behold, Faustus will come to explain everything!' " Or he says, " 'Ah, what great men are the Academic philosophers! Nothing certain can be found for the conduct of life! But no, we must search more diligently; we must not fall into despair!' " (6.11.18). Yet then the pressures of space, time, and eternity become almost unbearable:

> But where shall [the truth] be sought? When shall it be sought? Ambrose has no leisure. There is no time for reading. Where do we look for the books? Where or when can we get them? From whom can we borrow them? Times must be set and hours must be assigned for the health of our soul. (6.11.18)

> Our students take up my morning hours, but what do we do during the rest of the day? Why not do this? When will we pay calls on our more powerful friends, whose help we need? When can we prepare books for students to buy? When can we repair our strength by relaxing our minds from these persistent cares? (6.11.18)

> Perish all such things! Let us put away these vain and empty concerns. Let us turn ourselves to search only for the truth. Life is hard, and death is uncertain. It may carry us away suddenly. In what state shall we leave this world? Where must we learn what we have neglected here? Or rather, must we not endure punishment for our negligence? What if death should cut off and put an end to all care? This too must be investigated. Far be it, that this should be so! (6.11.19)

When Augustine attempts to cope with his hysteria by setting a schedule for his activities (6.11.18), it becomes clear that he does not have command of his destiny. Indeed, his desire for self-control cannot mask the discovery that his life is out of control; and as a consequence, he begins to wonder where to turn.

Driven by compulsions that threaten to destroy him, Augustine continues to vacillate: first, he decides to devote himself entirely to the search for truth; then he remembers his fear of dying and of the punishment that he might receive for neglecting the path of truth while he is alive; and finally, he considers the view that death will simply issue in oblivion, only to turn aside from this position because he is convinced that the soul will not perish with the death of the body. Yet even then the pendulum swings once more; and the rhetorician exclaims that his present life is pleasant and has a sweetness of its own, not to be abandoned lightly (6.11.19).

While Augustine tosses back and forth, time is slipping away. An earlier time comes to him as if he were an empty container; later it brings strange associations to his mind and does not glide by smoothly; gradually, it heals the wounds he suffers from the death of his closest friend; but now it slips away as he postpones his conversion. Yet Augustine cannot postpone the daily death in himself; and though he wants a happy life, he fears to seek it in its proper place, and flees from it as he seeks it somewhere else. The young philosopher cannot imagine that he can ever be happy without a woman, and he does not have the strength to embrace continence as a desirable way of living (6.11.20).

The concept of continence is broader than the concept of chastity: the first suggests moderation and self-control, while the second points to sexual restraint. This distinction is important; for though Augustine will embrace chastity eventually, he understands from the outset that continence is the more inclusive category. Yet at this stage of his life, Augustine is capable of neither continence nor chastity, not only because he is enslaved by addiction to a lasting habit, but also because he does not realize that he can overcome them only by renouncing his abortive quest for self-control and by opening himself to the grace of God.

Alypius prevents Augustine from marrying, arguing that if he does so, they could no longer live together and share the love of wisdom. Yet the irony of Augustine's description of the chastity and the self-control of Alypius is inescapable:

> He was even then living a life of strictest chastity, so that it was a source of admiration to me. In early adolescence, indeed, he had some experience with sex, but had not persisted in it. On the contrary, he had repented of it, turned away from it, and from that time on had lived in complete continence. (6.12.21)

To persuade Alypius to abandon asceticism, Augustine reminds him that many married men are lovers of wisdom and still loyal and affectionate to their friends. Thus, he rejects the counsel of his friend, telling his readers that the serpent begins to speak to Alypius through him, tempting his follower to imitate his teacher's behavior. (6.12.21)

As his teacher speaks, Alypius begins "to desire to marry, not because he was overcome by lust for such pleasure, but out of curiosity" (6.12.22). Here we find once more the fundamental difference between Augustine and Alypius. Augustine's erotic consciousness seeks sexual satisfaction because a sexual addiction drives him toward it, while Alypius contemplates marriage out of curiosity.

The future bishop admits that marriage and the opportunity to bring up children interests him and his closest friend only slightly. Instead, what makes Augustine a slave of sexuality is "the habit of satisfying an insatiable appetite," while what disturbs Alypius is that he is about to be enslaved by "an admiring wonder" (6.12.22). However different they may be, the problem for both Augustine and Alypius is not sexuality, but bondage to something that controls the pattern of their lives. In Augustine's case, the issue is bondage to an insatiable lust; in the case of Alypius, it is curiosity. Yet both problems reveal actual or incipient addictions, and they point to distorted wills that lie behind the behavior in which they express themselves.

Augustine's friends make active efforts to get him a wife; and in response, "[He] wooed, [he] was engaged, and [his] mother took the greatest pains in the matter" (6.13.23). Monica hopes that marriage will encourage her son to be cleansed in the waters of baptism; but when she asks God to disclose what they should do about Augustine's marriage, he does not respond. On this occasion, Monica has dreams that her strong preoccupations motivate, but has no confidence in them; for she insists that she can distinguish God's revelations from dreams of her own by a certain feeling that is almost impossible to describe. This feeling is not merely a subjective state, but the interpretation of a sign that points to an objective state of affairs.[36] Earlier, Monica has such an experience when she dreams that a young man is standing before her on a wooden rule, pointing to the conclusion that her son will be converted to Christianity. However, in the attempt to settle the matter of matrimony, no objective sign appears. Nevertheless, Monica presses on with her plans, proposing that Augustine become engaged to a ten-year-old girl who is too young to marry; and since the child who is also an heiress pleases Augustine, he agrees to wait for her.

Meanwhile, Augustine must face one of the most traumatic experiences of his life: his mother tears his mistress from him because she is an impediment to his marriage, and his heart that continues to cling to her is torn and wounded until it bleeds. The mistress goes back to North Africa, vowing never to live with another man and leaving their son with Augustine (6.15.25). As we read these lines, we cannot fail to notice the radical asymmetry between men and women in the late Roman Empire, and the suffering women undergo so the careers of the men they love will flourish.[37] On the other hand, we can scarcely accept the view that Augustine does not love the companion to whom he has been faithful for so long.[38] Though Augustine's mistress is no match for the power of Monica, and though Augustine permits his mothers ambitions to dominate him, the face of his unnamed mistress continues to haunt him, leading the Bishop to confess that he can scarcely bare his separation from her.

In spite of his bleeding heart, Augustine cannot wait two years to obtain the bride he seeks; and he informs us, "Since I was not so much a lover of wedlock as a slave of lust, I procured another woman, but not, of course, as a wife" (6.15.25). The emerging philosopher remains addicted to a lasting habit; and as in so many similar cases, this habit points, not primarily to a determinate problem, but to the deeper predicament of the bondage of the will. As he formulates the crucial point himself, the wound caused by cutting away the one he loves has not healed; and "it festered, and still caused [him] pain, although in a more chilling and desperate way" (6.15.25).

While Augustine continues to wallow in the abyss to which his addiction calls our attention, the love that he continues to feel for his mistress permits God to approach him. Yet even though God is a fountain of mercy that is ready to save him, Augustine does not know it; and nothing calls him back from plunging more deeply into the maelstrom of the search for pleasure but the fear of death and judgment, which remains with him at every stage of his development. He discusses the nature of good and evil with his friends, concluding that Epicurus would have been correct about the value of a life of pleasure if he had he not been wrong about life after death. Even at this stage of his development, Augustine believes that the soul survives death and that it must face judgment for its actions (6.16.26).

Augustine does not realize why he finds such delight in discussing problems about his ultimate destiny with his friends; but the author of the text insists that even if he had been able to lead a life of perpetual pleasure, he could not have been happy without them (6.16.26).[39] As this remark suggests, friendship remains a crucial theme throughout the *Confessions*. It first expresses itself in a negative form in the pear-stealing episode and in the "unfriendly friendship" that makes it possible. Then Augustine joins a group of friends called "the Wreckers," even though he insists that he does not approve of their demonic behavior. Next, he mourns the death of his closest philosophical companion and reflects about his need to love all things in God. Finally, the author describes the character of his friend, Alypius; speaks briefly about Nebridius; has his heart ripped open by the loss of his mistress; and as he contemplates the face of death, affirms the value of friendship for its own sake. In all these ways, the communal dimension of Augustine's experience reveals itself as a crucial element in his journey toward God and as an indispensable way of developing what it means for faith to engage in the distinctively philosophical task of seeking understanding.

Augustine concludes Book VI by chastising his soul for falling away from God, but he also introduces a cluster of bodily metaphors that bind his soul and his body together. In doing so, and in focusing on the soul that has led his body astray, he exclaims, "It turned and turned again, upon its back, sides, and belly, but all places were hard to it, for [God] alone [is] rest" (6.16.26). Finally, Augustine gives utterance to his strongest expression of hope by allowing the Prodigal Son to speak through his voice:

> Behold, you are present, and you deliver us from all wretched errors, and you put us on your way, and you console us, and you say to us, "Run forward! I will bear you up, and I will bring you to the end, and there also will I bear you up!" (6.16.26).

In this single sentence, the father Augustine has deserted reaches out his arms; and the journey that begins in a garden, moves through an ocean, becomes a wasteland, and is to be redeemed by the wood of the cross, begins to reach its culmination.

Notes

NOTES TO PREFACE

1. All references to the *Confessions* and Augustine's other writings are given in parentheses in book, chapter, and paragraph form. The purpose of this convention is to permit readers to find the references in any Latin edition and in any translation.

2. Carl G. Vaught, "Theft and Conversion: Two Augustinian Confessions," in *The Recovery of Philosophy in America: Essays in Honor of John Edwin Smith*, ed. Thomas P. Karsulis and Robert Cummings Neville (Albany, NY: State University of New York Press, 1997), 217–249.

NOTES TO INTRODUCTION

1. G. W. F. Hegel, *Lectures on the Philosophy of Religion*, vol. 1, trans. R. F. Brown, P. C. Hodgson, and J. M. Stewart (Los Angeles: University of California Press, 1984), 113.

2. Alfred North Whitehead, *Religion in the Making* (Cleveland: The World Publishing Company, 1963), 16.

3. Francis Petrarch, *Petrarch: The First Modern Scholar and Man of Letters*, ed. and trans., James Robinson (New York: G. P. Putnam, 1898), 316–318.

4. I use the familiar phrase from Paul Tillich, not because it is to be found in the *Confessions*, but because it expresses Augustine's fundamental intentions. It is not by accident that Tillich locates himself within the Augustinian tradition. See "Two Types of Philosophy of Religion," in *Theology of Culture*, ed. Robert C. Kimball (New York: Oxford University Press, 1959), 10–29.

5. *The Confessions of Saint Augustine*, F. J. Sheed, trans. (Indianapolis and Cambridge: Hackett Publishing Co., 1993), xxvii.

6. *Ibid.*, xxix.

7. Augustine makes all these dimensions explicit without ever binding them together in an overarching framework. He does this with respect to time by distinguishing

155

stages of the life cycle. He does it with respect to space d" describing the communities of which he is a part in the course of his development. And he does it with respect to eternity by pointing to the ultimate significance of many of the experiences that he undergoes. By holding all of these dimensions together, I am pointing to ways in which they intersect at various stages of Augustine's development.

8. Augustine, *On Free Choice of the Will,* trans. Anna S. Benjamin and L. H. Hackstaff (Englewood Cliffs, NJ: Prentice Hall, 1964), (1.1.11). Augustine never uses the more familiar Anselmian phrase, *"fides quarens intellectum"* Cf. Anselm, *Monologion and Proslogion, with the Replies of Gaunilo and Anselm,* trans. with an intro. Thomas Williams (Indianapolis and Cambridge: Hackett Co., 1995), 93. However, Augustine's motto and Anselm's formula are related closely, not only because Anselm is an Augustinian monk, but also because both thinkers insist that in religious matters faith must always precede understanding.

9. *The Retractations,* trans. Sister Mary Inez Gogan (Washington, DC: The Catholic University of America Press, 1968), (2.32).

10. Colin Starnes, *Augustine's Conversion: A Guide to the Argument of Confessions I–IX.* (Waterloo, ONT: Wilfrid Laurier University Press. 1990), xi–xii.

11. Erik H. Erickson, *Identity and the Life Cycle* (New York: W. W. Norton & Company, 1980), 52.

12. *Ibid.,* 60, 66.

13. *Ibid.,* 68–69, 78.

14. *Ibid.,* 87.

15. *Ibid.,* 119.

16. Robert J. O'Connell, *St. Augustine's Confessions: The Odyssey of Soul* (New York: Fordham University Press, 1989), 5 and John J. O'Meara, *The Young Augustine: The Growth of St. Augustine's Mind up to his Conversion* (New York and London: Longmans, Green and Co., 1954), 131–155.

17. Genesis 2.8.

18. Mark 14.32; Luke 22.39, 22.44; John 18.1.

19. Luke 23.43; Revelation 2.7.

20. The garden that Augustine enters is analogous to the biblical account of Jesus' prayers in the garden. In order to find privacy, Jesus would often rise early in the morning or spend all night in prayer. The garden of Gethsemane at the Mount of Olives was one of Jesus' beloved places (Luke 22.39). It is apparent that Augustine also found solitude and refuge in a garden. Like Augustine, Jesus also falls to the ground in distress and displays fear and anguish in the garden of Gethsemane as he commenced his prayers (Luke 22.44; Mark 14.35). Courcelle goes on to note that the fig tree in the garden can be identified with the fig tree that Christ saw Nathanael under (John 1.48), and he also identifies the tree with the darkness of human sin. (See Pierre Courcelle, *Recherches sur les Confessions de S. Augustin.* (Paris: E. de Boccard, 1950), 193).

21. Augustine, *Soliloquies*, trans. Thomas F. Gilligan, in *The Fathers of the Church*, vol. 1 (NY: Cima Publishing Co., 1948), (1.2.7).

22. *The Retractations*, (1.4).

23. *Ibid.*

24. Augustine writes,

I did not know that other being, that which truly is, and I was as it were subtly moved to agree with those dull deceivers when they put their questions to me: "Whence is evil?" "Is God confined within a corporeal form?" . . . Ignorant in such matters, I was disturbed by these questions, and while actually receding from the truth, I thought I was moving towards it. (3.7.12)

25. This familiar pattern is adumbrated in one of Augustine's earlier dialogues. In *Divine Providence and the Problem of Evil*, trans. Robert P. Russell, in *The Fathers of the Church*, vol. 1 (New York: CIMA Publishing Co., 1948), he speaks of the *ordo Dei* (2.7.23), the *ordo vitae* (2.8.25) and the *ordo naturae* (2.14.12). The point of these reflections is that order in nature can lead us to an ordered soul and ultimately to God (1.9.27).

26. Augustine, *Two Books on Genesis against the Manichees*, trans. Roland J. Teske, (Washington, DC, Catholic University of America Press, 1990), (2.8.11). It is important to notice that even the Neoplatonists try to preserve a separation between the One and later hypostases. However, the One is only relatively transcendent; the other hypostases are not created, but come to be through self-assertion. See Maria Boulding's formulation of the difference between the Augustinian and Neoplatonic accounts in her new translation of the *Confessions*, in *The Works of St. Augustine: A Translation for the Twenty-First Century*, vol. I.1, 2nd ed., ed. John E. Rotelle (Brooklyn: New City Press, 1996), 18–19. There is also a greater degree of otherness in creation *ex nihilo* than in emanation.

27. Augustine says this in some of his early writings. *The Greatness of the Soul*, trans. and annotated Joseph M. Colleran (Westminster, MD: Newman Press, 1950), (13.22).

28. *The Trinity*, trans. with an intro. and notes Edmund Hill in *The Works of Saint Augustine: A Translation for the Twenty-First Century*, vol. I.5, 2nd ed. (Brooklyn: New City Press, 1991), (15.11). See N. Cipriani, "L'influsso di Varrone sul pensiero antropologico e morale nei primi scritti di s. Agostino," StEphAug 53 (1996), 375–376 for a discussion of this issue.

29. *On the Immortality of the Soul*, trans. with a preface by George G. Leckie (New York and London: D. Appleton-Century Co., 1938), (2.2); *Soliloqies*, (1.12.20); and *The Greatness of the Soul* (13.22).

30. Augustine uses the term "body" to refer both to the physical body and to corruptive inclinations of the will. *On Genesis: Two Books on Genesis against the Manichees*, (2.7.8) and *Select Letters*, trans. James Houston Baxter, in *The Loeb Classical Library*, vol. 239 (Cambridge, Harvard University Press, 1980), (164.5.16).

31. Vernon J. Bourke, *Augustine's Love of Wisdom: An Introspective Philosophy* (West Lafayette, IN: Purdue University Press, 1992), 27.

32. This is the first reference to the (finite-infinite) structure of the soul that I make in this book to express the transitions from creation to the fall, from the fall to conversion, and from conversion to fulfillment. As I will attempt to indicate, this concept is not imposed on the text, but are ways of pointing to crucial distinctions that emerge from it.

33. Augustine was committed to the doctrine of the resurrection of the body even in his early writings. *The Greatness of the Soul* (33.76) and Margaret Miles, *Augustine on the Body* (Missoula, MT: Scholars Press, 1979), 108.

34. Wilfrid Sellars, "A Semantical Solution of the Mind-Body Problem," in *Pure Pragmatics and Possible Worlds: The Early Essays of Wilfred Sellars*, ed. Jeffrey Sicha (Reseda, CA: Ridgeview Publishing Company, 1980), 211–256.

35. I develop these distinctions in *The Quest for Wholeness* (Albany, NY: State University of New York Press, 1982), 213 and in the following essays: "Signs, Categories, and the Problem of Analogy," in *Semiotics*, 1985, ed. John Deely, Lanham, MD: The University Press of America, 1986, 64–82; "Metaphor, Analogy, and the Nature of Truth," in *New Essays in Metaphysics*, ed. Robert C. Neville (Albany, NY: State University of New York Press, 1986) 217–236; "Participation and Imitation in Plato's Metaphysics," in *Contemporary Essays on Greek Ideas: The Kilgore Festschrift*, ed. Robert M. Baird, William F. Cooper, Elmer H. Duncan, Stuart E. Rosenbaum (Waco, Texas: Baylor University Press, 1987), 17–31; "Hegel and the Problem of Difference: A Critique of Dialectical Reflection," in *Hegel and His Critics*, ed. William Desmond (Albany, NY: State University of New York Press, 1989), 35–48; "Categories and the Real Order: Sellar's Interpretation of Aristotle's Metaphysics," *The Monist*, 66 (1983): 438–449; "The Quest for Wholeness and Its Crucial Metaphor and Analogy: The Place of Places," *Ultimate Reality and Meaning*, 7 (1984): 156–165; "Metaphor, Analogy, and System: A Reply to Burbidge," *Man and World*, 18 (1984): 55–63; "Semiotics and the Problem of Analogy: A Critique of Peirce's Theory of Categories," *Transactions of the Charles S. Peirce Society*, 22 (1986): 311–326; and "Subject, Object, and Representation: A Critique of Hegel's Dialectic of Perception," *International Philosophical Quarterly*, 22 (1986): 117–135.

36. With regard to his exposure to Aristotle's *Categories*, Augustine writes:

The book seemed to me to speak clearly enough of substances . . . and the innumerable things that are found in these nine categories, of which I have set down some examples, or in the category of substance. (4.16.28).

37. David Chidester, *Word and Light: Seeing, Hearing, and Religious Discourse*, Urbana: University of Illinois Press, 1992), 53–67.

38. *Ibid.*, 55–56.

39. In his discussion of vision in *On Free Choice of the Will* (2.7.63–64), Augustine says that "one object is before both of us and is viewed by both of us at the same time"

and of hearing he says that "whatever sound occurs is present in its entirety, to be heard by both of us."

40. *Ibid.*

41. An example of an auditory image can be found in Augustine's numerous quotations from the Bible, for example, his use of the Psalms where he states:

> "Say to my soul: I am your salvation" (Psalms 34.3). Say this, so that I may hear you. Behold, my heart's ears are turned to you, O Lord: open them, and "say to my soul: I am your salvation" (Psalms 142.7). I will run after that voice, and I will catch hold of you. (1.5.5)

Augustine not only uses auditory images when he quotes the Bible, but also when he uses his own voice, as illustrated at the beginning of Book 10:

> But with what benefit do they wish to hear me? Do they wish to share my thanksgiving, when they hear how close it is by your gift that I approach to you, and to pray for me, when they hear how I am held back by my own weight? To such men I will reveal myself. (10.4.5)

42. Leo Ferrari, *The Conversions of Saint Augustine* (Augustinian Institute, Villanova University, 1984), 53–55.

43. Kenneth Burke, *The Rhetoric of Religion* (Berkeley: University of California Press, 1970), 43–171.

NOTES TO CHAPTER 1

1. Virgil, *The Aeneid of Virgil*, trans. Robert Fitzgerald (New York: Vintage Books, 1990).

2. Dante, *Hell: The Comedy of Dante Alighieri*, trans. Dorothy L. Sayers (London and New York: Penguin Books, 1949); *Purgatory*, trans. Sayers, 1955; and *Paradise*, trans. Sayers and Barbara Reynolds, 1962.

3. Romans 10.14.

4. James J. O'Donnell, *Augustine: Confessions*, vol. 2 (Oxford: Clarendon Press, 1992), 14, who tries to solve the problem of the relation between faith and knowledge in this way.

5. I follow O'Donnell in identifying the two preachers with Paul and Ambrose. *Ibid.*, 17.

6. Augustine believes that spiritual beings like God and the soul are not contained in a determinate place. See *Divine Providence and the Problem of Evil*, trans. Robert P. Russell in *The Fathers of the Church*, vol. 1 (New York: CIMA Publishing Co., 1948), (2.11.30).

7. For Augustine, the weight of the soul is not the way it fills up space, but its positive or negative orientation toward God. As he writes in (13.9.10), "My love is my weight! I am borne about by it, wheresoever I am borne."

8. John J. O'Meara, *The Young Augustine: The Growth of St. Augustine's Mind up to His Conversion* (New York: Longmans, Green and Co., 1954), 65.

9. I should point out once more that this phrase is Anselmian rather than Augustinian. However, there can be little doubt that it is connected closely with Augustine's claim that "Unless we believe, we shall not understand." It is also important to notice that the relation between faith and understanding is mediated by the healing of the soul. Augustine suggests that we will never understand God unless we are transformed by him. In fact, he discloses his need for transformation (7.1.1–7.1.2) and for cleanliness of soul (1.1.1), (1.5.6), (6.1.1), (6.4.5), (8.12.28) at numerous places in the text.

10. Rudolf Otto, *The Idea of the Holy* (New York: Oxford University Press, 1958), 10.

11. In our discussion of Augustine's way of dealing with the problem of origins, it is important not to claim that we know more than he does about the issue in question. It is noteworthy that he never decides which theory of the origin of the soul to embrace throughout his lengthy philosophical career. *On Free Choice of the Will*, trans. Anna S. Benjamin and L. H. Hackstaff, (Englewood Cliffs, NJ: Prentice Hall, 1964), (3.21.59); *The Literal Meaning of Genesis*, vols. 1–2, trans. John H. Taylor, in *Ancient Christian Writers*, vols. 41–42 (New York: Newman Press, 1982), (1.1.2–3), (10.1.1); *Select Letters*, trans. James Houston Baxter, in *The Loeb Classical Library*, vol. 239, Cambridge: Harvard University Press, 1980, (1.66); and *The Retractations*, trans. Sister Mary Inez Gogan. (Washington, DC: The Catholic University of America Press, 1968), (2.32).

Augustine considers four theories as possible explanations for the origin of the soul. The first theory, traducianism, presupposes that the souls of human beings evolve from the one soul that God created. Second, creationism claims that souls are created individually at birth. The third theory maintains that God sends the existing souls to the bodies when they are born. The soul then governs the individual. Finally, in the fourth theory, souls are not sent by God, but fall into bodies of their own accord.

12. Robert J. O'Connell, "Isaiah's Mothering God in St. Augustine's Confessions," *Thought*, (1983): 197–198.

13. Again, it is important to notice that original innocence is as important as original sin in giving us access to Augustine's approach to the problem of origins. This does not mean that there ever is a time when we are completely innocent or completely guilty. Rather, it means that from an eternal point of view, we participate in original innocence and original sin simultaneously.

14. Starnes claims that Augustine's account of origins is exclusively historical, and O'Connell claims that it is exclusively metaphysical. In the course of my analysis, I am trying to bind both dimensions together. Colin Starnes, *Augustine's Conversion: A Guide to the Argument of Confessions I–IX* (Waterloo, ONT: Wilfrid Laurier Univer-

sity Press, 1990), 277 and Robert J. O'Connell, *St. Augustine's Confessions: The Odyssey of Soul*, 41.

15. G. W. F. Hegel, *Science of Logic*, trans. A. V. Miller (New York: Humanities Press, 1969), 67–78.

16. See citation of Aristotle in Starnes, 3.

17. John Fisher, *From Baby to Toddler* (New York: Perigee Books, 1988), 73.

18. It is important to notice that finitude must be distinguished from fallenness, where the first condition is positive and the second is negative. Finitude points to limitations in virtue of which we are able to stand in contrast with God, while fallenness points to the negative orientation of the soul in virtue of which it turns away from him. The difficulty in drawing this distinction comes from two directions. First, it is easy to assume that finitude is a negative condition, where finitude is sufficient to separate us from God. Second, finitude and fallenness are interlaced so inextricably that it is difficult to separate them, even for the purposes of philosophical analysis.

However difficult it may be for us to draw the distinction before us, it is essential for us to do so if we are to preserve both sides of Augustine's discussion of the problem of origins. On the one hand, he claims that God creates the world and says that it is good. On the other hand, he is equally preoccupied with the problem of original sin. One way to do justice to both poles is to distinguish finitude from fallenness, the first of which points to original innocence and the second of which points to original sin.

19. O'Donnell, *Augustine: Confessions*, vol. 2, 37.

20. The clearest place where Augustine manifests this view is in (10.20.29). In that context, he says that all of us have been happy either as individuals or insofar as we participate in the created Adam. This is not to deny that we also participate in original sin (13.20.17), but only to claim that original innocence must also be taken into account.

21. Benedict Spinoza, *The Ethics*, trans. R. H. M. Elwes (New York: Dover Publications, 1955), 45.

22. Once more, it is of crucial importance to distinguish finitude from fallenness. Though they are always combined in Augustine's account of his development, finitude points to original innocence, while fallenness points to original sin.

23. This is the juncture at which Augustine begins to focus on the transition from finitude to fallenness. Finitude is "prior" to fallenness from an ontological point of view, for the first word to be said about the relation between God and the soul is creation. However, from the perspective of Augustine's tangled origins, original innocence and original sin stand side by side as explanatory principles.

24. In a later book, I will take up the question of how Augustine's inability to understand his life before conception is to be related to his claim in (10.20.27) that he can remember the happy life.

25. The most well-known defense of this view is to be found in O'Connell, *St. Augustine's Confessions: The Odyssey of Soul*, 1, 4, 11–12, 32, 81, 101, 151, and 159.

26. *Ibid.*, 26–28.

27. Plato, *Meno* in *Five Dialogues*, trans. G. M. A. Grube (Indianapolis: Hackett Publishing Company, 1981), (82a–86c).

28. Robert J. O'Connell, *The Origin of the Soul in Augustine's Later Works* (New York: Fordham University Press, 1987), 44.

29. Starnes, 8.

30. O'Connell, *St. Augustine's Confessions: The Odyssey of Soul*, 24.

31. Robert J. O'Connell, "Augustine's Rejection of the Fall of the Soul, *Augustinian Studies* 4 (1973): 9.

32. The evidence for this is the dual claim of Augustine that God fashions us in time (1.6.7), but that even the infant who has lived but a day on the earth is not free of sin (1.7.11). The first of these claims points to original innocence and the second points to original sin. Once more, the crucial problem is how to hold these aspects of the person together. This can be done, not by adopting one of the four theories of the origin of the soul that Augustine never embraces, but by developing a sophisticated analysis of what it means for us to exist in Adam.

As Michael Mendelson says in his article about Augustine [*The Stanford Encyclopedia of Philosophy* (Fall 2000 Edition), Edward N. Zalta (ed.), URL = *http://plato.stanford.edu/archives/fall2000/entries/augustine/*],

> it is . . . not surprising that there is an unofficial fifth hypothesis that can be found elsewhere in Augustine's works. In *De Civitate Dei*, for example, Augustine suggests that God created only one soul, that of Adam, and subsequent human souls are not merely genealogical offshoots (as in traducianism) of that original soul, but they are actually identical to Adam's soul prior to assuming their own individual, particularized lives [*De Civitate Dei*, 13.14]. Not only does this avoid the mediation of the traducianist hypothesis, but it also manages to provide a theologically satisfying account of the universality of original sin without falling into the difficulties of God's placing an innocent soul into a sin-laden body, as would be the case in a general creationism. To what extent this constitutes a serious contender for Augustine's attention remains a matter of controversy [O'Connell 1987, esp. pp. 11–16; Rist 1989; Rist 1994, pp 121–9; Teske 1999, p. 810].

The difficulty with these views is that they fail to mention the fact that Augustine considers this fifth hypothesis in the *Confessions* (10.20.29) and that when he does so, he sees it as a way of dealing with original innocence and original sin simultaneously.

33. Augustine identifies human beings as having two parts (the soul and the body) that make up one composite whole. For Augustine, the composite "does not make two persons, but one human being." *Tractates on the Gospel of John*, trans. John W. Rettig (Washington, DC: Catholic University of America Press, 1988), (19.5.15).

34. Vernon Bourke, *Augustine's Love of Wisdom* (West Lafayette, IN: Purdue University Press, 1992), 46–47.

35. *On the Immortality of the Soul*, trans. with a preface by George G. Leckie, (New York and London: D. Appleton-Century Co., 1938), (2.2); Augustine, *Soliloquies*, trans. Thomas F. Gilligan, in *The Fathers of the Church*, vol. 1 (NY: Cima Publishing Co., 1948), (1.20.20); and *The Greatness of the Soul* trans. and annotated Joseph M. Colleran, Westminster, MD: Newman Press, 1950, (13.22).

36. *The Greatness of the Soul*, (13.22) and *The Catholic and the Manichaean Ways of Life*, trans. Donald A. Gallagher and Idella J. Gallagher (Washington, DC: Catholic University of America Press, 1966), (1.4.6).

37. *Teaching Christianity*, trans. Edmund Hill in *The Works of Saint Augustine: Translations for the Twenty-First Century*, vol. I.11, ed. John E. Rotelle (Brooklyn: New City Press, 1996), (1.19.1).

38. I have profited immensely from the work of Gareth Matthews about the problem of the ego in Augustine's writings. See *Thought's Ego in Augustine and Descartes* (Ithaca, NY: Cornell University Press, 1992). However, I have found his early essay about the inner man in Augustine to be even more interesting and valuable. In this essay, Matthews goes a long way toward elaborating the kind of complex semantics that I am developing here. See Gareth Matthews, "The Inner Man," in *Augustine: A Collection of Critical Essays*, ed. R. A. Markus (Garden City, NY: Anchor Books, 1972), 176–190.

39. For a discussion of this issue see Starnes, 31, 103 and O'Donnell, *Augustine: Confessions*, vol. 2, 42.

40. *Ibid.*

41. See Starnes, 6–7 and O'Donnell, *Augustine: Confessions*, vol. 2, 44.

42. Romans 5.12.

43. Albrecht Diehl, *The Theory of the Will in Classical Antiquity* (Berkeley: University of California Press, 1982), 82.

44. It is important to notice that Augustine is pointing to original sin rather than to individual acts of sin in this reference to life in the womb. Augustine embraced Paul's claim in Romans 9.11 that unborn infants have never sinned. See *On Free Choice of the Will*, (3.21.59).

45. My reason for making this claim is twofold. First, if the person that God creates is good, and if this person has both a soul and a body, it can scarcely be the case that the soul falls into the body as a punishment for sin. Second, to speak of the "paradise," in which souls and bodies are created is not to mention a place in a literal sense of the term, but to point to a positive dimension of the person that is never effaced. *The Happy Life*, trans. Ludwig Shopp in *The Fathers of the Church*, vol. 1 (New York: CIMA Publishing Co., 1948), (2.7); *The Greatness of the Soul*, (8.5); *The Literal Meaning of Genesis*, (3.19.29); and *The Trinity*, trans. with an introduction and notes Edmund Hill, in *The Works of Saint Augustine: A Translation for the Twenty-First Century*, vol. I.5, 4th ed. (Brooklyn: New City Press, 1991), (15.11).

46. An adequate analysis of space and time as they are understood in the *Confessions* requires us to distinguish among created, fallen, converted, and fulfilled spatiotemporality. In his book about Augustine, John Rist expresses part of what I have in mind by distinguishing created from fallen temporality. In *Augustine: Ancient Thought Baptized* (Cambridge: Cambridge University Press, 1994), 84–85, he writes:

> If we "fell" into times or into time, was there no time before the fall? If there was, and to the mature Augustine it seems that there must have been, then we did not fall into it, but rather transformed it, or rather deformed it by our own fall.

47. For a contemporary account of this standard picture, see Ludwig Wittgenstein, *Philosophical Investigations*, 3rd ed. trans. G. E. M. Anscombe (Upper Saddle River, NJ: Prentice Hall), 1958.

48. *Ibid.*, 1–3.

49. *Ibid.*, 4–7.

50. For the debate about Wittgenstein's critique of Augustine, see Anthony Kenney, "The Ghost of the *Tractatus*," in *Understanding Wittgenstein*, ed. Godfrey Vesey (Ithaca, NY: Cornell University Press, 1974), 1–13; Patrick Bearsley, "Augustine and Wittgenstein on Language," *Philosophy*, 58 (1983): 229–236; and M. F. Burnyeat," "Wittgenstein and Augustine's *De Magistro*," *The Aristotelian Society*, 6 (1987): 1–24.

51. Cf. W. V. O. Quine, *Word and Object* (New York: MIT Press, 1960), 274.

52. Wittgenstein, 16.

53. Wilfrid Sellars, "Empiricism and the Philosophy of Mind," in *Science, Perception and Reality* (New York: The Humanities Press, 1963), 189.

54. Kenny, 2.

55. For examples of Augustine's use of symbolism see *Teaching Christianity*, (1.13.12).

56. Once again, the "paradise" to which I refer is not a place, but the positive dimension of the world that reflects the creative goodness of God. At this stage of my argument, I am claiming that the positive dimension of creation is reflected in the positive linguistic community in which Augustine participates.

57. Burnyeat, 1.

58. O'Donnell, *Augustine: Confessions*, vol. 2, 57.

59. A paradoxal problem is pointed out in *On the Teacher*, trans. Peter King in *Against the Academicians and The Teacher* (Indianopolis and Cambridge: Hackett Publishing Co., 1995), 1. In this dialogue between Augustine and his son, Adeodatus, Augustine explains that in order to teach, one must use signs. However, unless the human being already understands the meaning of these signs, the use of them would

be meaningless. Augustine provides the solution to the enigma with the doctrine of the "inner teacher." The ability of humans to acquire knowledge is made possible by consultation with the inner teacher, that is to say, Christ.

60. Erik Erikson, *Identity and the Life Cycle* (New York: W. W. Norton & Company, 1980), 89.

61. *Ibid.*, 87.

62. The sea is Augustine's image for humanity alienated from God; the clay is his metaphor for natural humanity; and the imago Christi is his way of pointing to humanity remade by grace. Henry Chadwick, *Saint Augustine's Confessions* (Oxford: Oxford University Press, 1991), 14.

63. Peter Brown, *Augustine of Hippo: A Biography*, new edition with an epilogue (Berkeley: University of California Press, 2000), 207–208.

64. C. Kligerman, *Journal of the American Psychological Association*, 5 (1957): 469–484 and L. Daly, "Psychohistory and St. Augustine's Conversion Process," in *Collectanea Augusiniana*, ed. Joseph Schnaublet, Frederick Van Fleteran (Villanova, PA: Villanova University Press, 1978), 244. For a discussion of why such interpretations are at best one-sided, see O'Donnell, *Augustine: Confessions*, vol. 1, xxxi.

65. Brown, 24.

66. Porphyry, "On the Life of Plotinus and the Order of His Books," in Plotinus, *Enneads*, trans. A. H. Armstrong, vol. 1, in *The Loeb Classical Library* (Cambridge: Harvard University Press, 1966–1984), 1.

67. *Ibid.*

68. Plotinus, (3.7.11), (3.5.4).

69. Chadwick says that the veil at the entrance of a school of literature is a sign of the dignity of the person beyond it. See Chadwick, *Saint Augustine's Confessions*, 16.

70. It has been noted that students in Rome were permitted to study under grammarians and rhetoricians; further, the students were allowed to pursue these disciplines in a way that allowed the learning of a language in the fullest way possible. James J. Murphy, *Rhetoric in the Middle Ages* (Berkeley: University of California Press, 1974), 35–37.

71. Erikson, 87–89.

72. *Ibid.*, 91.

73. Plato, *Republic*, trans. G. M. A. Grube (Indianapolis and Cambridge: Hackett Publishing Co., 1992), (509a–511e).

74. Pierre Courcelle, *Rechercehes sur les Confessions de saint Augustin*, 2nd ed. (Paris: E. de Boccard, 1968), 128–129 and Chadwick, *Saint Augustine's Confessions*, 16.

75. O'Donnell, vol. 2, 95–98.

76. *Ibid.*

77. Chadwick, *Saint Augustine's Confessions*, 249.

78. The distinction between fallen and unfallen space and time is parallel to the distinction between negative and positive dimensions of the human situation. Just as original innocence stands in contrast with original sin, so created space and time stands in contrast with the fallen spatiotemporal matrix into which it degenerates.

79. These modifications of the distinction between the finite and the infinite might seem to be categories that are alien to Augustine's text. Yet as I am attempting to indicate, they illuminate Augustine's argument at every step of the way. The brambles of sexuality that were excluded from "Paradise" are those aspects of it that are not subject to voluntary control. *The Literal Meaning of Genesis,* (10.5.8).

80. The other episode is Augustine's conversion to the love of wisdom (3.8.15).

81. *Teaching Christianity,* (1.3.1) and Margaret Miles, *Desire and Delight: A New Reading of Augustine's Confessions* (New York: Crossroad, 1992), 25–26.

82. The Manicheans believed that "if [they] have stinted [their] alms, or have given food that should have been reserved for the Elect to [their] household or to wicked men or to evil animals, or have thrown it away, thus sending the divine Light to the Evil Place," they have sinned. F. C. Burkitt, *The Religion of the Manichees* (Cambridge: The University Press, 1925), 56; O'Donnell, vol. 2, 127; and Leo Ferrari, *Revue des études Augustiniennes* 16 (1970): 236.

83. Genesis 2.17.

84. At this juncture, I am beginning to enrich my use of the distinction between the finite and the infinite. To say that a person is a (finite-infinite) being is to say that limitations and self-transcendence intersect in our journey toward God. If we accept our limitations, we are (finite↑infinite) beings; and our souls stretch out toward God without denying our created limitations. On the other hand, if we attempt to encroach on the mystery and the majesty of God, we turn away from our finitude to accentuate our infinite dimension. As a consequence, we become (finite↓infinite) beings who are separated from God. Soren Kierkegaard makes a similar characterization of the condition of the self when he writes, "A human being is a synthesis of the infinite and the finite, of the temporal and the eternal, of freedom and necessity, in short, a synthesis." Søren Kierkegaard, *The Sickness Unto Death,* trans. Howard Vincent Hong and Edna H. Hong (Princeton, NJ: Princeton University Press, 1980), 13.

85. Augustine believed that Adam would have become immortal if he had not eaten the forbidden fruit. *The Literal Meaning of Genesis,* (6.25).

86. *On Free Choice of the Will,* (3.8.52).

87. Luke 15.15–16.

88. Augustine is presenting himself here, not simply as a sinner in the traditional sense, but even as more notorious.

89. Brown, *Augustine of Hippo,* 9, 11.

90. Murphy, *Rhetoric in the Middle Ages,* 12.

91. Oliver Wendell Holmes to Harold Laski, Jan. 5, 1921 in *Holmes–Laski Letters* (I), ed. M. de Howe (Cambridge: Harvard University Press, 1953), 300.

92. Starnes develops an analysis of this kind in 38–45.

93. I owe this phrase to one of my former graduate students, Janice M. Stabb. See her article, "Standing Alone Together: Silence, Solitude, and Radical Conversion," in *Contemporary Themes in Augustine's Confessions: Part I,* ed. Carl G. Vaught, *Contemporary Philosophy* 15 (1993): 16–20.

94. David Riesman, *The Lonely Crowd: A Study of the Changing American Character* (Yale University Press), 1950.

95. Genesis 1.26.

96. Genesis 1.3.

97. Genesis 1.4–5.

NOTES TO CHAPTER 2

1. F. Homes Dudden, *The Life and Times of St. Ambrose,* vol. 1 (Oxford: The Clarendon Press, 1935), 322–323.

2. The hunger Augustine feels when he comes to Carthage is the hunger expressed by the original claim in Book I that his heart is restless until it comes to rest in God (3.1.1).

3. Augustine uses metaphors to bind the soul and the body together, and he uses analogies to hold them apart. As a consequence, Augustine's rhetoric permits him to move back and forth between unity and separation.

4. Once more Augustine distinguishes between the soul and the body and implies that the soul is more important than the body on the ontological continuum. However, he also implies that the *entire person* falls into an abyss because of actions that the soul initiates.

5. Instead of embracing the Aristotelian theory of catharsis according to which the soul is cleansed in the theater by experiencing pity and fear [Aristotle, *Poetics* in *The Basis Writings of Aristotle,* ed. with an introduction by Richard McKeon (New York, Random House, 1941), (452²31–32)], Augustine emphasizes the bondage of the soul that can result from theatrical spectacles. In this way, he moves from an aesthetic to a moral and religious conception of what transpires in the theater.

6. The contrast between misery and mercy is the key to Augustine's analysis of our response to theatrical spectacles.

7. Once more we have a case in which a bodily metaphor binds the soul and body together. By contrast, analogies hold these two dimensions of the person apart in contexts where it is important to distinguish them.

8. Augustine's most detailed discussion of the three kinds of sin is to be found in Book X (10.30.41–10.36.59), where he uses them to organize his confession about the spiritual problems he encounters, even after his conversion.

9. In the epilogue to the recent revision of his biography about Augustine, Peter Brown has elaborated this point by quoting a passage from one of Augustine's sermons:

"When I went to vigils as a student . . . , I spent the night rubbing up beside women, along with other boys anxious to make an impression on the girls, and where, who knows, the opportunity might present itself to have a love-affair with them."

Peter Brown, *Augustine of Hippo: A Biography*, new edition with an epilogue (Berkeley: University of California Press, 2000), 456–457.

10. James J. Murphy, *Rhetoric in the Middle Ages* (Berkeley: University of California Press, 1974), 35–38.

11. Erik H. Erikson, *Identity and the Life Cycle* (New York: W.W. Norton & Co., 1980), 89.

12. John J. O'Meara, *The Young Augustine: The Growth of St. Augustine's Mind up to His Conversion* (New York: Longmans, Green and Co., 1954), 57.

13. Murphy, 61.

14. "The Hortesius stressed the importance of a liberal education as the basis for the study of philosophy. Cicero also included a sketch of the history of philosophy . . . [and] the four great ancient virtues (prudence, temperance, fortitude, and justice) are covered. Cicero, writing before the time of Christ, even suggests that the study of philosophy is an ideal preparation for death and the celestial life." Vernon Bourke, *Augustine's Love of Wisdom* (West Lafayette, IN: Purdue University Press, 1992), 3.

15. *Ibid.*, 34–40.

16. Whitney Oates, *Basic Writings of Saint Augustine* (New York: Random House, 1948), xxi.

17. Brown, 31.

18. Allen D. Fitzgerald, "Jerome," in *Augustine Through the Ages: An Encyclopedia*, ed. Allan D. Fitzgerald (Grand Rapids, MI: Eerdmans Publishing Co., 1999), 461.

19. *Against the Academics*, trans. Peter King in *Against the Academicians and The Teacher* (Indianopolis and Cambridge: Hackett Publishing Co., 1995), (2.40), (2.66).

20. Brown, 33, 485 and O'Meara, 62–65.

21. Brown, 34–36.

22. There are at least four reasons why Augustine is willing to become a Manichaean: (1) they emphasize reason rather than authority; (2) the name of Christ is a central element in their teaching; (3) Augustine could embrace this teaching without changing his lifestyle; and (4) they had a simple, but persuasive solution to the problem of evil.

23. *Meditations on First Philosophy* in *The Philosophical Writings of Descartes*, vol. 2, trans. John Cottingham, Robert Stoothoff, and Dugald Murdoch (New York: Cambridge University Press, 1984), 13.

24. *Ibid.*, 15.

25. *Ibid.*

26. Manichaeanism proposes a cosmology that unfolds in three stages. The first stage involves two basic principles, good and evil. These principles are both coeternal and radically separate. The principle of good is made up of positive qualities and is made manifest in light, its primary substance. The evil principle is made up of negative qualities and is manifest in darkness.

The second stage refers to the world's present condition. The realm of darkness, having approached the realm of light and developed a desire for it, invaded the light realm. The good principle evoked the "Mother of Light" for defense, who in turn evoked the "Primal Human." Both of these were composed of light, the substance of the good principle. During the ensuing battle between the demons from the realm of darkness and the defenders of the light, each side took prisoners and accidentally comingled. The present, visible world is a result of this comingling.

The struggle goes on to free the particles of divine light from their detention in the realm of darkness. The so-called "Great Father" set out a method for doing this by creating the sun and moon to collect the light substance, which would then pass it on into the realm of light. The Great Father also sent the "Third Messenger" to the realm of darkness to seduce the demons there by appearing as a member of the opposite gender. The evil principle retaliated by creating the biblical Adam, who served as a rival to the Primal Human. Both Adam and Eve were offspring of demons under the control of the evil principle, and they were sent to earth to entrap particles of light in darkness by generating offspring themselves. The good principle sent "Jesus," who was pure by not being born at all, to reveal divine knowledge to Adam and Eve in an effort to thwart the evil principle's plan. "Jesus" was to train the Elect, or high-ranking members of the Manichean religion, on how to free the light substance from the clutches of the evil principle.

The third and final phase of the cosmology involves a return to the first phase. This will happen when the Elect free as much light substance as possible and the two principles are separated once again. O'Meara, 69–79 and Gerald Bonner, *Augustine of Hippo: Life and Controversies* (New York and Rome: Canterbury Press, 1986), 162–175.

27. Brown, 43–44.

28. *Ibid.*

29. G. R. Evans, *Augustine on Evil* (Cambridge: Cambridge University Press, 1982), 12–13.

30. Plotinus, *Enneads*, vol. 1, trans. A. H. Armstrong (Cambridge: Harvard University Press, 1989), xiv.

31. Within a Christian context, our fall away from God toward absolute nonbeing is the explanation for the fact that we are less than we were meant to be.

32. Plato, *Republic*, trans. G. M. A. Grube (Indianapolis and Cambridge: Hackett Publishing Co., 1992), (514a).

33. Her answer to Augustine also inverts the statement of the bride during the Roman marriage rite, "Where you are, there I will be." Henry Chadwick, *Saint Augustine's Confessions* (Oxford: Oxford University Press, 1991), 50.

34. John 14.6.

35. Robert J. O'Connell, *St. Augustine's Confessions: The Odyssey of Soul* (Cambridge: Harvard University Press, 1989), 55.

36. Brown, 27–28.

37. The name Augustine gives his son is a variant of a traditional name given to children in North Africa. Even so, the concept of grace is present in the name itself. Brown, 128.

38. Colin Starnes, *Augustine's Conversion: A Guide to the Argument of Confessions I–IX* (Waterloo, ONT: Wilfrid Laurier University Press, 1990), 90 and Brown, 51–52.

39. Starnes, 90–91.

40. There have been a number of recent studies of Augustine's attitude toward women and toward marriage that fill out the picture of Augustine's mature position about the issues in question. K. E. Borresen, *Subordination and Equivalence: The Nature and Role of Woman in Augustine and Thomas Aquinas*, trans. Charles H. Talbot (Washington, DC: University of America, 1981); Margaret Miles, *Desire and Delight: A New Reading of Augustine's Confessions* (New York: Crossroad, 1992); and Kim Power, *Veiled Desire: Augustine's Writing on Women* (New York: Continuum, 1996). The conclusion that seems to be warranted is that Augustine thought of "paradise" as a place where perfect sexual relations obtained. In addition, both sexuality and the body became a problem only as a result of the fall. *The Literal Meaning of Genesis*, (9.37); *On Genesis: Two Books on Genesis against the Manichees*, trans. Roland J. Teske, (Washington DC, Catholic University of America Press, 1990), (2.11); and John H. Taylor, (1.2.4–6). Unlike many of his contemporaries (e.g., Jerome), he believed that sexual activity is not the sin par excellence, and unlike Plotinus, he regarded the fall as pertaining to the entire person as a psychosexual unity rather than to the soul falling into the body. Brown, 431.

41. Brown, 50.

42. The kind of nonbeing about which I am speaking is absolute rather than relative; and as a consequence, it does not stand in contrast with being as its polar opposite. This is what is meant by the claim that absolute nonbeing violates the law of excluded middle.

43. Martin Heidegger, *Being and Time*, trans. John Macquarrie and Edward Robinson (San Francisco: Harper Collins, 1962), 235–267.

44. *Teaching Christianity*, trans. Edmund Hill, in *The Works of Saint Augustine: Translations for the Twenty-First Century*, vol. I.11, ed. John E. Rotelle (Brooklyn: New City Press, 1996), (1.22.20).

45. Henry Johnstone, *The Problem of the Self* (University Park, PA: Pennsylvania State University, 1970), 15.

46. In the *Confessions*, Augustine blames his departure from Thagaste exclusively on the death of his friend. However, in one of his earlier writings, he admits that his desire for professional advancement also played a role in the decision. Brown, 129.

47. For a discussion regarding the world-soul see John Rist, *Augustine: Ancient Thought Baptized* (Cambridge: Cambridge University Press, 1994), 83; Hilary Armstrong, "St. Augustine and Christian Platonism," in *Collectanea Augusiniana* (Villanova: Villanova University Press, 1967): 14; and Roland Teske, "The World-Soul and Time in St. Augustine," *Augustinian Studies*, 14 (1989), 89.

48. See Hannah Arendt's discussion of these issues in *Love and Saint Augustine*, ed. Joanna Scott and Judith Stark (Chicago: University of Chicago Press, 1996). In the course of her argument, she distinguishes among three concepts of love in Augustine's thinking. First, she speaks about love for God in which everything finite is used for this purpose. Second, she mentions the love for finite things in which our love for them is referred to God. Finally, she says that loving our neighbor as ourselves is rooted in our sinful predicament and in the incarnation of God's historical response to it.

49. *The Literal Meaning of Genesis*, (9.3).

50. *Teaching Christianity*, (1.3.3).

51. It is also clear that when he writes the *Confessions*, Augustine holds the view that death results from sin. For example, in 1.1.1 he says,

You are great, O Lord, and greatly to be praised: great is your power and to your wisdom there is no limit. Any man, who is a part of your creation, wishes to praise you, man who bears about within himself his *mortality*, who bears about within himself testimony to his *sin* and testimony that you resist the proud. Yet man, this part of your creation, wishes to praise you. You arouse him to take joy in praising you, for you have made us for yourself, and our heart is restless until it rests in you.

52. I am attempting to synthesize the first two concepts of love distinguished by Arendt. First, she claims that Augustine understands love in terms of the contrast between use and enjoyment. Then she says that he characterizes it as a way of referring all things to God. It is important that these two ideas be distinguished. I am suggesting that both definitions can be construed as involving a symbolic relation between the finite and the infinite, thereby closing the chasm between them.

53. Rist, 107–108.

54. My analysis of these issues differs from Rist's account in two important respects. First, he does not distinguish on a spatiotemporal level, but only on levels of temporality. Second, he only mentions created and fallen time, and does not acknowledge the level of converted and fulfilled spatiotemporality.

55. Bourke, 38.

56. See for example, O'Connell, 135–144.

57. Gerard O'Daly, *Augustine's Philosophy of Mind* (London: Gerald Duckworth & Co., 1987), 10, 17.

58. This is my way of answering Arendt's question about how we can love all things in God without loving them instead of him. In his discussion of the incarnation of the soul.

59. In the formulation, I am unifying the second and the third of Arendt's definitions of love.

60. Romans 7:24.

61. Plotinus, xxi–xxii.

62. This remark might reflect the fact that actors, charioteers, and combatants in the amphitheater enjoyed a low social status and were thought to be morally disrespectable. Chadwick, 66.

63. Plato, *Republic*, trans. G. M. A. Grube (Indianapolis and Cambridge: Hackett Publishing Co., 1992), (509a–511e).

64. J. N. Findley, *The Discipline of the Cave* (New York: Humanities Press, 1966).

65. The transcendentals with which God is to be identified, both for the mature Augustine and for the late Medieval thinkers are being, goodness, truth, and unity.

66. There are a number of places in the first six books of the *Confessions* where Augustine clearly substitutes the concept of orientation for the concept of place and for the part-whole logic that this second concept presupposes (2.3.5), (3.1.1), (4.7.12), and (5.13.23).

NOTES TO CHAPTER 3

1. See Frederick Van Fleteran, "Augustine's Ascent of the Soul in Book VII of the Confessions: A Reconsideration," *Augustinian Studies* 5 (1974): 32.

2. Augustine says,

Your whole creation does not cease or keep silent from your praise, nor does every spirit through a mouth turned to you, nor do animals and corporeal things through the mouths of those who meditate upon them, so that our soul may arouse itself to you out of its weariness. (5.1.1)

3. As I have suggested earlier, an appropriate spatiotemporal matrix corresponds to each of the stages of creation, fall, conversion, and fulfillment. In the first stage, space and time are created and are just as good as the creatures who occupy it. Otherwise, it would be difficult to make sense of Augustine's view that whatever God creates is good (7.12.18). Analogous remarks can be made about each of the other options.

4. Both ascent and the fall are central themes. Here ascent corresponds to the first act of pride and the fall corresponds to the revolt.

5. By familiar correspondence theories of truth I mean theories that point to a correspondence between facts or states of affairs, on the one hand, and judgments, propositions, or statements on the other. For theories of this kind, judgments, propositions, and statements are true insofar as they correspond to facts on the one hand and states of affairs on the other. See my article, "Metaphor, Analogy, and the Nature of Truth," in *New Essays in Metaphysics*, Robert C. Neville, ed. (Albany, New York: State University of New York Press, 1986), 217–236.

6. *Teaching Christianity*, trans. Edmund Hill, in *The Works of Saint Augustine: Translations for the Twenty-First Century*, vol. I.11, ed. John E. Rotelle (Brooklyn: New City Press, 1996), (1.4.4), (1.22.20). Augustine hesitates to answer the question about whether we are to use other people as a means to God. When this questions arises, he usually shifts his attention from this means-ends relation to a way of referring all things to God.

7. Peter Brown, *Augustine of Hippo*, new edition with an epilogue (Berkeley: University of California Press, 2000), 45.

8. James J. Murphy, *Rhetoric in the Middle Ages* (Berkeley: University of California Press, 1974), 60.

9. The Manichaeans are proud of the fact that their beliefs are based on reason rather than authority by contrast with simple Christians who believe on the basis of authority. However, Augustine finds that Manichaeans are not only unable to answer questions, but are prepared to order their adherents to believe outrageous things on the basis of authority alone (5.5.8–9).

10. Murphy, 44.

11. On the radical separation between good and evil that the Manichaeans adopted, Peter Brown says:

[Augustine's] confidence was constantly eroded by the powerful myths of the sect itself, myths that made the good seem utterly abandoned and helpless before the onslaught of evil: oppressed, violated, messed-up, its God of so untarnished an innocence so as to be dangerously shorn of His omnipotence. (Brown, 42)

See also John Rist, *Augustine: Ancient Thought Baptized* (Cambridge: Cambridge University Press, 1994), 42.

12. Virgil, *The Aeneid of Virgil*, trans. Robert Fitzgerald (New York: Vintage Books, 1990).

13. C. Bennett, "The Conversion of Virgil: the *Aeneid* in Augustine's *Confessions*," *Revue des études Augustiniennes* (Paris: Etudes Agustiniennes), 34 (1988): 47–69.

14. Brown, 19.

15. Alice Miller, *The Drama of the Gifted Child*, trans. Ruth Ward (New York: Basic Books, 1981), 17–21.

16. Brown, 58.

17. As I have indicated already, Augustine never chooses among four theories of the origin of the soul: (1) that the soul falls into the body on its own initiative; (2) that the soul is sent on a mission to transform the body; (3) that we inherit our souls from the sinful dimension of our parents; and (4) that God creates every soul for the body to which it is conjoined. Even a cursory reflection on these options makes it clear that (1) and (3) are negative and (2) and (4) are positive and that to select any of them is to embrace either the negative or the positive dimension of our experience exclusively.

Only the claim that we exist in Adam enables him to hold both the negative and positive dimensions of the soul together in a single framework (10.20.29). According to this account, we remember God in Adam, which is positive; and we die in Adam, which is negative. In this way, Augustine is able to hold original innocence and original sin together in a single context to which figurative discourse gives us access.

If this account seems to be too speculative, we should notice that every theory about the issue in question is equally speculative. This one has the virtue of holding the positive and negative dimensions of our existence together in a single context. In addition, it permits us to distinguish three Adams: (1) the Adam in whom we are created; (2) the Adam in when we die; (3) the Adam in whom we are made alive. In doing so, a single theory enables us to point to three of the crucial stages of the drama of redemption.

18. This is not to say that Augustine never considers the "traducianist" theory according to which sin is inherited from our parents. However, his refusal to embrace this theory along with the others that he considers suggests that we need to elevate the discussion to the level of a "theory beyond theories." As a consequence, participation in the three Adams points to a "theoretical" level only in an extended sense of the term.

19. Henry W. Johnstone, *The Problem of the Self* (University Park, PA: Pennsylvania State University Press, 1970), xi.

20. G. W. F. Hegel, *Phenomenology of Spirit*, trans. A. V. Miller (New York: Oxford University Press, 1977), 47–50.

21. *Ibid.*, 50.

22. Colin Starnes provides one example of a scholar who reads the text as a logical pattern of development. He views the *Confessions* as "a single connected argument." See Colin Starnes, *Augustine's Conversion: A Guide to the Argument of Confessions I–IX* (Waterloo, ONT: Wilfrid Laurier University Press, 1990), xi.

23. Hegel, 55.

24. This is not to say that the stain of sin produced by the fall does not continue to haunt Augustine, even after his conversion. However, it is to say that Augustine's conversion will allow him to reject a negative way of living, even if it continues to have a negative effect on him.

Augustine came to understand this problem only gradually; for once his conversion to Christianity occurs, he expects to be free from the existential difficulties that had plagued him beforehand. This leads him to expect to have a vision of God as a result of his existential transformation (7.10.16), (7.17.23), (7.20.26). However, his confessions in Book X make it clear that sin remains a problem (10.41.66), even though Augustine has repudiated the way of living out of which it arises.

25. In his earliest writings on the subject, Augustine criticizes the idea of skepticism as unending inquiry. *Against the Academics*, trans. Peter King in *Against the Academicians and The Teacher* (Indianopolis and Cambridge: Hackett Publishing Co., 1995), (2.9.23). Later, he describes Academic skepticism as a cover for a more esoteric Platonic teaching, the purpose of which is to protect it from those without the intellectual maturity to understand it. *Against the Academics*, (3.17.38–3.18.40) and *Select Letters*, trans. James Houston Baxter, in *The Loeb Classical Library*, vol. 239, (Cambridge, Harvard University Press, 1980), (1.1).

26. Symmachus, the one who appoints him for the teaching position, has been in conflict with Ambrose, the Bishop of Milan, about the former's plea that the Altar of Victory and subsidies for pagan cults be restored (5.13.23). It is ironical that this conflict, which is the rationale for his appointment, leads him to Ambrose and to the religion that he represents.

27. Pierre Courcelle, *Rechercehes sur les Confessions de saint Augustin*, 2nd ed. (Paris: E. de Boccard, 1968), 98–132.

28. Dudden, 458 and Jacques Pepin, "Saint Augustin et la fonction protreptiquede l'allegorie," *Recherches Augustiniennes* 1(1958): 243–286.

29. Dudden, 459.

30. *Teaching Christianity*, (3.10.15).

31. *On the Profit of Believing* trans. C. L. Cornish in *Basic Writings of Saint Augustine*, vol. 2., ed. with an intro. and notes Whitney J. Oates (New York: Random House, 1948), (1.8).

32. There is a vast literature about the allegorical method of interpretation, both as Ambrose develops it and as Augustine uses it. For example, D. Dawson, "Transcendence as Embodiment: Augustine's Domestication of Gnosis," *Modern Theology* 1 (1994): 1–26; J. Pepin, "Saint Augustin et la fonction protreptique de l'allegori," *Recherches Augustiniennes* 1 (1958): 243–286; and L. M. Poland, "Augustine, Allegory, and Conversion," *Journal of Literature and Theology* 1 (1988): 37–48. However, the point I have just made about the concreteness of Augustine's use of language in contrast with the language of Ambrose must not be lost in the attempt to give a scholarly survey of it. Indeed, it is just this dimension of language that enables Augustine to write the *Confessions* with the same richness with which he preaches.

33. Acts 27.21–22.5.

34. See, for example, Ralph Flores, "Reading and Speech in St. Augustine's Confessions," *Augustinian Studies*, (6) 1975: 4–5.

35. Hegel, 47.

36. "The dreams by which [Monica] foresaw the course of her son's life were impressive, and she was confident that she could tell, instinctively, which of these dreams were authentic." Brown, 17.

37. K. E. Borresen, *Subordination and Equivalence: The Nature and Role of Woman in Augustine and Thomas Aquinas*, trans. Charles H. Talbot (Lanham, MD. University Press of America, 1981); Elaine Pagels, *Adam, Eve, and the Serpent* (New York: Vintage, 1988); and Kim Power, *Veiled Desire: Augustine on Women* (New York: Continuum, 1996).

38. Margaret Miles, *Desire and Delight: A New Reading of Augustine's Confessions* (New York: Crossroad, 1992), 27–28.

39. At this stage of his argument, Augustine also anticipates the two Neoplatonic visions that he describes in chapters ten and seventeen of Book seven. He says,

I did not know... that being drowned and blinded, I could not conceive the light of a virtue and beauty that must be embraced for their own sake. For this the body's eye does not see: it is seen only from within. (6.16.26)

Bibliography

SELECTED ENGLISH TRANSLATIONS OF AUGUSTINE'S WRITINGS, LISTED IN THE APPROXIMATE ORDER OF THEIR COMPOSITION:

Against the Academicians. Translated by Peter King in *Against the Academicians and The Teacher.* Indianapolis and Cambridge: Hackett Publishing Co. 1995.

The Happy Life. Translated by Ludwig Shopp in *The Fathers of the Church,* vol. 1. New York: CIMA Publishing Co., Inc., 1948.

Divine Providence and the Problem of Evil. Translated by Robert P. Russell in *The Fathers of the Church,* vol. 1. New York: CIMA Publishing Co., Inc., 1948.

Soliloquies. Translated with and introduction and notes by Kim Paffenroth in *The Works of Saint Augustine: Translations for the Twenty-first Century,* vol. 2. Edited by John E. Rotelle. Brooklyn: New City Press, 2000.

On the Immortality of the Soul. Translated with a preface by George G. Leckie in *Concerning the Teacher* and *On the immortality of the soul.* New York and London: D. Appleton-Century Co., 1938.

The Catholic and the Manichaean Ways of Life. Translated by Donald A. Gallagher and Idella J. Gallagher. Washington, D.C., *Catholic University of America Press,* 1966.

The Greatness of the Soul. Translated and annotated by Joseph M. Colleran in *The Greatness of the Soul* and *The teacher.* Westminster, MD: Newman Pres, 1950.

On Free Choice of the Will. Translated by Anna S. Benjamin and L. H. Hackstaff. Englewood edition, introduced by Peter Brown. Indianapolis and Cambridge: Hackett Publishing Co. Inc., 1993.

The Trinity. Translated with an introduction and notes by Edmund Hill in *The Works of Saint Augustine: A Translation for the 21st Century.* Brooklyn, NY: New City Press, 1995.

The Literal Meaning of Genesis. Translated by John H. Taylor in *Ancient Christian Writers,* vols. 41–2. New York: Newman Press, 1982.

The City of God against the Pagans. Translated by R. W. Dyson in *Cambridge Texts in the History of Political Thought.* Cambridge: Cambridge University Press, 1998.

Select Letters. Translated by James Houston Baxter in *Loeb Classical Library,* vol. 239. Cambridge, Mass.: Harvard University Press, 1980. In addition, there are some important, recently discovered Letters numbered 1*–29*. Translated by R. Eno in *The Fathers of the Church,* vol. 81. New York: CIMA Publishing Co. Inc., 1989.

The Retractations. Translated by Sister Mary Inez Gogan. Washington, D.C.: The Catholic University of America Press, 1968.

SELECTED GENERAL STUDIES:

Bonner, Gerald. *Augustine of Hippo: Life and Controversies.* New York and Rome: Canterbury Press, 1986.

Bourke, Vernon Joseph. *Augustine's Quest of Wisdom: Life and Philosophy of the Bishop of Hippo.* Milwaukee: The Bruce Publishing Co., 1945.

Burnaby, John. *Amor Dei: A Study of the Religion of St. Augustine.* Reissued with corrections and a new forward. New York and Rome: Canterbury Press, 1991.

Chadwick, Henry. *Augustine.* In *Past Masters Series.* Oxford: Oxford University Press, 1986.

Clark, Gillian. *Augustine: the Confessions.* Cambridge: Cambridge University Press, 1993.

Clark, Mary T. *Augustine.* Washington, DC: Georgetown University Press, 1994.

Gilson, Etienne. *The Christian Philosophy of Saint Augustine.* Translated by L. E. M. Lynch. New York: Random House, 1967.

Kirwan, Christopher. *Augustine.* In *The Arguments of the Philosophers.* New York and London: Routledge, 1989.

Meagher, Robert E. *Augustine: an Introduction.* New York: Harper Colophon Books, 1979.

Mendelson, Michael. "Augustine." *The Stanford Encyclopedia of Philosophy.* Fall 2000 ed. Edited by Edward N. Zalta.URL = http://plato.stanford.edu/archives/fall2000/entries/augustine/.

O'Donnell, James. *Augustine.* In *Twayne's World Author Series.* Boston: Twayne Publishers, 1985.

O'Meara, John J. *The Young Augustine, The Growth of St. Augustine's Mind Up to His Conversion.* New York and London: Longmans, Green and Co., 1954.

O'Meara, John Joseph. *Understanding Augustine.* Dublin, Ireland: Four Courts Press, 1997.

Otto, Rudolf. *The Idea of the Holy.* New York: Oxford University Press, 1958.

Portalie, Eugene. *A Guide to the Thought of Saint Augustine*, with an introduction by Vernon J. Bourke. Translated by Ralph J. Bastian. Chicago: H. Regnery Co., 1960.

Rist, John. *Augustine: Ancient Thought Baptized.* Cambridge: Cambridge University Press, 1994.

Scott, T. Kermit. *Augustine: His Thought in Context.* New York: Paulist Press, 1995.

Wills, Gary. *Saint Augustine.* New York: Viking, 1999.

SELECTED SECONDARY WORKS:

Alfaric, Prosper. *L'évolution intellectuelle de saint Augusti.* Paris, 1918.

Anselm. *Monologion and Proslogion, with the Replies of Gaunilo and Anselm.* Translated with an Introduction by Thomas Williams. Indianapolis and Cambridge: Hackett Co., 1995.

Arendt, Hanna. *Love and Saint Augustine.* Edited by Joanna Scott and Judith Stark. Chicago: University of Chicago Press, 1996.

Aristotle. *Categories.* Translated by E. M. Edghill in *The Basic Works of Aristotle.* Edited with an introduction by Richard McKeon. New York: Random House, 1941.

Aristotle. *Poetics.* Translated by Ingram Bywater in *The Basic Works of Aristotle*, edited with an introduction by Richard McKeon. New York: Random House, 1941.

Armstrong, Hilary. "St. Augustine and Christian Platonism." In *Collectanea Augustiniana.* Villanova, PA: Villanova University Press, 1967.

Augustine: A Collection of Critical Essays. Edited by Markus, R. A. Garden City, NY: Anchor Books, 1972.

Augustine, Saint, Bishop of Hippo: The Confessions of Augustine. Edited by John Gibb and William Montgomery. Cambridge: Cambridge University Press, 1908.

Augustine Through the Ages: An Encyclopedia. Edited by Allen D. Fitzgerald. Grand Rapids, MI: Eerdmans Publishing Co., 1999.

Augustinian Studies. Villanova, PA: Villanova University Press.

The Augustinian Tradition. Edited by Gareth B. Matthews. Berkeley: University of California Press, 1999.

Babcock, William S. "Augustine's Interpretation of Romans (A.D. 394–396)." *Augustinian Studies* 10 (1979): 55–74.

Bearsley, Patrick. "Augustine and Wittgenstein on Language." *Philosophy* 58 (1983): 229–236.

Bennett, C. "The Conversion of Virgil: the *Aeneid* in Augustine's *Confessions.*" *Revue des études Augustiniennes* 34 (1988): 47–69.

Borresen, K. E. *Subordination and Equivalence: The Nature and Role of Woman in Augustine and Thomas Aquinas.* Translated by Charles H. Talbot. Lanham, MD. University Press of America, 1981.

Bourke, Vernon J. *Augustine's View of Reality.* Villanova, PA: Villanova University Press, 1963.

Bourke, Vernon J. *Augustine's Love of Wisdom: An Introspective Philosophy.* West Lafayette, IN: Purdue University Press, 1992.

Brown, Peter. *Augustine of Hippo: A Biography.* New edition with an epilogue. Berkeley: University of California Press, 2000.

Burke, Kenneth. *The Rhetoric of Religion: Studies in Logology.* Berkeley: University of California Press, 1970.

Burkitt, F. C. *The Religion of the Manichees.* Cambridge: Cambridge University Press, 1925.

Burnaby, John. *Amor dei: A Study of the Religion of St. Augustine.* Reissued with corrections and a new foreword. New York and Rome: Canterbury Press, 1991.

Burnyeat, M. F. *The Skeptical Tradition.* Berkeley: University of California Press, 1983.

Burnyeat, M. F. "Wittgenstein and Augustine's *De Magistro.*" *Proceedings of the Aristotelian Society.* Supplementary Volume 61 (1987): 1–24. Reprinted in *The Augustinian Tradition.*

Chidester, David. *Word and Light: Seeing, Hearing, and Religious Discourse.* Urbana: University of Illinois Press, 1992.

Colish, M. *The Mirror of Language: A Study in the Medieval Theory of Knowledge.* New Haven and London: Yale University Press, 1968.

Contemporary Themes in Augustine's Confessions: Part I. Edited by Carl G. Vaught. *Contemporary Philosophy* 15 (1993).

Contemporary Themes in Augustine's Confessions: Part II. Edited by Carl G. Vaught. *Contemporary Philosophy* 15 (1993).

Courcelle, Pierre. *Le Confessions de Saint Augustin dans la tradition littéraire, antecedents et posterite.* Paris: Études Augustiniennes, 1963.

Courcelle, Pierre. *Rechercehes sur les Confessions de saint Augustin.* 2nd ed. Paris: E. de Boccard, 1968.

Curley, Augustine J. *Augustine's Critique of Skepticism: A study of Contra academicos.* New York: Peter Lang, 1996.

Daly, L. "Psychohistory and St. Augustine's Conversion Process." In *Collectanea Augusiniana.* Edited by Joseph Schnaublet and Frederick VanFleteran. Villanova, PA: Villanova University Press, 1978.

Dante. *Hell: The Comedy of Dante Alighieri.* Translated by Dorothy L. Sayers. London and New York: Penguin Books, 1949; *Purgatory.* Translated by Sayers, 1955; and *Paradise.* Translated by Sayers and Barbara Reynolds, 1962.

Dawson, D. "Transcendence as Embodiment: Augustine's Domestication of Gnosis." *Modern Theology* 1 (1994): 1–26.

Descartes, René. *Meditations on First Philosophy*. In *The Philosophical Writings of Descartes*, vol. 2. Translated by John Cottingham, Robert Stoothoff, and Dugald Murdoch. Cambridge: Cambridge University Press, 1984.

Diehl, Albrecht. *The Theory of the Will in Classical Antiquity*. Berkeley: University of California Press, 1982.

Djuth, Marianne. "Will." In *Augustine Through the Ages: An Encyclopedia*, 1999.

Dudden, F. Homes. *The Life and Times of St. Ambrose*, vol. 1. Oxford, The Clarendon Press, 1935.

Erikson, Erik H. *Identity and the Life Cycle*. New York: W. W. Norton and Company, 1980.

Evans, G. R. *Augustine On Evil*. Cambridge: Cambridge University Press, 1982.

Ferrari, Leo C. *The Conversions of Saint Augustine*. Villanova, PA: Villanova University, 1984.

Findlay, J. N. *The Discipline of the Cave: Gifford Lectures Given at the University of St. Andrews*. New York: Humanities Press, 1966.

Fisher, John. *From Baby to Toddler*. New York: Perigee Books, 1988.

Fitzgerald, Allan D. "Jerome." In *Augustine Through the Ages: An Encyclopedia*, 1999.

Flores, Ralph. "Reading and Speech in St. Augustine's Confessions." *Augustinian Studies* 6 (1975): 1–13.

Harnack, Adolf. "*Die Hohepunkte in Augustins Konfessionen.*" Reprinted in his *Redens und Aufsätze*, vol. 1. Giessen: Ricker, 1904.

Hegel, G. W. F. *Phenomenology of Spirit*. Translated by A. V. Miller. Oxford: Oxford University Press, 1977.

Hegel, G. W. F. *Science of Logic*. Translated by A. V. Miller. New York: Humanities Press, 1969.

Hegel, G. W. F. *Lectures on the Philosophy of Religion*, vol. 1.Translated by R. F. Brown, P. C. Hodgson, and J. M. Stewart. Los Angeles: University of California Press, 1984.

Heidegger, Martin. *Being and Time*. Translated by John Macquarrie and Edward Robinson. San Francisco: Harper Collins, 1962.

Holmes–Laski Letters. Vol. 1. Edited by M. de Howe. Cambridge: Harvard University Press, 1953.

Holscher, Ludger. *The Reality of the Mind: Augustine's Philosophical Arguments for the Human Soul as A Spiritual Substance*. New York and London: Routledge and Kegan Paul, 1986.

Johnstone, Henry. *The Problem of the Self*. University Park, PA: Pennsylvania State University Press, 1970.

Kenney, Anthony. "The Ghost of the *Tractatus*." In *Understanding Wittgenstein*. Edited by Godfrey Vesey. Ithaca, NY: Cornell University Press, 1974.

Kierkegaard, Søren. *The Sickness Unto Death*. Translated by Howard Vincent Hong and Edna H. Hong. Princeton, NJ: Princeton University Press, 1980.

Kligerman, C. *Journal of the American Psychological Association* 5 (1957): 469–484.

Mallard, William. *Language and Love: Introducing Augustine's Religious Thought through the Confessions Story*. University Park, PA: Pennsylvania State University Press, 1994.

Matthews, Gareth B. "*Si Fallor, Sum*." In *Augustine: A Collection of Critical Essays*.

Matthews, Gareth B. "The Inner Man." *Ibid*.

Matthews, Gareth B. *Thought's Ego in Augustine and Descartes*. Ithaca, NY: Cornell University Press, 1992.

Matthews, Gareth B. "Augustine and Descartes on Minds and Bodies." In *The Augustinian Tradition*.

McMahon, Robert. *Augustine's Prayerful Ascent: An Essay on the Literary Form of the Confessions*. Athens, GA: University of Georgia Press, 1989.

Mendelson, Michael. "The Dangling Thread: Augustine's Three Hypotheses of the Soul's Origin in the *De Genesi ad Litteram*." *British Journal of the History of Philosophy* 3 (1995): 219–247.

Mendelson, Michael. "The Business of Those Absent, The Origin of the Soul in Augustine's *De Genesi ad Litteram* 10.6–26." *Augustinian Studies* 29 (1998): 25–81.

Mendelson, Michael. "Augustine." *The Stanford Encyclopedia of Philosophy*. Edited by Edward N. Zalta. Fall 2000 Edition. URL = *http://plato.stanford.edu/archives/fall2000/entries/augustine/*.

Miles, M. R. *Augustine on the Body*. Missoula, MT: Scholars Press, 1979.

Miles, Margaret R. "Vision: The Eye of the Body and the Eye of the Mind in Saint Augustine's De Trinitate and Confessions." *Journal of Religion* 63.2 (1983): 125–142.

Miles, Margaret R. *Desire and Delight: A New Reading of Augustine's Confessions*, New York: Crossroad, 1992.

Miller, Alice. *The Drama of the Gifted Child*. Translated by Ruth Ward. New York: Basic Books, 1981

Murphy, James J. *Rhetoric in the Middle Ages*. Berkeley: University of California Press, 1974.

Nash, Ronald H. *The Light of the Mind: St. Augustine's Theory of Knowledge*. Lexington, KY: The University Press of Kentucky, 1969.

Newman, John Henry. *A Grammar of Assent*. South Bend, IN: University of Notre Dame Press, 1992.

Nygren, Anders. "The Structure of Saint Augustine's Confessions." *The Lutheran Church Quarterly* 21 (1948): 214–230.

O'Connell, Robert J. *St. Augustine's Early Theory of Man.* Cambridge: Harvard University Press, 1968.

O'Connell, Robert J. *St. Augustine's Confessions: The Odyssey of Soul.* Cambridge: Harvard University Press, 1969.

O'Connell, Robert J. "Augustine's Rejection of the Fall of the Soul." *Augustinian Studies* 4 (1973): 1–32.

O'Connell, Robert J. "Isaiah's Mothering God in St. Augustine's Confessions." *Thought* (1983): 188–206.

O'Connell, Robert J. *The Origin of the Soul in St. Augustine's Later Works.* New York: Fordham University Press, 1987.

O'Daly, Gerard. *Augustine's Philosophy of Mind.* London: Gerald Duckworth & Co., 1987.

O'Donnell, James J. *Augustine, Confessions. Text and Commentary,* 3 vols. Oxford: Oxford University Press, 1992.

Pagels, Elaine. *Adam, Eve, and the Serpent.* New York: Random House, 1988.

Pepin, J. "Saint Augustin et la fonction protreptique de l'allegori," *Recherches Augustiniennes* 1 (1958): 243–286

Petrarch, Francis. *The First Modern Scholar and Man of Letters.* Edited and translated by James Robinson. New York: G. P. Putnam, 1898.

Plantinga, Alvin. "Augustinian Christian Philosophy." *Monist* 75 (1992): 291–320. Reprinted in *The Augustinian Tradition.*

Plato. *Meno.* In *Five Dialogues.* Translated by G. M. A. Grube. Indianapolis and Cambridge: Hackett Publishing Co., 1981.

Plato. *Republic.* Translated by G. M. A. Grube. Indianapolis and Cambridge: Hackett Publishing Co., Inc., 1992.

Plotinus. *Enneads.* Translated by A. H. Armstrong, 7 vols. In *The Loeb Classical Library.* Cambridge: Harvard University Press, 1966–1984.

Poland, L. M. "Augustine, Allegory, and Conversion." *Journal of Literature and Theology* 1 (1988): 37–48.

Power, Kim. *Veiled Desire: Augustine's Writing on Women.* London: Darton, Longman, Todd, 1995.

Quine, W. V. O. *Word and Object.* New York: MIT Press, 1960.

Riesman, David. *The Lonely Crowd: A Study of the Changing American Character.* New Haven: Yale University Press, 1950.

Rigby, Paul. *Original Sin in Augustine's Confessions.* Ottawa: University of Ottawa Press, 1987.

Rist, John. *Augustine: Ancient Thought Baptized.* Cambridge: Cambridge University Press, 1994.

Robbins, Jill. *Prodigal Son/Elder Brother: Interpretation and Alterity in Augustine, Petrarch, Kafka, Levinas.* Chicago: University of Chicago Press, 1991.

Sellars, Wilfrid. "Empiricism and the Philosophy of Mind." In *Science, Perception and Reality.* New York: The Humanities Press, 1963.

Sellars, Wilfrid. "A Semantic Solution of the Mind-Body Problem." In *Pure Pragmatics and Possible Worlds: The Early Essays of Wilfred Sellars.* Edited by Jeffrey Sicha. Reseda, CA: Ridgeview Publishing Company, 1980.

Solignac, Aime. *Bibliotheque Augustinienne. Oeuvres de saint Augustin.* Paris: Desclee de Brouwer. Vols. 13 and 14, 1962.

Spence, Sarah. *Rhetorics of Reason and Desire: Vergil, Augustine, and the Troubadours.* Ithaca, NY: Cornell University Press, 1988.

Spinoza, Benedict. *The Ethics.* Translated by R. H. M. Elwes. New York: Dover Publications, 1955.

Stabb, Janice M. "Standing Alone Together: Silence, Solitude, and Radical Conversion." *Contemporary Themes in Augustine's Confessions: Part I.* Edited by Carl G. Vaught. *Contemporary Philosophy,* 1993.

Starnes, Colin. *Augustine's Conversion: A Guide to the Argument of Confessions I–IX.* Waterloo, ONT: Wilfrid Laurier University Press, 1990.

Stock, Brian. *Augustine the Reader: Meditation, Self-knowledge, and the Ethics of Interpretation.* Cambridge: Harvard University Press, 1996.

TeSelle, Eugene. *Augustine, the Theologian.* New York: Herder and Herder, 1970.

Teske, Roland. "The World-Soul and Time in St. Augustine." *Augustinian Studies,* 14 (1989).

Teske, Roland J. "St. Augustine's View of the Original Human Condition in *De Genesi contra Manichaeos.*" *Augustinian Studies* 22 (1991): 141–155.

Teske, Roland J. "Soul." In *Augustine Through the Ages: An Encyclopedia,* 1999.

Testard, M. "Cicero," *AugLex* 1: 913–930.

Testard, M. *Saint Augustin et Cicero,* 2 vols. Paris: Etudes Augustiniennes, 1958.

Tillich, Paul. "Two Types of Philosophy of Religion." In *Theology of Culture.* Edited by Robert C. Kindall. Oxford: Oxford University Press, 1959.

Van Fleteran, Frederick. "Augustine's Ascent of the Soul in Book VII of the Confessions: A Reconsideration." *Augustinian Studies* 5 (1974): 29–72.

Vaught, Carl G. *The Quest for Wholeness.* Albany, NY: State University of New York Press, 1982.

Vaught, Carl G. "Categories and the Real Order: Sellar's Interpretation of Aristotle's Metaphysics." *The Monist,* 66 (1983): 438–449.

Vaught, Carl G. "Metaphor, Analogy, and System: A Reply to Burbidge." *Man and World*, 18 (1984): 55–63.

Vaught, Carl. G. "The Quest for Wholeness and its Crucial Metaphor and Analogy: The Place of Places." *Ultimate Reality and Meaning*, 7 (1984): 156–165.

Vaught, Carl. G. "Metaphor, Analogy, and the Nature of Truth." In *New Essays in Metaphysics*. Edited by Robert C. Neville. Albany: State University of New York Press, 1986.

Vaught, Carl. G. "Semiotics and the Problem of Analogy: A Critique of Peirce's Theory of Categories." *Transactions of the Charles S. Peirce Society*, 22 (1986): 311–326.

Vaught, Carl G. "Signs, Categories, and the Problem of Analogy." In *Semiotics*, 1985. Edited by John Deely. Lanham, MD: The University Press of America, 1986.

Vaught, Carl G. "Subject, Object, and Representation: A Critique of Hegel's Dialectic of Perception." *International Philosophical Quarterly*, 22 (1986): 117–135.

Vaught, Carl G. "Participation and Imitation in Plato's Metaphysics." In *Contemporary Essays on Greek Ideas: The Kilgore Festschrift*. Edited by Robert M. Baird, William F. Cooper, Elmer H. Duncan, and Stuart E. Rosenbaum. Waco, TX: Baylor University Press, 1987.

Vaught, Carl G. "Hegel and the Problem of Difference: A Critique of Dialectical Reflection." In *Hegel and His Critics*. Edited by William Desmond. Albany, NY: State University of New York Press, 1989.

Vaught, Carl G. "Theft and Conversion in Augustine's Confessions." In *The Recovery of Philosophy in America: Essays in Honor of John Edwin Smith*. Edited by Thomas P. Karsulas and Robert Cummings Neville. Albany: NY: State University of New York Press, 1997.

Virgil, *The Aeneid of Virgil*. Translated by Robert Fitzgerald. New York: Random House, 1990.

Wetzel, James. *Augustine and the Limits of Virtue*. Cambridge: Cambridge University Press, 1992.

Wittgenstein, Ludwig. *Philosophical Investigations*. 3rd edition. Translated by G. E. M. Anscombe. Upper Saddle River, NJ: Prentice Hall, 1958.

Index

Adam and Eve, 1, 34, 35, 36, 42, 47,
  51, 53, 57, 58, 60, 65, 101, 103,
  106, 129, 142, 161n, 162n, 166n,
  169n, 174n
Adeodatus, 91, 164n
adolescence, 5, 7, 21, 43, 52, 54, 67,
  80, 141, 151,
  mischief, 52, 60
Aeneas, 45, 46, 126, 127, 130
aesthetic, 55, 56, 59, 61–64, 167n
Alexandrians, 136
Alypius, 147, 148, 149, 151–153
ambiguity, 10, 73, 111, 125
Ambrose, 24, 49, 116, 134–141, 143,
  145, 146, 147, 150, 159n, 175n
Aeneid, 22, 130
Anselm, 156n
anxiety, 96, 97, 107, 116, 128
Aquinas, Thomas, 3
Aristotelian categories, 112
Aristotelian tradition, 13
ascension of Christ, 105
astrology, 67, 89–93
attitude
  negative, 46
  positive, 100
auditory images, 13, 159n

Babylonian exile, 54
beautiful things, 100, 107
beautiful, the, 68, 107, 109, 111, 112
beggar, 146–147

being
  continuum of, 72
beings
  continuum of, 72
belief, 11, 50, 91, 130, 139, 144, 145
body
  as a prison house, 11
bondage, 76, 80, 85, 87, 92, 125, 129,
  131, 134, 139, 143, 152, 153, 167n
Burke, Kenneth, 18, 159n

Carthage, 47, 67, 68, 70, 98, 115, 119,
  126, 127, 129, 130, 148, 149, 167n
Catiline, 158n
chance, 67, 92, 93
charity, 71, 72, 93
childhood companion, 93
Christian faith, 11, 116, 134, 135, 137,
  143
chronology, 6
Cicero, 3, 22, 48, 58, 67, 74–79, 110,
  115, 124, 132, 138, 145, 168n
City of God, 52
cognition, 12, 13, 26, 32, 35, 40
community
  historical, 31
  linguistic, 41
  mythological, 31
  negative, 32
  of willfulness, 64,
  of wills, 64
  positive, 29

187

Confessions
  relevance of, 15
consciousness
  content of, 10
  self-transcendent structure of, 2
  static contents of, 17
containment, 25–27, 99
conversion, xi, 1, 6, 9, 14, 44, 75, 76,
    92, 94, 98, 100, 102, 103, 104,
    105, 111, 117, 130, 139, 140, 142,
    144, 146, 149, 151, 158n, 166n,
    172n
conversation
  between God and soul, 14
Courcelle, Pierre, xi, 48, 156n
created beings, 36, 101
creation
  ex nihilo 2
Creationism, 160n, 162n
crisis, 6, 7, 73, 139
crying, 14, 106
custom, 27, 35, 44

Dante, 159n
darkness, 56, 61, 87, 112, 118, 139,
    156n, 169n
death, ix, 6, 7, 28, 32, 36, 47, 58, 67,
    68, 73, 74, 75, 88, 90, 94, 95, 96,
    98, 99, 100, 101, 102, 105, 106,
    107, 110, 127, 129, 130, 139, 146,
    150, 151, 153, 168n, 171n
death of father, 75
decentered self, 8
desert, 49, 125, 145
desire, 21, 22, 23, 24, 27, 30, 44, 53,
    54, 55, 56, 58, 64, 65, 76, 79, 90,
    95, 112, 113, 127, 128, 140, 150,
    151, 169n, 171n
destiny, 18, 45, 91, 126, 129, 150, 153
dialogical logic, 6
Dido, 45, 46, 68, 126, 127, 129, 130
discontinuity, 7, 21, 29, 32, 60, 61, 98,
    117, 133
discourse
  analogical, 6
  figurative, 2

intelligible, 2
  metaphorical, 2
  peformative, 2
  reflective, ix
Divine Comedy, 22,
downward, 4, 5, 54, 71, 75, 117, 145
dwelling place, 100

embodied Christ, 105
embodied existence, 11, 103, 120
encounter, 1, 81
enigma, 19, 165
enjoyment, 7, 55, 64, 71, 73, 121, 171
eternal, ix, 2–9, 13, 19, 31, 34, 43, 44,
    50, 52, 65, 68, 82, 105, 115, 116,
    119, 125, 150, 160n, 166n
eternity, 2, 7, 8, 12, 13, 18, 33, 34, 44,
    51, 113, 126, 129, 150, 156n
  stability of, 13
ethical, 48, 55, 56, 59, 61, 63, 64, 74,
    87, 121
evil, 9, 11, 50, 56, 57, 58, 59, 60, 61,
    74, 79, 80, 81, 83, 84, 85, 86, 87,
    92, 94, 110, 130, 131, 133, 134,
    143, 148, 149, 153, 157n, 166n,
    168n, 169n, 173n
existential development, 6
experience
  vertical dimension of, 16

faith seeking understanding 22, 24, 26,
    27, 125, 139, 144
fall, 1, 6, 11, 33, 42, 46, 48, 49, 52, 60,
    69, 70, 89, 90, 98, 100, 101, 102,
    103, 104, 105, 110, 117, 118, 120,
    130, 142, 146, 158n, 164n, 169n,
    170n, 172n, 174n
fallenness, 2, 31, 32, 36, 42, 51, 102,
    143, 161n
father, 29, 32, 44, 49, 54, 75, 77, 88,
    104, 105, 133, 135, 139, 144, 145,
    148, 154, 169n
Faustus, 116, 119, 122, 123, 124, 125,
    126, 130, 131, 135, 141, 146, 147,
    150
feeling, 18, 96, 146, 152

finitude, 2, 14, 29, 30, 31, 32, 36, 46,
    51, 56, 60, 65, 98, 100, 101, 102,
    143, 161n 166n
first being, 33
first book, 67, 107, 109, 111
flesh, 53, 90, 100, 105, 110, 130, 131,
    133
fleshly sense, 103
flogging by teachers 42
fornication, 11, 12, 45, 46, 54, 69, 134
fragmentation, 13, 17, 21, 73, 89, 116,
    146
freedom, 10, 13, 64, 76, 79, 87, 92, 93,
    98, 109, 125, 166n
fruit of death, 73
fulfillment, 1, 2, 6, 52, 53, 69, 70, 98,
    102, 103, 104, 105, 106, 111, 117,
    128, 130, 142, 146, 158n, 172n
future, 2, 3, 4, 120, 147, 152

gardens 7
    Garden of Eden, 7, 58, 63
    Garden of Gethsemane, 8, 156n
    in center of house, 8
    orchard, 7, 58, 60, 62, 63
gathering, 4, 25, 28, 38, 53
God
    access to, 9
    and the soul, 1–19, 22, 24–27, 33,
        37, 38, 40, 42, 43, 50, 51, 60, 61,
        67, 72, 73, 83, 100, 112, 113, 115,
        117, 124, 125, 128, 159n, 161n
    calling on, 23
    City of, 52
    determinate attributes of, 27
    dynamism of, 2, 22, 25
    father, 44
    greatness of, ix, 22
    knowledge of, 23, 24
    mystery of, 2, 24
    paradoxical adjectives of, 22
    part-whole relationship with soul, 26
    positive concept of, 42
    power of, 2
    providential hand of, 16
    richness of, 11, 104

separation of God and the soul, 2
    transforming activity of, 22
    unspoken presence of, 30
    Word of, 2, 24
grace, 29, 52, 105, 113, 117, 128, 130,
    151, 165, 170
Greek, 45, 46, 47, 50, 77, 158n
grief, 70, 71, 72, 97, 98, 101
ground of existence, 1

healing, 70, 144, 160
hearing, 2, 13, 23, 24, 27, 31, 40, 48,
    111, 116, 140, 141, 149, 159n
heart, ix, 2, 3, 9, 13, 14, 19, 22, 23, 24,
    28, 48, 49, 51, 53, 61, 69, 75, 88,
    92, 95, 96, 97, 106, 108, 109, 119,
    120, 125, 126, 129, 130, 134, 137,
    138, 139, 140, 141, 145, 146, 152,
    153, 167n, 171n
Hegel, 29, 132, 133, 144
highest good, 9, 43, 110, 113
Holmes, Oliver Wendall, 60, 61
Holy of Holies, 18, 46, 145
Holy Spirit, 105, 122
Hortensius, 74, 77, 115, 124, 132, 138,
    145
human being, 11, 101, 108, 109, 130,
    162n, 164n, 166n
    development of, 130
    predicament of, 8
hysteria, ix, 116, 150

identity, 7, 73, 104, 105, 115, 117, 146
ignorance, 28, 51, 124, 125
illegitimate son, 73
image, 21, 23, 30, 43, 44, 48, 51, 52,
    60, 64, 73, 81, 83, 90, 97, 101,
    102, 117, 142, 159n, 165n
    false, 45, 46, 47, 48, 50, 68, 73, 76,
        83, 145
imagination, 30, 42, 43, 78, 81
imitation, 30, 60, 65
incarnated word, 15
incarnation, 24, 105, 120, 130, 133,
    171n, 172n

individual, 1, 2, 5, 6, 11, 12, 22, 31, 32, 37, 63, 67, 97, 102, 104, 108, 111, 113, 131, 132, 148, 160n, 162n
infancy, ix, 5, 6, 21, 22, 28–37
infant, 6, 30, 31, 32, 35, 36, 37, 41, 42, 44, 50, 71, 88, 90, 142, 145, 162n
instinctive affection, 29
intellect, 3, 5, 8, 14, 16, 23, 43, 45, 46, 47, 60, 73, 77, 82, 87, 116, 119, 120, 121, 123, 135, 139, 140, 141
intellectual ascent, 5
interpretation, 16, 86, 111, 127, 128, 129, 136, 152
  allegorical 17, 77, 78, 135, 137, 141, 143, 145, 175n
intuition, 18, 78
inward, 4, 9, 12, 95

Jesus, 88, 130, 137, 156n, 169n
John, 88
joy, 65, 70, 71, 73, 95, 96, 99, 111, 136, 139, 147, 171n
justice, 27, 56, 86, 118, 168n

knowledge, 23, 24, 28, 33, 43, 46, 57, 58, 72, 120, 121, 124, 141, 144, 159n, 165n, 169n

language
  auditory, 13
  ecstatic, 3
  existential, 3
  experiential, 8
  learning signs, 37
  learning to speak, 37
  linguistic community, 41, 47, 164n
  natural, 38
  of God and the soul, 2
  of redemption, 8
  performative use of, 2
  reflective, 47
Latin, 17, 45–47, 50, 77, 107
Latin orator, 107
laughter, 30, 61, 62, 136, 137
law, 56, 60, 73, 84, 86, 91, 100, 101, 134, 136

levels of interpretation, 136
liberal arts, 67, 89, 111, 112, 124
light, 1, 3, 5, 29, 33, 41, 53, 55, 65, 110, 112, 118, 120, 169n, 176n
love, 52, 53, 63, 65, 67, 68, 69, 70, 71, 72, 75, 76, 77, 78, 79, 82, 91, 93, 96, 99, 100, 101, 104, 105, 106, 107, 108, 109, 117, 127, 128, 134, 135, 145, 148, 151, 152, 153, 160n, 166n, 171n, 172n
love of wisdom, 11, 67, 75, 76, 77, 78, 79, 82, 151, 166n

Manichees
  critique of Old Testament, 135
  dualism of, ix, 54, 67, 68, 76, 80, 83, 85, 93, 94, 116, 124, 131, 143, 145
marriage, 54, 91, 146, 152, 170n
memory, 10, 15, 16, 32, 33, 37, 38, 41, 51
Meno, 33
metaphysics, 97
  of presence, 83
method of inquiry, 8
Middle Ages
  development of, 3
mistress, 91, 152, 153
modern philosophy, 16
Monica, 44, 54, 75, 88, 89, 116, 126, 128, 129, 130, 139, 147, 152, 175n
monologue, 9
mortality, ix, 23, 34, 35, 110, 111, 171n
mother, 8, 28, 29, 32, 36, 44, 49, 54, 68, 75, 87, 88, 94, 116, 125, 126, 127, 128, 129, 130, 138, 139, 149, 152, 169n
mouth, 14, 38, 96, 106, 107, 139, 172n
mythology, 80, 82, 124

names, 39, 40, 46, 137
narrative, 5, 8, 28, 30, 43, 65, 73, 90, 102, 107, 108, 111, 116, 122, 123, 130, 138, 147
natural consciousness, 89, 132
natural philosophers, 119

nature, 9, 10, 22, 86, 92, 100, 101, 104,
    115, 119, 121, 122, 138, 157n
    symbolic status of, 121
Nebridius, 92, 147–149, 153
negativity, 30, 59, 74, 89, 110, 132, 145
    absolute, 74, 89
Neoplatonic commentators, 7
Neoplatonic ladder, 43, 45, 50
Neoplatonism, 14, 33, 45, 85, 110, 123,
    132, 136
nihil, 65, 72, 74, 82, 85, 87, 90, 110
nonbeing, 61, 62, 63, 74, 82, 85, 87,
    94, 96, 110, 132, 169n, 170n
    human face of, 94
nothingness, 28, 59, 61, 62, 69, 82, 85,
    87, 90, 95, 101
nurses, 4, 28, 29, 30, 31, 32, 35, 36,
    38, 40, 41, 42, 47, 94, 95, 127,
    142

O'Connell, Robert, 33
ocean metaphor, 47
Odysseus, 48, 49
old age, 5, 6, 113
omnipotence, 21, 60, 62, 173n
ontological continuum, 60, 82, 84, 112,
    167
ontology, 35, 59, 60, 62, 72, 82, 84, 87,
    99, 105, 108, 110, 112, 114, 142,
    146, 161n, 167n
orientation, 8, 11, 25, 45, 46, 57, 62, 64,
    69, 74, 75, 99, 101, 105, 110, 114,
    117, 118, 124, 146, 160n, 161n, 172n
Origen, 136
original innocence, 22, 28, 29, 34, 36,
    51, 53, 54, 80, 95, 102, 142, 145,
    160n, 161n, 162n, 166n, 174n
original sin, 21, 28, 34, 36, 37, 51, 80,
    95, 102, 129, 145, 160n, 161n,
    162n, 163n, 166n, 174n
Otto, Rudolph, 28
outward, 4, 9, 73, 148

paradise, 8, 30, 31, 33, 36, 41, 42, 47,
    50, 51, 58, 106, 163n, 164n, 166n,
    170n

paradox, 27, 28, 108
Parmenidean questions, 26
particular, x, 2, 67, 76, 86
part-whole framework, 26
past, ix, 2, 4, 86
Patricius, 54, 75
Paul, 24, 36, 105, 138, 155n, 159n
pear-stealing episode, 21, 51–65
perception, 13, 132
Petrarch, 1
phantasia, 81
phantasma, 81
phenomena, 13, 120, 122, 124
Philo, 136
philosophy, 1, 3, 16, 39, 40, 67, 74, 76,
    78, 79, 86, 136, 149, 168n
physician, 92, 143
Platonic tradition, 13
Plotinus, 45, 49, 78, 108, 170n
poisoned fingernail, 73
political, 55, 57, 61, 63, 64, 68
Porphyry, 45
postmodern predicament, 15
prayer, 89, 100, 129, 130, 139, 156n, 159n
preaching, 24, 135
preexistence, 33
primordia, 33
privation doctrine, 84–85
Prodigal Son, 48, 49, 58, 113, 135, 154
profession and confession, 121
professional disappointments, 7
progress, 7, 83, 87, 116, 124
prophets, 86, 136
publicity, 13
punishment, 42, 49, 53, 103, 150, 163n

radical opposition 15, 36
reading aloud, 140
reason, 9, 10, 83, 93, 122, 132, 142,
    144
recollection, 4, 16, 23, 24, 33, 61, 98,
    125
reconciliation, 15
reconstruction, 15, 16, 98
redemption, 8, 18, 25, 27, 54, 89, 105,
    106, 116, 119, 123, 124, 129, 174n

relative absence, 87
religious, 5, 11, 18, 22, 41, 43, 55, 61, 74, 78, 79, 111, 138, 167n
representation, 45
rest, ix, 14, 46, 68, 69, 96, 97, 98, 100, 101, 104, 105, 113, 117, 125, 129, 139, 147, 154, 167n
restless heart, 2, 22, 23, 24, 69
return to God, 54, 75, 76, 100, 102, 106, 113
rhetoric, 7, 8, 9, 14, 43, 54, 67, 68, 73, 74, 75, 90, 93, 109, 112, 119, 122, 123, 124, 126, 127, 134, 135, 167n
  negative uses of, 123
  Positive uses of, 123
Roman Empire, 16, 75, 91, 126, 127, 130, 152
Rome, 47, 115, 126, 127, 128, 129, 130, 134, 148, 165n

salvation, 12, 27, 44, 49, 50, 88, 95, 106, 117, 126, 144, 146, 159n
Scholasticism, 43
self-accentuation, 36, 57, 64, 87, 88
self-denunciation, 74
self-transcendence, 23, 31, 65, 78, 106, 125, 129, 166n
sensation, 10, 11, 103
sensory metaphors, 13
separation, 31, 34, 35, 64, 69, 73, 96, 97, 120, 126, 127, 129, 146, 153, 157n, 167n, 173n
  from God, ix, 2, 12, 21, 54, 60, 67, 73, 85, 97, 117,
serpent, 41, 151
sexual addiction, 7, 12, 46, 70, 76, 112, 152
signifier and signified, 17
sin, 7, 12, 21, 22, 23, 28, 34, 35, 36, 37, 49, 51, 52, 54, 56, 57, 58, 59, 60, 61, 65, 73, 74, 80, 87, 91, 95, 98, 101, 102, 103, 105, 110, 120, 121, 129, 130, 131, 145, 156n, 160n, 161n, 162n, 163n, 166n, 167n, 170n, 171n, 174n, 175n
  three classes of, 120

skepticism, 115, 116, 123, 131, 132, 133, 137, 175n
Soliloquies, 9
son, 44, 48, 49, 54, 58, 73, 88, 89, 91, 104, 105, 113, 125, 126, 128, 129, 130, 133, 135, 138, 139, 152, 154, 164n, 170n
soul
  bodily entanglements of, 11
  corrupted, 11
  disembodied, 33, 34, 90
  separation from God, See God
space, 2, 4, 6, 7, 8, 16, 24, 31, 33, 42, 44, 48, 51, 52, 53, 56, 68, 70, 72, 75, 78, 82, 86, 95, 99, 103, 113, 115, 124, 125, 126, 128, 129, 139, 142, 143, 150, 156n, 160n, 164n, 166n, 172n
speaking, 2, 9, 13, 14, 15, 17, 18, 24, 27, 39, 51, 67, 82, 90, 97, 101, 106, 116, 123, 125, 131, 134, 135, 137, 138, 140, 141, 144, 146, 149
Spinoza, 161n
stoicism, 11, 78, 148
stolen fruit, 55
students, 46, 48, 73, 77, 89, 90, 93, 117, 126, 134, 147, 148, 150, 165n
substance, 13, 63, 75, 77, 78, 83, 84, 109, 110, 111, 133, 137, 138, 142, 158n, 169n
superstition, 83, 90

temporal, ix, 2, 4, 5, 6, 7, 8, 9, 13, 18, 19, 22, 28, 29, 31, 37, 41, 48, 50, 51, 52, 55, 65, 67, 68, 87, 94, 95, 96, 102, 103, 108, 111, 115, 116, 119, 125, 141, 150, 166n
temptation, 46, 85, 87
Ten Commandments, 56
Thagaste, 98, 171n
theoretical issues, 9, 107
thinking, x, xi, 3, 4, 8, 14, 18, 40, 48, 76, 80, 125
Tillich, Paul, 155n
time, 2, 6, 7, 8, 13, 28, 31, 33, 34, 42, 44, 51, 52, 53, 58, 68, 95, 98, 102,

103, 113, 115, 126, 129, 142, 150, 151, 155n, 162n, 164n, 166n, 168n

tongue, 14, 42, 47, 99, 116, 140

Traducianism, 160n, 162n

Trinity, 64, 104, 122

truth, 3, 5, 10, 13, 14, 15, 16, 32, 33, 39, 46, 50, 51, 57, 73, 75, 78, 81, 88, 104, 109, 110, 111, 112, 119, 120, 121, 122, 123, 124, 125, 131, 132, 133, 134, 135, 139, 141, 143, 144, 145, 149, 150, 157n, 172n, 173n

Two Great Commandments, 86

ultimate issues of life, 1, 2, 8

understanding, 22, 23, 24, 26, 27, 32, 35, 41, 125, 132, 139, 144, 153, 156n

unfallen world, 102

unity, 2, 12, 21, 31, 34, 35, 51, 62, 73, 97, 98, 99, 108, 110, 117, 146, 167n, 170n, 172n

universal, 2, 43, 44, 46, 69, 132

upward, 4, 5, 10, 48, 49

utility, 43

vertical relationship, 3

Virgil, 127, 130

visual metaphors, 13, 14

voice
of God, 9, 14, 27, 48, 54, 73, 111
of heart, 14
of reason, 9

volition 87, 95

wasteland, 65, 68, 97, 113, 117, 118, 128, 154

weeping, 96

Whitehead, Alfred North, 155n

wife, 53, 58, 152, 153

will, 3, 5, 11, 13, 16, 21, 23, 24, 29, 31, 32, 35, 36, 41, 43, 45, 46, 47, 49, 50, 51, 52, 57, 58, 59, 60, 75, 85, 87, 91, 92, 108, 109, 120, 121, 123, 137, 139, 144, 148, 153, 157n

willfulness, 5, 11, 21, 36, 42, 43, 44, 49, 58, 59, 60, 64, 87, 95, 127

Wittgenstein, Ludwig, 38, 39, 47, 164n

wooden rule, 88, 152

word, 2, 15, 19, 24, 38, 40, 120, 141
two senses of, 14

Wreckers, 67, 73, 74, 93, 113, 153